Contempor

Bibliographic Information published by the Deutsche Nationalbibliothek
The Deutsche Nationalbibliothek lists this publication in the Deutsche Nationalbibliografie; detailed bibliographic data is available on the internet at <http://www.d-nb.de>.

This book has been published with part support from English Heritage.

Front cover photo:
"A car wreck as vanitas symbol."
© Åsa Nyhleń,
reproduced with kind permission.

Back cover photo:
© Cornelius Holtorf

Cover design:
Olaf Glöckler, Atelier Platen
(Friedberg)

ISBN 978-3-631-57637-3

© Peter Lang GmbH
Internationaler Verlag der Wissenschaften
Frankfurt am Main 2009
All rights reserved.

All parts of this publication are protected by copyright. Any utilisation outside the strict limits of the copyright law, without the permission of the publisher, is forbidden and liable to prosecution. This applies in particular to reproductions, translations, microfilming, and storage and processing in electronic retrieval systems.

Printed in Germany 1 2 3 4 5 7

www.peterlang.de

Introduction: Fragments from a Conversation about Contemporary Archaeologies

Angela Piccini and Cornelius Holtorf

'How can you see something that isn't there?' yawned the Humbug, who wasn't fully awake yet.
'Sometimes it's much simpler than seeing things that are.' Alec said. 'For instance, if something is there, you can only see it with your eye s open, but if it isn't there, you can see it just as well with your eyes closed. That's why imaginary things are often easier to see than real ones.'
'Then where is Reality?' barked Tock.
'Right here,' cried Alec, waving his arms...
'I don't see any city,' said Milo very softly.
'Neither do they,' Alec remarked sadly, 'but it hardly matters, for they don't miss it at all ....one day someone discovered that if you walked as fast as possible and looked at nothing but your shoes you would arrive at your destination more quickly.....Because nobody cared, the city slowly began to disappear. Day by day the buildings grew fainter and fainter, and the streets faded away, until at last it was entirely invisible.'

Norton Juster (1961) *The Phantom Tollbooth*

Cornelius: To some, an archaeology studying contemporary periods may sound like a contradiction in terms: isn't archaeology dealing with precisely what comes *before* the contemporary? But there is no reason why archaeologists, studying material remains, should not be studying objects from the recent pasts of the twentieth and twenty-first centuries. To a large extent, our surroundings are literally made of artefacts, sites and monuments from this period. Yet, it can take an archaeologist to realise the potential of rendering a scrap of yesterday into archaeological material. As Colleen Beck and her co-writers remember (this volume, p. 104), 'permission to conduct a field study of the Peace Camp was granted to us even though we were told that we really didn't need it because we were not doing archaeology'.

Contemporary archaeologists, however, have understood that the field of archaeology itself is changing. Accordingly, Dan Hicks has already proclaimed archaeology's 'loss of antiquity':

Archaeology has previously consistently chalked out a field of study separate from the present. As a diversity of archaeologies has proliferated around the world, 'buffer-zones' of varying lengths between past and present have been established and maintained. ... The loss of a delimited archaeological past, of that generalized disciplinary time bounded from the present, has occurred. ... No longer simply foreign countries, the moment of confluence between past and present develops quickly from bilateral exchange into oceans of material interactions. (2003: 316-17)

Having lost a 'delimited archaeological past', archaeologists are increasingly researching the interface between the past behind us and the fleeting moment of the present. Typical for this trend is the title of a session organised by David A. Gadsby and Jodi Barnes at the 2008 annual conference of the Society for Historical Archaeology:

'The Archaeology of Ten Minutes Ago: Material Histories of the Burgeoning Past and the Vanishing Present'. By historicising the present, archaeologists effectively suggest that we are living in the past. A recently excavated Ford Transit van is another project at the same interface (Newland et al 2007). The discussion that accompanied this forensic archaeological investigation was revealing. Whereas some maintained that the project had more general methodological implications and would raise profound issues, for example about remembering and forgetting, others replied that it was 'mad' and 'a waste of time and resources' since very little new could possibly be discovered

Of course, archaeologists do not have an academic monopoly on questions of matter and time, and that applies to the study of the contemporary past, too. Historians, sociologists, ethnologists and many others study the twentieth and twenty-first centuries. As archaeologists, we have our own perspectives and approaches, complementing those of other fields with whom we must work together. Surely William Rahtje (2001) was right in arguing that the best kind of archaeology integrates a whole range of different sources and approaches. In studying the contemporary world archaeology can make use of ethnographical, textual, oral and material evidence.

Angela: For me, that 'loss of antiquity' is grounded in Walter Benjamin's assertion that 'history is the subject of a structure whose site is not homogeneous, empty time, but time filled by the presence of the now' (Benjamin 1970: 263); Benjamin understood the impossibility of speaking about the past in any other terms than the present. And this is why the opening quotation from a popular children's book is apposite, specifically in the context of archaeology's contribution to matters of time: unless we make 'visible' the physical reality of the presence of the past in 'the now', we effectively erase the materialities of everyday life.

So, how best to define the shape of archaeological practices if we take on Rathje's argument for a multi-disciplinary approach to archaeology that embraces a wide range of data-producing research practices? How do we grasp that past in the present? While a popular way of defining archaeology may be grounded in the notion of the Ancient, archaeologists themselves perhaps locate the specificity of their subjects in a set of specialised techniques that differ from the toolkits of geographers, anthropologists and others (Lucas 2005: 119). That toolkit facilitates a practice of material attention involving detailed processes of measurement and analysis, of weight, height, length, colour, texture, chemical composition, spatial relation.

Like anthropologists, archaeologists are concerned with the evidence for human behaviours; like geographers, archaeologists are interested in the spatial analysis of human phenomena; like historians, archaeologists rely on archives and other material traces that point towards past events; like artists, archaeologists actively shape materials in a process of transformation. With their photographic, writing, measuring and analytical tools, however, archaeologists produce Geertzian 'thick descriptions' of the lives of things in a microscopic mapping of the Earth's material culture. For archaeologists archives are more than sources of information: their objects tell us about the processes by which humans have come to value some stories as evidence and not others. And whereas art may be held to announce truths, archaeologists aim to connect their individual practices to a bigger picture, to elaborate upon 'truth' (Badiou, 2005). It is through the use of the archaeological toolkit in what we may term the contemporary world — the right-about-now — that we can work through the specific qualities of archaeology and identify how it might operate in an uncertain future.

Cornelius: Indeed — materiality and material evidence usually are the starting point and focus of archaeological research, and the same applies to archaeologies of the contemporary period (see Gould and Schiffer 1981; Graves-Brown 2000). Yet besides these tools, there are certain questions and approaches that are distinctively, although perhaps not exclusively, archaeological too.

Archaeology is a way of looking at the past. We are asking about change over time, often in a long-term perspective of hundreds or thousands of years, but we are also asking about the ways in which people's views and ideas, social structures, and material culture are interlinked within different historical circumstances. Moreover, as archaeologists we believe that it is important to reveal what lies below the surface, and that — like detectives — we must extremely carefully record our data in the field (Holtorf 2005).

Angela: Yet, the contribution that archaeology can make to studies of the contemporary world is not obvious. A student once asked 'what does archaeology add to our understanding that you can't get from documents?' This is a question often put to archaeologists. It underlies the still frequently cited description of archaeology as the 'handmaid of history' — what you do if you do not have books. In response I raised Victor Buchli and Gavin Lucas's chapter in *Archaeologies of the Contemporary Past* (2001a), in which they discuss their study of the abandonment of a council house in England. The point they made so very clearly is that while the documents pertaining to the case provided an interesting and useful insight into the management of people on state benefits, it was only through the use of archaeological techniques that 'normalising civic discourse' (*pace* Foucault) could be identified and woven together into a story that evoked the materialities of discursive everyday life.

Cornelius: Yes, material culture does more than provide illustrations for what we already know from disciplines such as history. Rathje's Garbage project has shown convincingly how material evidence can correct other kinds of evidence such as interview-surveys (2001). Focussing on things can also raise new questions about familiar issues. A brilliant example is Nick Saunders' study of 'Trench Art' from the early twentieth century, which in an entirely new way makes you realise what the experience of taking part, and then remembering, the horrors of World War I trench warfare must have been like (2000). I think that your paper in this volume, Angela, has a similar effect. I found it fascinating to be made aware of links between rubbish in the gutter and slavery in Bristol.

Angela: What I wanted to do with *Guttersnipe* — both the initial performance-video piece and my chapter in this book, as a reflexive dissemination of a series of events — was to work archaeologically with a contemporary assemblage. That is to say, I worked with a video record of material to raise questions about the relationship of the 'field document' to archaeological event. At the same time, I used that record to generate an archaeological story that went beyond what was documented, in either my video piece or the written documents that I used as source material, to stimulate a devising process. Not only does this practice potentially raise new questions about familiar issues, my concern with contemporary decay shares similarities with Mats Burström's argument in his chapter on car cemeteries that this provides the 'potential for existential reflection concerning the passage of time, the perishability of the material world, and the conditions of our human existence.... It is as if the car wrecks are sufficiently young to strike us with the full power of ruination' (this volume, p. 141).

Cornelius: In many cases the people whose remains are being studied by archaeologists of the contemporary world are still around too, and archaeologists can talk to them directly. This not only contributes to academic knowledge but also the social relevance of archaeological research. Opportunities to empower people through archaeological research are rare, but contemporary archaeologies regularly offer to assist people in their own quests for the contemporary past (Wilkie 2001; Casella 2005). In this way, archaeology can give a voice to those silenced in or by society. A particularly vivid example is the growing field of forensic archaeology, where archaeologists are assisting the families of victims to secure justice and find closure by identifying individuals within mass graves (see Cox 2001; Crossland 2002). Similarly, Alfredo González-Ruibal (2008) has been arguing that one of the tasks of an archaeology of the contemporary past is to perform a therapeutic function and bring healing to those who have suffered violence in contemporary society. These are very important concerns.

Angela: To return to your point, Cornelius, about what archaeology is not — not simply the study of material culture nor the use of material to illustrate history — I want to suggest that together, the chapters in this book describe the field of archaeologies of the recent past as they exist in the present. They approach their material through a series of overt, embodied practices aimed at detailing the dynamic production of matter, its 'performativity', rather than simply decoding its meaning. They tell stories *through* material culture rather than reducing the material to an illustrative or explicative function. In this way, too, these archaeologies give voice not only to people who are silenced, but to material culture itself. This was one of Pearson and Shanks' arguments in *Theatre/Archaeology* (2001) and it is the contemporary attempts by archaeologists to write *in proximity* of matter that suggests for me an important relationship between archaeological practice and 'practice-led research'.

Drawing on scholarship in 'tacit' knowledges (see Csikszentmihalyi 1980; Harrison 1978; Schön 1983), practice-led research has been concerned with the production of scholarly knowledges in modes other than archive- and library-based research in the arts and humanities. As more and more professional artists teach and research in the global higher education sector, there has been concern to find ways in which to embrace research-driven creative practice alongside critical-analytical writing. These practices might include directing plays, devising site-specific performances, making video documentaries, designing stage environments, dancing and choreographing, painting, sculpting, writing TV drama scripts — all as formal research practices (Jones, Kershaw, Piccini forthcoming; Piccini 2003a; b).

Archaeologists should find this relevant in that we 'do' a variety of activities within complex ecologies of practice and then have to find ways of describing those practices to take into account both the process and materiality of archaeology (archaeology as the 'stuff' we unearth and archaeology as the 'event' of excavation). Archaeology and creative practice have in common a combination of lab- and field-based practices with material storytelling. We require specialist equipment and expertises, particular environments and audiences. Like other field- and lab-based disciplines we share ethico-philosophical concerns with the ways in which subject and object, self and other, representation and translation have been constructed. For me, Foucault's understanding of discourse as material event informs this relationship: 'eventualization means rediscovering the connections, encounters, supports, blockages, plays of forces, strategies and so on which . . . count . . . as being self-evident, universal and necessary' (Foucault 1981: 6). Archaeology is particularly useful in exposing the experiential gaps between what people may say they do and how they perform. Archaeologists have therefore to pay particular attention to their own writing practices, practices that seek to translate, to transform, the events of archaeology into text. Where archaeologists might all agree that their in-the-field practices are both 'performance', in terms of structured, repeated and often ritual acts (Schechner 1985), and 'performative', in the sense of speech acts (Austin 1962; Derrida 1988; Butler 1990) it is less common for archaeologists to consider writing as performative, material event.

While Gavin Lucas writes of archaeological writing as a process of translation, a 'double materialisation' (2004: 117), it is perhaps more helpful to think about writing as one material practice in a symmetrical relationship with the other material practices and outcomes of archaeology. Instead of framing our practices as translation from one language into another we might consider instead the potential for writing, talking, photographing, drawing in proximity to the archaeological event. Here in this introduction we wanted to preserve our distinct voices to indicate that both the on/in-the-ground practices of archaeology and its subsequent transformations are part of a community of practice. We wished to preserve something of the dialogical nature of our own research practices involved in producing this book, to explore how this process mirrors the archaeological 'working out' from material remains. On the one hand this conversational structure may seem overly informal. However, we felt strongly that we did not wish to erase the differences between us in tone, language and practice. Whether this interest in relationality is traced specifically to Wittgenstein (Pleasants 1999), to Benjamin's radical particularities of historical materialism (1970), to Foucault's genealogies of materialised knowledge / power or to the processes by which 'the relations of the outside [are] folded back to create a doubling, allow[ing] a relation to oneself to emerge' (Deleuze 1988: 100), it suggests a commitment to resisting a narrative drive that would result in setting up a 'contemporary archaeology' to sit alongside 'the Neolithic' or 'the Iron Age'. By maintaining those spaces between us, as editors we hope to keep alive the sense of archaeology as event, as potential.

Cornelius: I agree that in this book we are not necessarily trying to promote a new period specialisation. You are right when you imply that, in a way, all archaeologies are contemporary archaeologies. Although archaeologists can do work *about* other periods they cannot work *in* other periods. As Gavin Lucas put it: 'Prehistoric artefacts are contemporary objects, as much as the latest Nokia cell phone or BMW' (2004: 117). That is a truism. Yet, there are not that many studies that take archaeology seriously as a phenomenon of our own present. Among those few that exist, some focus on archaeology as a distinctive field with its own topics, traditions, and techniques (e.g. Edgeworth 2003, 2006; Holtorf 2005; McGuire and Shanks 1996; Thomas 2004). Others focus on the way archaeology is implicated in the politics of the past in the present (e.g. Gathercole and Lowenthal, 1994; Graves-Brown, Jones and Gamble, 1996).

Angela: In this way archaeology is both a craft (McGuire and Shanks 1996) and a powerful narrative in a global politics of power, domination and resistance. What it can never be is a window into another time or mindset. Yet many of us still operate as though there were an indexical link between artefact and the past. We all too often work through an assumption that artefacts serve as indexes of past events — that they can somehow stand in for events. Through archaeological practices that focus on the remains of the contemporary past the argument that all archaeology only ever exists in the lived moment is powerfully made. It perhaps also suggests that archaeology is as much a spatio-temporal philosophy of matter as it is a science. Archaeology makes us think and behave differently; the archaeology of the contemporary teaches us that that difference is not generated by the innate otherness of the remains of past human activity, but in the performativity of material culture itself as it calls out to us for a response.

Cornelius: Absolutely! Archaeology can never escape from the present. Instead, archaeology reveals what the present quite literally consists of. The existence of archaeology in turn is a direct consequence of that composition of the present (Russell 2002; Thomas 2004). Vice versa, it is impossible to understand the contemporary Western world without coming to terms with the existence and widespread popularity of archaeology today. Among the things most characteristic for the contemporary world must be its preoccupation with the past (Holtorf 2005; 2007). These are some paradoxes this book is about.

Figure 1: The Annual Dig of the Institute of Contemporary Archaeology, February 1966. Courtesy of Boyle Family

The Institute of Contemporary Archaeology

The Institute of Contemporary Archaeology was founded in 1966 by artists Joan Hills and Mark Boyle, otherwise known for taking random samples of places anywhere on earth. In a telegram to Mike Jeffries, sent in August 1967, Boyle explained the idea behind their work and the 'Institute' (all quotes from *www.boyle family.co.uk*):

THE INSTITUTE OF CONTEMPORARY ARCHAEOLOGY AND THE RANDOM SAMPLES WE TAKE OF OUR ENVIRONMENT ARE DEVICES TO EXPAND OUR ABILITY TO ABSORB BECOMING INCREASINGLY UNNECESSARY UNTIL IF WE'VE THE CAPACITY WE BECOME ONLY SENSITIVE BEINGS TOTALLY PERMANENTLY OPEN TO EVERYTHING ... DISCOVERING JUST HOW MUCH REALITY HUMAN KIND CAN BEAR = MARK BOYLE =

Whereas even contemporary archaeologies may be struggling with these rather grand aims, in practice the activities of the 'Institute' were considerably more down to earth. In a letter from October 1977, Mark Boyle remembered what happened:

In February 1966 we sent our invitations asking people to attend the Annual 'Dig' of the Institute of Contemporary Archaeology. They were to assemble on the steps of the ICA in Dover Street one Sunday morning. (...) We piled them all into trucks and cars and drove them off to a demolition site in Shepherd's Bush, which I knew was the site of an ornamental garden statue factory that had been burnt down a short time before. We put them to work on the site digging inside a roped-off square. It was rather cold and I was fairly relieved when someone found a statue after about 20 minutes. This galvanised the whole party into activity. Everybody got in then and dug with a will. To avoid police aggravation I had asked friends with film cameras to come, as though it was an episode in a picture that we were shooting. In fact, they had film in their cameras, so the whole piece was recorded. In the course of the afternoon we excavated hundreds of broken statues, moulds and tools from the ornamental garden statue factory. Also we collected a large number of other items, sinks, bottles, cans, a large collection of printing blocks used in advertising the porcelain filters that were apparently made in this factory as well, and a bundle of newspapers circa 1965 that we are only just how beginning to open and separate for examination. The next day a second party worked on a site selected at random in the Watford area. This turned out to be an allotment garden, where we gathered, for example, a string of cans, lampshades and rags used to keep birds off seeds, ornamental iron bedheads used for training climbing plants, a more traditional scarecrow, tins of sea-shells, broken tools, and so on. Both collections were later exhibited.

At the time, Boyle found it necessary to take the additional precaution against unwelcome questioning by carrying a spurious letter from the Institute of Contemporary Archaeology authorising him to clear the site. Today it would seem entirely possible to carry out a similar investigation in earnest. As Boyle Family knew early on, contemporary archaeologies are indeed DEVICES TO EXPAND OUR ABILITY TO ABSORB ... DISCOVERING JUST HOW MUCH REALITY HUMAN KIND CAN BEAR.

Boyle Family's explorations over the past three decades powerfully demonstrate the ways in which contemporary archaeologies provide new ways of experiencing and understanding our built environment. That is, they help us to apprehend everyday realities that we are usually expert at ignoring. Their work brings us face to face with both the conditions and the limits of reality.

Cornelius and Angela: One of us — we cannot quite remember who — came up with the sentence that made it into all our project descriptions: contemporary archaeologies marry archaeology *in* the modern world with the archaeology *of* the modern world. We like to think of it as an arranged marriage. We can see the economic sense of this coupling, but it is not an essential link, borne out of romantic love. It requires work to keep both partners in sight and on site, each contributing 100% to the union. This is an interesting perspective for our project here. Each author in this volume was instructed to present not only their research on an aspect *of* the contemporary world but, while doing so, also to reveal something about archaeology *in* the contemporary world.

Julian Thomas meditates on archaeology *qua* archaeology to explore its genealogy in the context of modernity. He traces the significance of archaeology — specifically the depth metaphor — in the work of Sigmund Freud, which leads him to a critique of the 'essentialist' conception of archaeology in search of hidden, primordial truths.

Cornelius Holtorf looks at representations of archaeology and the archaeological past in theme parks and other themed environments in the Western world. He discusses some of the characteristics of the contemporary 'Experience Society' while at the same time he considers the implications of the popularity of archaeological themes for the role that archaeology plays, and maybe should play in society.

Sarah May writes about the material culture of tigers — in zoos, in performance and as pets — and in so doing not only sheds light on the potential for archaeologies of human/animal interaction but also asks whether archaeologists are effectively domesticating and thus trivialising the past by caring for it.

Mike Pearson explores the freeze-dried remains of British Antarctic expeditions. He points to the various ways of interpreting archaeological remains and considers how a building that has often shifted use and meaning can be recreated without losing that sense of fluidity and movement. In so doing he asks how a range of performance practices might activate all the non-discursive, inarticulate, delinquent and disregarded elements of the history of a given site.

Colleen Beck, John Schofield and Harold Drollinger give an account of their work documenting the Peace Camp near the site in Nevada where the US tested nuclear weapons during the Cold War period. This is as much an account of a previously neglected site of political controversy as it is a case-study illustrating the complexities of an archaeological project that has to negotiate multiple interests including those of their peers, the local native population, the government and the people whose remains are being studied.

Louise K Wilson discusses her own creative practice in the military landscape of Orford Ness, which suggests exciting possibilities of documenting corporeal memories and sensory accounts of the built environment beyond text-based interpretation. For Wilson 'there was a desire to make audible what is absent or intangible or cannot be said' (this volume, p. 118), where the transient sonic residues that litter the site are given materiality via electronic manipulation.

Mats Burström writes about industrialised car production and discard in contemporary Sweden, which sheds light on the complicated administrative process of validating heritage and the powerful existential dimension that remains from the past can exert on human beings.

Jonna Ulin illuminates aspects of Swedish domestic life in the early twentieth century, while her methods raise fascinating questions about archaeology as embodied and embodying practice. How does one explore archaeologically the emotional landscapes contained in one's own body? How might the specific sensibilities and ways of writing inform archaeological practice more generally?

Alice Gorman provides a fascinating account of the material relationships between the 'Space Race' and global telecommunications. At the same time she illuminates the potential for archaeology to disrupt 'official' histories by focussing on the relations between science and technology of the Western states and indigenous populations in areas of the world that seem remote from Europe and North America but were central to space exploration.

Angela Piccini discusses her observations while walking, with a video camera, along a street gutter in Bristol. On one level the paper is about the way in which an archaeological focus on material remains effortlessly evokes social and historical issues of global significance. But it also engages with the potential of media to articulate academic research in ways that both nod towards conventional methods of archaeological recording and trouble our easy acceptance of record as documented event.

Paul Graves-Brown contributes to our understanding of the contemporary significance of 'privacy' by focussing on homes and means of transport through time, effectively asking about archaeology's potential to reveal long-term processes.

These unions produce something far greater than the sum of their parts. In the future, an archaeology of the present and archaeology in the present may come to love each other even more than perhaps they do now.

Angela: This may be a good point to talk a little more about how this book originated. Although both of us have been working on aspects of contemporary archaeology for some time, we were inspired to bring together writers and practitioners in this area following the inaugural CHAT (Contemporary and Historical Archaeology in Theory) conference in 2003 and follow-on session at the December 2003 TAG (Theoretical Archaeology Group) conference. I might locate the origins of CHAT in conversations that I was having with Dan Hicks at the time about the need to disrupt the constructed boundaries between medieval, post-medieval, historical, industrial and contemporary archaeologies — what Gavin Lucas considers to be the 'ontological' historic period (2004: 110). That is to say, not the 'historic' as closely defined by archaeologists working either in the US or in the UK, but 'historic' in its performative connotations as that which occurs through the writing of history and historiography.

Hicks, who was himself working on archaeologies of the Atlantic world (2002; 2005), identified the exciting potential for archaeologists working in a range of historic-contemporary areas to come together to build intellectual partnerships. Despite recognising the fact that use of the word 'contemporary' alongside 'historical' reified that split, suggesting that there is a locatable past that is different from now, he and I decided to retain its use partly due to our desire to have an easy, friendly-sounding acronym. More significantly, CHAT was a way to draw together all of those archaeologies of the recent and not-so-recent past with research into archaeology as contemporary practice. A more serious point was our attempt to locate contemporary archaeology within the mainstream of historical archaeology.

I was involved as a co-founder of CHAT due to my own awkward positioning halfway between departments of Archaeology and Theatre, Film and Television — a location due as much to accident as design. Teaching into Bristol University's Archaeology for Screen Media masters course built upon my earlier research into mediatised archaeologies (TV, museums, souvenirs, curricula) as performative of multiple, contemporary group identities (Gruffudd et al 1999; Piccini 1999). This was, in turn, informed by Julian Thomas's (in)famous 1993 TAG session 'Performing Places' (participants included David Austin, Mark Edmonds, Clifford McLucas, Mike Pearson, Heike Roms and Michael Shanks), and the evening's Brith Gof performance. My 'official' job exploring practice-led research later contributed to a growing concern with how various creative practices apprehend the materialities of the contemporary world in distinctively archaeological ways.

The first CHAT conference was a huge success, with over 100 international delegates — academic and professional, historic and contemporary, student and teacher — all of whom felt challenged and inspired by the range of ideas and approaches and the avowedly 'democratic' approach to participation (see McAtackney, Palus and Piccini 2007). Subsequent CHAT conferences were hosted in Leicester (2004), Dublin (2005), Bristol (2006) and Sheffield (2007).

Cornelius: Angela and I had this volume already in mind while we were co-organising the TAG session in 2003. To see this project through to publication was, however, not easy. The academic book market is highly competitive and in constant flux on a global level: at different points in time we were expecting this volume to be published by four different publishers based in three different countries. What is more, contemporary archaeologies are — as we have indicated earlier — a field at the interface of several disciplines including archaeology, history, anthropology and material culture studies. Scholars feel protective about defending the boundaries of their fields and inclined to keep off intruders. They also have directly contradicting views on which papers may or may not make worthwhile contributions, especially when their authors address somewhat unusual topics or use creative writing styles, as many of the papers in this book do. Eventually we found a home for this project at Peter Lang. Thanks to a generous subsidy by English Heritage the book is published at a price that will hopefully make it affordable to readers at all academic ages and in all forms of employment (or lack thereof).

Some of our authors are part of the CHAT movement whereas others have been recruited elsewhere. However, we are all united in our belief that contemporary archaeologies are one of the most exciting fields of archaeological research right now. And all the chapters in this book demonstrate the intellectual excitement and the variety in research interests, approaches and presentation formats that characterise the field.

Of course this book is not the first archaeological perspective on the recent past and the present. The single most important bibliographic ancestor of the field, though still very much alive today, has got to be Victor Buchli and Gavin Lucas' edited volume *Archaeologies of the Contemporary Past* from 2001 — not older than that. Another topical volume is Paul Graves-Brown's edited volume on *Matter, Materiality and Modern Culture* (2000), which inhabits an intermediate space between contemporary archaeologies on the one hand and anthropological and philosophical material culture studies on the other. There is also an older tradition of 'modern material culture studies', including

Rathje's classic Garbage project and various ethno-archaeological studies that have been conducted in the past decades (Gould and Schiffer 1981; cf. Buchli and Lucas 2001b: 3-8). In large parts, these studies were, however, conducted mainly in order to inform 'proper' archaeology concerned with gaining knowledge about periods much longer ago. A useful overview of all the various academic lineages in the field is now available in a Swedish book that also makes an original contribution to the field itself (Burström 2007).

Angela: I suggest that we also owe much to what might be referred to as the transdisciplinary field of contemporary material culture studies pioneered by such figures as Arjun Appadurai and Daniel Miller. 'Stuff' is not merely by-product, not merely expressive of culture, but is actively constitutive of social life. We live our lives materially: matter is performative in that it produces the terms by which we engage with it and use it to perform social relations. If all things that we term past can only be named because they exist in some way right now, so too is nothing ever really 'new'. It is therefore worth citing early attempts to re-think 'history' from a material culture perspective: in William Rathje's 'Garbology' project operating out of the University of Arizona since the 1970s; in Mike Parker Pearson's ethnoarchaeology of twentieth-century British mortuary practices (1982); in Michael Shanks' and Christopher Tilley's work on the semiotics of Swedish beer cans (1987); and in Julian Thomas's and Mike Pearson's initial articulations of 'Theatre/Archaeology' (1994). While they may not all employ the archaeological toolkit in the way in which we discussed above, their work has inspired useful questioning of disciplinary boundaries and of spatial and temporal distinctions.

Cornelius: You are right, of course, Angela! In fact your comments made me re-read Gould and Schiffer's *Modern Material Culture: The Archaeology of Us* (1981). I was actually surprised by the quality of the papers, especially those about contemporary America. Quite a few contributions in that volume demonstrate not only an amazing creativity and academic courage but also a degree of methodological sophistication that probably has not been surpassed since then. It is quite wonderful to read there in considerable detail, for example, about fences around houses in Mormon communities; about the function and meaning of pennies in Denver; and about the material culture of a modern supermarket.

Angela: Yet, I would agree with you that those self-confident archaeologies in and of the contemporary really only gain currency at the turn of this present century. While on the European side of the Atlantic we may feel that our North American colleagues have been doing contemporary archaeology longer than we have, what we share is the constant call for us to justify this as archaeology. From a focus on the history of a contemporary archaeological sensibility (Schmidt 2001; Thomas 2004) to the popularity of residue in the contemporary urban landscape (Alexander 2000; Edensor 2005; Lucas 2002; Platt 2005) archaeologists have sought to demarcate an intellectual territory that is differentiated from material culture studies *per se* through a focus on method.

Cornelius: As I see it, archaeologies of the contemporary world have thus far tended to follow one of a few overlapping strands — or maybe these are the roots from which the field has been growing most vigorously. The present volume makes at least a minor contribution to each of these existing lines of discussions.

One strand has been industrial archaeology, which, since its origins in the 1960s, has established itself as a field concerned with valuing the remains of the industrial age, including machines, means and systems of transport, factories and mines. In recent years, that research has even embraced twentieth-century industrial architecture and associated sites (Stratton and Trinder 2000; Symonds and Casella 2006).

Another focus has been the attempts by various national heritage authorities to determine which of the numerous sites and monuments of the twentieth and indeed twenty-first centuries ought to be managed and preserved as heritage for the future (Schofield and Johnson 2006; Schmidt and von Preuschen 2005). By now, even recently closed nuclear power stations such as Barsebäck in southern Sweden are considered by some as worthy of preservation for the benefit of future generations.

Recently, twentieth-century conflict and military sites have been catching the particular attention of archaeologists and heritage managers. That is a third line of enquiry within current archaeologies of the contemporary world. These sites include anything from concrete bunkers throughout Europe to the missile test site in Nevada (see also Beck et al, this volume), from Japanese military headquarters of the 1940s to the Berlin Wall before 1989, and from battle fields of World War I to mass graves of genocide in Cambodia. Sites such as these are increasingly the object of archaeological fieldwork concerned with identifying, investigating, recording, and preserving remains (Schofield et al 2002; Schofield 2005a; Schofield et al 2006; Schofield and Cocroft 2007).

Finally, archaeologists have been studying a wide range of other distinctive twentieth-century sites and artefacts using them as original historical sources that throw new light on topics also studied by historians, geographers and others. Some examples of this broad trend are contained in many of the edited volumes already referred to, but especially in those edited by Gould and Schiffer (1981) and Buchli and Lucas (2001a). However, there are many other stimulating new studies investigating, among other original topics,

- zoos (Holtorf 2008)
- football courts (Karlsson 2004)
- 1950s–70s youth culture (Schofield 2000)
- car cemeteries (Burström this volume)
- 1990s road protests (Schofield 2005b)
- a transit van (Newland et al 2007)
- robot heritage (Spennemann 2007)
- space exploration (Gorman 2005).

Angela: From the examples above there appears a narrative of loss, the sense in which as sites and landscapes disappear, they call out for preservation. There is clearly something in the relationship between trauma, nostalgia, melancholy and loss that captures archaeological imaginations. The current interest in late industrial landscapes, the structures of the Cold War, the archaeologies of the motorway all seek to employ archaeology to understand the more painful sites of the twentieth and early twenty-first centuries. Of course, such sites hold fascination for a range of scholars across disciplines. In the UK, the major funding body for the arts and humanities recently launched its Landscape and Environment strand. Among the many projects funded that explore contemporary landscapes, historians Peter Coates and Tim Cole are leading research into militarised landscapes of twentieth-century Europe, with a specific focus on human and non-human activity.

Problematically in this context, no one can do this sort of archaeology now without also referencing the World Trade Centre events of 2001. Shanks, Platt and Rathje (2004) opened this out as an intellectual debate for archaeologists. The events of 11 September 2001 have generated a number of archaeological responses. At CHAT 2005, Charles Orser questioned some archaeologists' tendencies to accept US 9/11 ideology and over-determine the cultural impact of the bombing and the deaths of nearly 3,000 people. Yet, surely the point is that the cultural impact of those events rather than the raw fatality numbers — of course grotesquely overshadowed by the numbers of civilians and military personnel killed as a result of ongoing US/UK-led military activities — has opened up archaeological practices. As Shanks, Platt and Rathje suggest, around Ground Zero are coalesced archaeology's various concerns: conservation, garbage, classification, composition and decomposition (2004). Archaeology is ever more clearly a way of negotiating loss due to the affective power of the material trace recognisable as haunting (Stewart, 1993) and enchantment (Bennett, 2001). Through preservation and conservation, through its practice, archaeology constantly reminds us of everything that is in excess of that endeavour. Archaeology holds in tension the dyadic relationship between loss and preservation, remembering and forgetting, and is thus sustained.

Cornelius: Ground Zero obviously still catches the public imagination. Intriguingly, many of the new studies into our contemporary pasts engage with themes that are widely appreciated and appear to be very popular indeed. As John Schofield (2000: 139) pointed out, Jim Morrison's grave at Père Lachaise cemetery attracts more visitors and flowers than the Mur des Fédérés where the martyred dead of the Paris commune are buried. In Berlin, the exhibition *Topography of Terror*, incorporating some original remains of buildings used by Gestapo and SS has been extremely popular ever since it opened in 1987 (*www.topographie.de*). Elsewhere, TV programmes like Discovery Channel's *Finding the Fallen* (2005) about archaeological research on the battle fields of the First World War, Five's (UK) excavation of a World War 2 plane on *Fighter Plane Dig: Live!* (2003) and the Swedish series *Utgrävarna* (Excavators) about archaeological investigations at ten sites associated with twentieth-century Swedish history have been popular too (Burström 2007: 21–24).

Having said that, one of the problems of some archaeologies of the contemporary world is that they are largely limiting themselves to being concerned with conservation issues, i.e. the identification, study and scheduling of recent sites. Ever more kinds of sites, ever closer to our own present, are being suggested as urgently requiring research and protection. Yet this desire to conserve needs in itself to be seen in the context of a contemporary preoccupation with (safe-guarding) the past. It is, however, an entirely open question whether future generations will in fact benefit from the twentieth- and twenty-first-century sites many archaeologists are so eager to protect for them. What kinds of historical consciousness and memorial practices will it take to render our buildings and battlefields meaningful for them? How certain can anybody be that such sites will remind people living in the twenty-second century of something other than merely our own obsession with conservation and heritage? What options do we preclude by leaving an extensive material heritage (at considerable cost) rather than leaving absences, gaps, holes, or constructing new buildings as it suits us best? What benefits might be gained from destroying (forgetting, not preserving) parts of the heritage? Such questions, although elementary, are seldom asked (but see Huyssen, 1995; Holtorf 2006; González-Ruibal 2008).

In an excellent essay, Zoë Crossland (2002) has done contemporary archaeologies a great favour by problematising archaeological excavations and the preservation of heritage. She contrasted two very different strategies as to what to do regarding the physical remains of those who 'disappeared' during the Argentinean military dictatorship in between 1976 and 1983. Whereas some people involved have been advocating the excavation of the unmarked graves to provide closure for themselves and as forensic evidence in trials against those responsible, some of the mothers and relatives of the disappeared have been opposing these excavations. Their arguments are interesting. They prefer to remember their loved ones as living individuals rather than as dead bodies. They prefer to maintain public absences rather than allow excavated physical remains to reside in tightly enclosed spaces. Arguably, filling such spaces, now empty, with the bones of the deceased, gained from formalised excavations to be drawn on in the law courts, reproduces the structures of institutionalised power that created the absences in the first place. The question raised is ultimately whether maybe some historical events or processes might be remembered better through the absence of material remains than through their presence. Arguably, the cultural memory of apartheid, genocide and possible nuclear devastation ought to be based on a notion of huge absences and not on some poorly preserved remote sites and rusty artefacts. In this sense, less (preservation) could be more (memory).

Angela: Your point about memory and its complex relationship to materiality is particularly salient, Cornelius. Paradoxically perhaps, these very real and pressing issues of archaeological ethics bring me back to questions of creative practice, touched on above. That sense of archaeology as creative cultural production (Joyce 2002) reminds me of another major strand within contemporary archaeologies: the long-standing links between archaeologists and the creative and performing arts. There is a significant literature around the use of archaeological themes, materials and landscapes by artists that is beyond the scope of our introduction (eg., Ackling, 1991; Jameson, Ehrenhard, Finn, 2003; Renfrew, 2003; Schofield, 2006). However, you have suggested, Cornelius, that a significant difference between artistic and archaeological approaches to material residue and taxonomy is that artists working with archaeological themes and material tend to focus on collecting 'evidence' whereas archaeologists attempt to interpret it (Holtorf 2005: 65–72).

However, I want to suggest that while our expressive modes may differ we must be wary of locating interpretation solely within conventional publication. I thus return to the issue of practice-led research. While creative practices may not 'interpret' through critical-analytic writing, these acts of collecting are performative in that art as materialised cultural discourse is already understood to be a critical apprehension of the world. We 'know' the difference between artist Mark Dion's *Tate Thames Dig* (1999) and undigested finds. As supplementary praxes (Smiles 2004, following Derrida), archaeology and the creative and performing arts look to detail, the everyday, the castaway to materialise discursive realities that intervene in the continuing textual economies of power. So, in fact, the creative use of archaeological practice interrupts our archaeological belief in the distinction between 'neutral' data sets and their interpretation. These practices question regimes of conservation, the production of official knowledges and spaces. Following Hamilakis, both archaeologists and artists 'select and valorise, but also ignore and destroy; they produce material realities' (2004: 56).

Thus, it is not simply the case that artists exist in some kind of parasitical relationship with archaeologists. For me the supplementary relationship between the arts and archaeology is evidenced, too, by the personal relationships enjoyed between archaeologists and artists. This of course stretches back to the earliest antiquarian endeavours accompanied by sketches and continues through to the interwar relationships between Stuart Piggott, Jacquetta Hawkes, O. G. S. Crawford and Cyril Fox and neo-Romantic British artists such as Paul Nash and Alan Sorrell (Mellor 1987). Contemporary personal relationships between archaeologists and artists are numerous — including the collaborations between Michael Shanks and Mike Pearson, English Heritage's support for artists such as Louise K Wilson, and the contributions of archaeologists to contemporary arts events.

Angela and Cornelius: Our exploration of archaeological practices through case studies in contemporary material relations positions this book as a reflexive account of archaeologists as material cultural producers who investigate material cultural production. We argue on two parallel tracks, through three sections. Each chapter develops one case study as a contribution to an archaeology of the modern world, and through that case study develops a creative and critical argument about one key aspect of archaeology in the modern world.

As Thomas so elegantly demonstrates (this volume, p. 33–36), as a practice originating in and quickly accelerating during the nineteenth century, archaeology is a modern project. Its repertoire of aims, questions, procedures and methodologies as well as terminology, but also its material manifestations (protected sites, public museums, archives, etc) and its popular appeals are specific to modern (mostly) Western societies. We have suggested that contemporary archaeologies marry archaeology *in* the modern world with the archaeology *of* the modern world. As such, their strengths lie in opportunistic excavations of interdisciplinary fields surrounding archaeology, and in a stimulating mix of a range of mixed-mode practices across academic, public sector and cross-art contexts.

By discussing sites of the contemporary world contributors at the same time throw light on some of the foundations on which the discipline of archaeology rests in that world. We seek to demonstrate archaeology's entanglements in the modern world and to analyse the multiple ways in which archaeological practice is engaged with aspects of contemporary, modern life. If archaeology is always-already contemporary, of the present, then we cannot get away from the fact that archaeological practice is affected by and affects contemporary lives. There are ramifications for which we need to take responsibility. Our archaeological toolkit literally manipulates our world in ways that we cannot predict. In this way we perhaps approach the radical utopianism of the injunction to 'Try again. Fail again. Fail better' (Beckett 1995). What contemporary archaeologies produce is an understanding that while lived experience always exceeds its material records and while archaeology will always 'fail' to *reveal* the past, the performative power of material culture and the built environment is such that archaeologists are driven always and more creatively to try again.

Bibliography

Ackling, R (1991) *From Art to Archaeology*, London: South Bank Centre

Alexander, C (2000) 'The factory: fabricating the State' *Journal of Material Culture* 5 (2): 177–95.

Austin, J L (1962) *How to Do Things With Words*, Oxford: Clarendon Press.

Badiou, A (2005) *Handbook of Inaesthetics*, Stanford: Stanford University Press.

Beckett, S (1995) *Nohow On: Company, Ill Seen Ill Said, Worstward Ho*, New York: Grove Press.

Benjamin, W (1970) 'Theses on the philosophy of history', in *Illuminations*, London: Jonathan Cape, 255–66.

Bennett, J (2001) *The Enchantment of Modern Life: Attachments, Crossings and Ethics*, Princeton, N J: Princeton University Press.

Buchli, V (1999) *An Archaeology of Socialism: the Narcomfin Communal House*, Oxford: Berg.

Buchli, V and Lucas, G (eds) (2001a) *Archaeologies of the Contemporary Past*, London and New York: Routledge.

Buchli, V and Lucas, G (2001b) 'The absent present: archaeologies of the contemporary past', in Buchli, V and Lucas, G (eds), *Archaeologies of the Contemporary Past*, London and New York: Routledge, 3–18.

Burström, M (2007) *Samtidsarkeologi. Introduktion till ett forskningsfält*, Lund: Studentlitteratur.

Butler, J (1990) *Gender Trouble: Feminism and the Subversion of Identity*, London: Routledge.

Casella, E C (2005) 'The excavation of industrial era settlements in north-west England' *Industrial Archaeology Review* 27 (1): 77–86.

Cox, M (2001) 'Forensic archaeology: questions of socio-intellectual context and socio-political responsibility', in Buchli, V and Lucas, G (eds), *Archaeologies of the Contemporary Past,* London and New York: Routledge, 145–57.

Crossland, Z (2002) 'Violent spaces: conflict over the reappearance of Argentina's disappeared', in Schofield, J, Johnson W G and Beck, C M (eds), *Matériel Culture: the Archaeology of 20th-Century Conflict*, London: Routledge, 115–31.

Csikszentmihalyi, M (1990) 'Society, culture and person: a systems view of creativity', in Sternberg, R J (ed.), *The Nature of Creativity: Contemporary Psychological Perspectives*, Cambridge: Cambridge University Press, 325–39.

Deleuze, G (1988) *Foucault*, London: Athlone.

Derrida, J (1988) *Limited Inc.*, Evanston: Northwestern University Press.

Dion, M (1999) *Tate Thames Dig*, London, Tate Modern Gallery.

Edensor, T (2005) 'Waste matter: the debris of industrial ruins and the disordering of the material world' *Journal of Material Culture* 10 (3): 311–32.

Edgeworth, M (2003) *Acts of Discovery: an Ethnography of Archaeological Practice*, BAR Int. Ser. 1131, Oxford: Archaeopress.

Edgeworth, M (ed.) (2006) *Ethnographies of Archaeologies' Practice: Cultural Encounters, Material Transformations*, Lanham: Altamira.

Finn, C (2005) 'A life on line: Jacquetta Hawkes, archaeo-poet (1910–1996)', http://humanitieslab.stanford.edu/ChristineFinn/Home (01.11.2007).

Foucault, M (1981) 'Questions of method' *Ideology and Consciousness* 8: 3–14.

Gathercole, P and Lowenthal D (eds) (1994) *The Politics of the Past*, London and New York: Routledge.

González-Ruibal, A (2008) 'Time to destroy. An archaeology of supermodernity' *Current Anthropology* 49 (2).

Gorman, A (2005) 'The cultural landscape of interplanetary space' *Journal of Social Archaeology* 5(1): 85–107.'

Gould, R and Schiffer, M B (eds) (1981) *Modern Material Culture Studies: the Archaeology of Us,* New York: Academic Press.

Graves-Brown, P, Jones, S and Gamble, C (eds) (1996) *Cultural Identity and Archaeology: the Construction of European Communities,* London: Routledge.

Graves-Brown, P (ed.) (2000) *Matter, Materiality and Modern Culture*, London and New York: Routledge.

Gruffudd, P, Herbert, D and Piccini, A (1999) '"Good to think": social constructions of Celtic heritage in Wales' *Environment and Planning 'D': Society and Space* 17 (6): 705–21.

Hamilakis, Y (2004) 'The fragments of modernity and the archaeologies of the future' *MODERNISM/modernity* 11 (1): 55–59.

Harrison, A (1978) *Making and Thinking: a Study of Intelligent Activities,* Hassocks: Harvesters Press.

Hicks, D (2002) *'The Garden of the World': a Historical Archaeology of Eastern Caribbean Sugar Plantations, AD 1600–2000,* unpublished PhD thesis, University of Bristol.

Hicks, D (2003) 'Archaeology unfolding: diversity and the loss of isolation' *Oxford Journal of Archaeology* 22: 315–29.

Hicks, D (2005) 'Places for Thinking' from Annapolis to Bristol: Situations and Symmetries in "World Historical Archaeologies"' *World Archaeology* 37 (3): 373–91.

Holtorf, C (2005) *From Stonehenge to Las Vegas: Archaeology as Popular Culture,* Lanham: Altamira.

Holtorf, C (2006) 'Can less be more? Heritage in the age of terrorism' *Public Archaeology* 5: 101–09.

Holtorf, C (2007) *Archaeology is a Brand! The Meaning of Archaeology in Contemporary Popular Culture,* Oxford: Archaeopress.

Holtorf, C (ed.) (2008) 'Zoos as heritage' special issue *International Journal of Heritage Studies* 14.

Huyssen, A (1995) *Twilight Memories: Marking Time in a Culture of Amnesia,* London: Routledge.

Jameson, J H Jnr, Ehrenhard, J E and Finn, C A (eds) (2003) *Ancient Muses: Archaeology and the Arts,* Tuscalooosa and London: University of Alabama Press.

Jones, S, Kershaw, B and Piccini, A (eds) (forthcoming) *Practice-as-Research: in Performance and Screen Media,* London: Palgrave-Macmillan.

Joyce, R (2002) *The Languages of Archaeology: Dialogue, Narrative and Writing,* Oxford: Blackwell.

Juster, N (1961) *The Phantom Tollbooth,* New York: Bullseye Books.

Karlsson, H (2004) *Försummat Kulturarv. Det Närliggande Förflutna och Fotbollens Plaster,* Lindome: Bricoleur.

Lucas, G (2002) 'Disposability and dispossession in the twentieth century' *Journal of Material Culture* 7 (1): 5–22.

Lucas, G (2004) 'Modern disturbances: on the ambiguities of archaeology' *MODERNISM/modernity* 11 (1): 109–20.

Lucas, G (2005) *The Archaeology of Time,* London and New York: Routledge.

McAtackney, L, Palus, M and Piccini, A (eds) (2007) *Contemporary and Historical Archaeology in Theory,* B.A.R International Series 1677, Oxford: Archaeopress.

McGuire, R H and Shanks, M (1996) 'The craft of archaeology', *American Antiquity* 61: 75–88.

Mellor, D (1987) *A Paradise Lost: The Neo-Romantic Visual Imagination in Britain, 1935–1955,* London: Lund Humphries.

Newland, C, Bailey, G, Schofield J and Nilsson, A (2007) 'Sic Transit Gloria Mundi' *British Archaeology* issue 92 (Jan/Feb 2007), 16–21. Also available at http://www.britarch.ac.uk/ba/ba92/feat2.shtml (18.10.2007).

Parker Pearson, M (1982) 'Mortuary practices, society and archaeology: an ethnoarchaeological study', in Hodder, I (ed.), *Symbolic and Structural Archaeology,* Cambridge: Cambridge University Press, 99–112.

Pearson, M and Thomas, J (1994) 'Theatre/Archaeology' *The Drama Review* 38: 133–61.

Pearson, M and Shanks, M (2001) *Theatre/Archaeology,* London and New York: Routledge.

Piccini, A (1999) *Celtic Constructs: Heritage Media, Archaeological Knowledge and the Politics of Consumption in 1990s Britain,* unpublished PhD thesis, University of Sheffield.

Piccini, A (2003a) 'An historiographic perspective on practice as research' *Studies in Theatre and Performance* 23 (3): 191–207.

Piccini, A (2003b) 'Practising the RAE: the performance of research assessment', http://www.bris.ac.uk/parip/piccini.htm (01.11.2007).

Platt, D (2005) 'Where London stood', http://traumwerk.stanford.edu:3455/71/Home (01.11.2007).

Pleasants, N (1999) *Wittgenstein and the Idea of a Critical Social Theory: a Critique of Giddens, Habermas and Bhaskar,* London: Routledge.

Rathje, W (2001) 'Integrated archaeology: a garbage paradigm', in Buchli, V and Lucas, G (eds), *Archaeologies of the Contemporary Past,* London and New York: Routledge, 63–76.

Renfrew, C (2003) *Figuring it Out,* London: Thames and Hudson.

Russell, M (ed.) (2002) *Digging Holes in Popular Culture. Archaeology and Science Fiction,* Oxford and Oakville: Oxbow / The David Brown Book Company.

Saunders, N J (2000) 'Bodies of metal, shells of memory: "Trench Art", and the Great War re-cycled' *Journal of Material Culture* 5 (1): 43–67.

Schechner, R (1985) *Between Theater and Anthropology,* Philadelphia: University of Pennsylvania Press.

Schmidt, D (2001) 'Refuse archaeology: Virchow – Schliemann – Freud' *Perspectives on Science* 9 (2): 210–32.

Schmidt, L and H von Preuschen (2005) *On Both Sides of the Wall. Preserving Monuments and Sites of the Cold War Era,* Berlin and Bonn: Westkreuz.

Schnapp, J, Shanks, M and Tiews, M (2004) 'Archaeology, Modernism, Modernity' *MODERNISM/modernity* 11 (1): 1–16.

Schofield, J (2000) 'Never mind the relevance? Popular culture for archaeologists', in Graves-Brown, P (ed.), *Matter, Materiality and Modern Culture,* London and New York: Routledge, 131–55.

Schofield, J (2005a) *Combat Archaeology: Material Culture and Modern Conflict,* London: Duckworth.

Schofield, J (2005b) 'Discordant landscapes: managing modern heritage at Twyford Down, Hampshire (England)' *International Journal of Heritage Studies* 11: 143–59.

Schofield, J (2006) 'Constructing place: when artists and archaeologists meet' *Diffusion,* http://diffusion.org.uk/?p=98 (1.11.2007)

Schofield, J and Cocroft, W (eds) (2007) *A Fearsome Heritage: Diverse Legacies of the Cold War*, Walnut Creek: Left Coast Press.

Schofield, J and Johnson, W G (2006) 'Archaeology, heritage and the recent and contemporary past', in Hicks, D and Beaudry, M (eds), *The Cambridge Companion to Historical Archaeology*, Cambridge: Cambridge University Press, 104–22.

Schofield, J, Johnson, W G and Beck, C M (eds) (2002) *Matériel Culture: the Archaeology of Twentieth Century Conflict*, London and New York: Routledge.

Schofield, J, Klausmeier, K and Purbrick, L (eds) (2006) *Re-mapping the Field: New Approaches in Conflict Archaeology*, Berlin and Bonn: Westkreuz.

Schön, D A (1983) *The Reflective Practitioner: How Professionals Think in Action*, London: Temple Smith.

Shanks, M, Platt, D and Rathje, W L (2004) 'The perfume of garbage: modernity and the archaeological' *MODERNISM/modernity* 11 (1): 61–83.

Shanks, M and Tilley, C (1987) *Re-constructing Archaeology: Theory and Practice*, Cambridge: Cambridge University Press.

Smiles, S (2004) 'Thomas Guest and Paul Nash in Wiltshire: two episodes in the artistic approach to British Antiquity', in Smiles, S and Moser, S (eds.), *Envisioning the Past: Art and Archaeology*, Oxford: Blackwell, 133–57.

Spennemann, D H R (2007) 'On the Cultural Heritage of Robots', *International Journal of Heritage Studies* 13: 4–21.

Symonds, J and Casella, E C (2006) 'Historical archaeology and industrialisation', in Hicks, D and Beaudry, M (eds), *The Cambridge Companion to Historical Archaeology*, Cambridge: Cambridge University Press, 143–67.

Stewart, S (1993) *On Longing: Narratives of the Miniature, the Gigantic, the Souvenir, the Collection*, Durham: Duke University Press.

Stratton, M and Trinder, B (2000) *Twentieth Century Industrial Archaeology*, London: Spon.

Thomas, J (2004) *Archaeology and Modernity*, London and New York: Routledge.

Wilkie, L (2001) 'Black sharecroppers and white frat boys: living communities and the appropriation of their archaeological pasts', in Buchli, V and Lucas, G (eds), *Archaeologies of the Contemporary Past*, London and New York: Routledge, 108–18.

Part 1: On the character of archaeology/heritage

Sigmund Freud's Archaeological Metaphor and Archaeology's Self-understanding

Julian Thomas

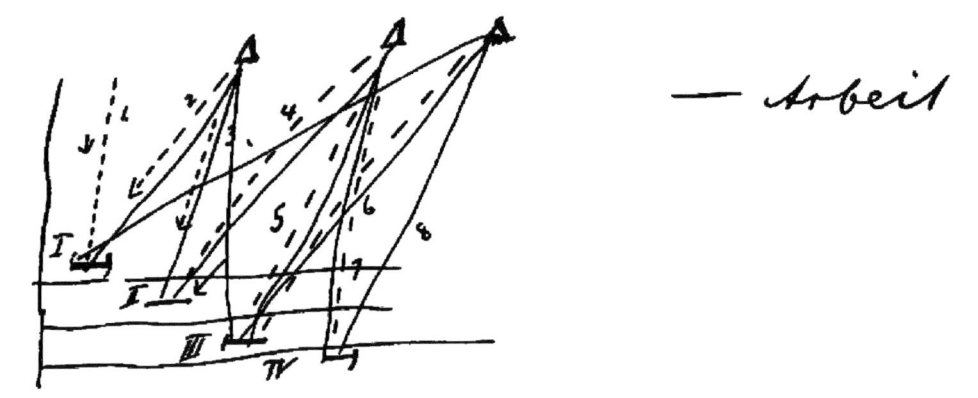

Figure 1.1 Freud's sketch of the analytic work showing penetrations into deeper and deeper layers (Freud 1950: 217). Reproduced with permission.

Introduction: archaeology and the depth metaphor

Archaeology has long been recognised as a product of the modern era, emerging in its antiquarian guise with the Renaissance, and gaining recognition as a scientific discipline at the start of the nineteenth century (Trigger 1989: 27). But it is also arguable that archaeology embodies and condenses the modern condition, and would have been unlikely to develop under other historical circumstances. This is the argument that I develop in *Archaeology and Modernity* (Thomas 2004), and here I will reprise and extend some of the arguments of that book. Archaeology relies upon the distinctively modern understanding that new knowledge can be created from material things, that the past differed in significant ways from the present, and that tradition and myth are not adequate sources of information about the past. In the modern world, the legitimacy of nation-states and their rulers has been vested in accounts of the past substantiated through scholarly inquiry, and archaeology has formed part of the apparatus through which modern states have sought their ancient origins. Furthermore, because it embodies so much of the modern attitude, archaeology is continually drawn on by other discourses as an image or a metaphor. Archaeology encapsulates a series of evocative themes: of repression, of loss and concealment, of discovery and revelation. These share the common element of being understood in spatial terms through the relationship between depth and surface. These preoccupations began to occupy a central place in the Western imagination at the end of the eighteenth century. It was at this point that the atomistic outlook that had been fostered by the Scientific Revolution, in which the things of the world were understood as free-standing, isolated entities that could be ordered on a great classificatory table, began to be eroded by the notion that deeper structures were concealed beneath outward appearances (Foucault 1970). This general shift in modern thought from visible attributes to hidden essences coincided precisely with the transformation of antiquarianism into archaeology.

One source of the growing concern with hidden depths was a changing conception of the person, which increasingly stressed interiority. As far back as St Augustine, it had been argued that introspection provided the most direct route to God, so that a radical reflexivity was promoted, in which the contemplation and experience of the inner self led to the deity (Taylor 1989: 129). By the time of the Council of Trent (1545–63), the institution of the confessional had come to focus on concealed desires and urges rather than sinful acts, indicating that this inner self now needed to be monitored and policed. As Michel Foucault has argued, the therapeutic relationship with the inner person seen in confession is one that would later be picked up and elaborated by psychoanalysis (1978: 20). Increasingly, the inner person was understood as experiencing feelings of turmoil, anxiety, isolation and loneliness resulting from external influences, and requiring a cathartic expression (Jameson 1984: 61). Clearly, this is one of the great themes of modern art and literature, where streams of consciousness and inner monologues create a very different image of the person from that found in, say, pre-modern heroic literature.

From the late eighteenth century onwards scholars in many different fields began to suggest that there were aspects of reality that were not immediately visible, but which served to explain the character of more readily accessible phenomena. As a result, interiority began to be an attribute of the *objects* of knowledge as well as the knowing subject. We can see this development most clearly in the biology of Cuvier, who argued that animals could no longer be classified exclusively according to their outward appearance, but that the internal functions of their bodies, their behaviour, and their habitat had also to be taken into account (Foucault 1979). Turned back onto humanity, this produced a conception of a person who was at once a subject and an object, and who possessed two different kinds of interior. For, although humans were containers of consciousness and reason, they also had a body interior. As Foucault demonstrates, one of the consequences of this reformulation was a shift from a 'nosological' medicine concerned with the classification of symptoms to a renewed interest in pathological anatomy, and the *depths* of the body (1973: 136).

As a representative of the new 'Sciences of Man' that emerged around this time, clinical medicine demonstrated a concern with what Frederic Jameson has called 'depth models', which appear to be characteristic of high modernity (Jameson 1984: 62). Other examples would include Hegel's historical idealism, which suggested that happenings in the world are the manifestation of thoughts in the mind. It is here that we can identify the ultimate origin of Collingwood's distinction between the 'inside' and the 'outside' of events (Collingwood 1946: 297). Similarly, Jameson points to the Marxist distinction between essence and appearance, where the true nature of social reality is obscured by a shell of ideology, which needs to be penetrated by critique. Further candidates are the couplings of latent and manifest, or authentic and superficial: in each case, there is the implication that truth or profundity is deeper than superficial appearances, which may be deceptive. However, the clearest example of the modern conviction that surface conditions are underlain by a more significant reality are the structural linguistics of Ferdinand de Saussure (1959). For structuralism, speech can be observed, but the deep structures of language are hidden and have to be reconstructed from our observations on people's communication. Saussure draws the analogy with watching two people playing a game of chess, in which we can observe the moves that they make, but have to infer the rules of the game which underlie those rules. Importantly, structuralist approaches generally propose that speech is only the momentary expression of a single person, but that language is bound up with the collective consciousness of the group.

These arguments begin to connect more obviously with archaeology when we recognise that the beginnings of this 'structural revolution' in Western thought were absolutely contemporary with the 'stratigraphic revolution' which Glyn Daniel identified in geology and archaeology (1950: 29). For centuries, it had been recognised that distinct layers of rock and soil overlay archaeological sites, but the probability that these had been laid down in an ordered sequence was not fully grasped prior to the publication of James Hutton's *Theory of the Earth* in 1788 and William Smith's *Strata Identified by Organised Fossils* in 1816. These two works laid the foundations for Charles Lyell's uniformitarianism (1830), by demonstrating that geological strata could be the products of forces that could still be observed in the present. These included heat, pressure, and erosion. Moreover, each stratum could be distinguished by the fossils that it contained, which could be presumed to represent organisms which had lived at the time of deposition, and their vertical sequence reflected the temporal changes of depositional environments through time. It seems highly likely that Smith's observations in the canal cuttings were to some extent informed by the more general belief that the forces responsible for the appearance of things could be found below the surface. In this case, scenery and topography were the outcome of geological processes that could be understood through stratigraphy, which opened a window into the distant past. It has been noted that William Smith kept his geological specimens in a cabinet in which separate shelves were assigned to sequential strata (Harris 1989: 3). This would appear to demonstrate that by the start of the nineteenth century, spatial depth had come to be identified with change through time, and that objects could be sorted according to their position within such a spatio-temporal ordering.

In the first instance, the significance of Hutton's and Smith's arguments was that by demonstrating that geological deposits had formed over very long periods of time they indicated that the human remains or stone tools that they sometimes contained were of great antiquity. Consequentially the short chronologies of human existence based upon Biblical scholarship could be contested. But in philosophical terms it is equally important that 'slices' of geological time were now identified as the contexts within which relics of one kind or another might be contained. This is conceptually rather similar to Christian Thomsen's archaeological application of the 'three age system', which was being developed at precisely the same time (Lucas 2001: 75). Hitherto, the notion of mann's discovery of Troy is identified as the paradigm of the fulfilment of a childhood wish, while Freud's own visit to the Acropolis is so desirable as to promote a sense of unreality, a derealization. Arriving in Athens, he experienced an incredulity at the very existence of the ancient structures, so passionate had his desire to travel been during childhood (Freud 1936: 308). The enjoyment both of the Acropolis and of Rome were connected for him with the guilt of having achieved more professionally than his father, who had never had the opportunity to travel abroad. Indeed, he identified in himself a 'Rome neurosis', which involved a recurrent failure to fulfil his 'passionate wishes'. As a Jew, he compared himself to Hannibal, whose own success or failure in life (in comparison to his own father, Hamilcar Barca) was epitomised by the effort to arrive in Rome, the symbol of both the ancient empire and Christian society (Ferris 1997: 147). In both cases (Athens and Rome), the deferral or denial of pleasure is understood as a means of avoiding the guilt and self-evaluation that would attend the enjoyment. Similarly, while Freud did use his collection of antiquities for didactic purposes, the thrill of collecting was singularly important to him, and comparable only with the pleasure of smoking a cigar (which, in turn, he understood in sexual terms). Moreover, his collection began in the 1890s as a source of comfort following his father's death and at a time of professional isolation and rising anti-Semitism in Vienna (Flem 2003: 29). In a sense, Freud's collection mania can be compared with the complex pleasures and consolations that are today found by many in shopping, and yet because the artefacts that he collected were archaeological in character they suggest a kind of pleasure that was never entirely removed from psychological unease. In this respect, his antiquities collection is potentially instructive on a number of levels, from the drive to acquire commodities as a source of ontological security to the nexus of relationships between museums, the authenticity of the past, objectification and shopping arcades.

Depths of the unconscious

Psychoanalysis had its foundation in a reaction against Cartesian thought, which had prioritised consciousness and reason, and sought to speak the unvarnished truth without any recourse to metaphor (Spence 1987: 3). Freud argued that the psychic world of human beings extended beyond consciousness, and indeed that much of what concerns us is unconscious. Therefore, we are never fully aware of the contents of our own minds. Some ideas slip freely from consciousness to the unconscious and back again, but others are held down by the force of repression. It is the notion of repression in particular that suggests a spatial idiom for the expression of these ideas: consciousness is understood as being on the surface, and the unconscious is 'below' or 'inside', while repression restricts the upward movement of thoughts and images. This already suggests stratification, but the archaeological element is emphasised in Freud's view that the repression not only holds the material in place, but also preserves it, like an archaeological deposit. At the same time, the concept of the unconscious taps into more general themes of depth, for like Saussure's deep structures of language it cannot be directly observed

(Spence 1987: 17). The unconscious has to be reconstructed from outward signs and symptoms. And like the structuralist conception of language, the unconscious is connected with the collective or the species rather than the singular person. So just as Augustine advocated a journey deep into the self in order to connect with God, psychoanalysis and structuralism both looked into the depths for that which transcended the individual. The difference, perhaps, was that Freud also identified the unconscious with the distant past, while structuralism prioritised the synchronic system of language over history and change.

Freud was doubly preoccupied with the past, both in his fascination with antiquity and in his belief that the explanations for psychological pathologies could be found in his patient's early lives. As his career progressed, these concerns increasingly intersected, particularly once the insights that he had gathered from his self-analysis and his clinical work began to be extended to the human race in general. All of this was ultimately underwritten by the *epistemological* theory of the mind that Freud had inherited from Descartes by way of Brentano, whose lectures he attended as a student in Vienna (Ferris 1997: 31). This presents the mind as a container of representations and intentional states, which may or may not harmonise with the outside world, and the person's outward behaviour as the upshot of motivations held within the mind (see, for example, Taylor 1985; 2000). Brentano had added to this the understanding that thought is always directed, so that every mental state is of or about something (Dreyfus and Wakefield 1988: 273; Schuhmann 2004: 281). Where Freud broke with earlier views was in proposing that the mind is not like a cupboard into which ideas can be placed for later retrieval, but contains an unconscious which is not directly accessible. The unconscious may contain ideas that were at one time conscious, but have now been repressed. Moreover, we also have a phylogenetic inheritance of drives and fantasies that may at any time erupt into consciousness. While the conscious mind interacts with the outside world through the senses, the unconscious is 'deeper' — and hence the stratigraphic metaphor. While hidden, the unconscious parts of the mind are still understood as containing representations, in the same way that archaeological deposits contain artefacts, and hence the sources of neurosis can be conceived as located within the mind (Spence 1987: 13).

If the unconscious is composed of representations that are inaccessible, this content can none the less still be causally active, manifesting itself as neurotic symptoms, dreams, jokes, and parapraxes such as slips of the tongue (Dreyfus and Wakefield 1988: 274). Moreover, it is the task of the analyst to reduce the distress of the patient by removing the layers of repression and delving into the unconscious in search of repressed memories, in the way that Freud compares with archaeological excavation. Memories are thus the equivalents of archaeological 'finds', nuggets of information that form the basis for therapeutic reconstructive narratives. Like Schliemann's uncovering of Troy, psychoanalysis recovers that which has been long forgotten, and while for archaeology only rare sites like Pompeii reveal perfect preservation, the whole of a human life is hidden in indestructible form in the unconscious:

> [In psychoanalysis] we are regularly met by a situation which in archaeology occurs only in such rare circumstances as those of Pompeii or the tomb of Tutankhamun. All of the essentials are preserved, even things that seem completely forgotten are present, somehow and somewhere, and have merely been buried and made inaccessible to the subject (Freud 1937: 361).

While therapy might be aimed at resolving conflicts that were generated in a person's early years, the implication of Freud's theory is that the most deeply stratified parts of the mind contain material that derives from a much more distant past. In simplified terms, this means that while the Ego is that part of the mind concerned with selfhood and personal experience, the Superego is formed in relation to cultural inheritance and the species memory of significant events in the history of humankind, while the Id contains the pre-cultural, elemental drives of our primordial ancestors. As the unconscious part of the mind, it is not involved in cognition, but emotional motivation. While the Ego lives in proximity to the outside world and has access to it through the perceptual systems, the unconscious 'proliferates in the dark', and this means that the deeper parts of the mind are not subject to temporality. Effectively, the unconscious is timeless, in both senses.

The implication of this argument is that Freud's discussion of the depths of the mind is literal as well as metaphorical. His argument was that the human mind had gained its present form through a process of sedimentation, so that the deepest layers were also the most ancient. The strata of the mind had built up through the process of evolution, as humanity emerged from the background of more primitive species and underwent a series of formative crises and events. Indeed, the deepest parts of the mind could be identified with a pre-human past. Furthermore, just as each organism recapitulated the entire process of the evolution of its species in growing from a fertilised egg to a mature creature, so each human being achieved psychological maturity by re-living the principal psychic experiences of humanity (Bowdler 1996: 425). Given that it was ancient and pre-human, Freud was not specific about the origin of the Id. Yet the Superego or Ego-Ideal was a much more recent layer of the mental apparatus, laid down in a savage if human past.

Freud connected the creation of the Ego-Ideal, which contained those representations of the parents that human beings aspired to as figures of authority and moral rectitude, with the so-called 'primal crime'. This had the status of a quasi-historical explanation for aspects of human psychology, principally the Oedipus complex and its repression. He reasoned that at some time in the distant past, humanity had lived together as a patriarchal horde — a notion which harmonised to some extent with the evolutionary anthropology of the later nineteenth century (e.g. Morgan 1877: 505). This horde had been presided over by a primal father, who monopolised the women of the community and cast out his sons. The ambivalent feelings of the young men, who at once loved, feared and resented their father, culminated in their slaughtering and devouring him (Paul 1991: 275). Yet they were immediately stricken with remorse, and in their guilt created the twin institutions of the incest taboo and the totemic animal. The renunciation of incest meant that the sons could not gain from their crime, since they would not be able to have sexual relations with their mothers, while the totemic animal provided a symbolic substitute for the father, at once venerated and prohibited for everyday killing and eating as a symbol of the community, and yet consumed in the totemic feast as a means of enhancing community solidarity. These traumatic events at once destroyed the patriarchal horde and brought human society into being through the dual institutions of totem and taboo (Freud 1918: 189). In the process, a new element of the mind was created, specifically concerned with the identification of ethical values. In the process of severing their childhood sexual attraction to the parents, each individual human being re-lived this trauma, so that the formation of a growing child's mind recapitulated the evolution of the human species. So, when Freud wrote that his psychoanalytic 'excavation' was comparable with the activities of an archaeologist, he was *literally* claiming that by removing the layers of repression he could uncover the collective past of the human race.

Freud thus sees the mind as built up through a temporal process of sedimentation, with the deeper layers being the most ancient, as in a geological formation. Yet the deepest layers of all effectively transcend time altogether, and approach the condition of being archetypal or universal. So, both the psychoanalyst and the archaeologist dig down through that which is transient in order to arrive at that which is eternal, and here the depth metaphor takes the form of an opposition between the superficial to the profound. And indeed, another way in which Freud employs themes of antiquity and archaeology is in connection with the mythic or the essential, as with the very name of the Oedipus Complex. Tellingly, in a letter to his wife written from London, he described the Egyptian and Assyrian bas-reliefs in the British Museum as portraying a 'dream-like world' (Flem 2003: 31). This, from an author who connects dreams with wish-fulfilment and the play of the unconscious. It is arguable that this particular way in which Freud mobilised the image of the ancient past tapped into *and informed* the perception of archaeology in the earlier twentieth century, as a form of investigation capable of reaching beyond the transitory aspects of contemporary existence, and addressing some enduring human essence.

The psychoanalysis of civilisations

In Freud's later works psychoanalysis is increasingly identified as a means of investigating the origins and development of human culture, a task that might reasonably be seen as the responsibility of archaeology. However, Freud had now identified the preservation of psychic phenomena as superior to that of ancient ruins, while noting that the task of archaeology generally came to a halt with reconstruction. His so-called 'cultural books' make only sparing use of archaeological evidence. Freud's notions of the personal recapitulation or re-enactment of universal history were coupled with a universal evolutionism, which presented 'primitive' peoples as representative of the 'childhood' era of humankind (1993: 231). *Totem and Taboo* (1918) combines these elements, by comparing the mental lives of 'savages', children and neurotics. Conversely, the evolution of particular civilisations took a form that was comparable with a person's psychological development. Thus in *Civilisation and its Discontents* (1930) Freud describes the institutions of state societies as being engaged in a colossal repression of the primitive drives and instincts (Schorske 1991: 8), in a way that recalls Rousseau's arguments about the loss of freedom that attends the transformation of the 'noble savage' into the civilised citizen. For Freud, advanced civilisations are subject to a kind of mass neurosis, in which the aggressive drive is inhibited by the cultural formation of the Super Ego, which facilitates submission to dominant leaders (Deigh 1991: 299). None the less, the material that a person represses on the way to adulthood can return traumatically, and the same may be the case with civilisations, so that wars, revolutions and pogroms may erupt out of the collective unconscious.

It should be evident from what we have seen so far that Freud's relationship with archaeology and the ancient past was by no means a straightforward one. Sometimes he used the language of archaeology as a means of expressing the unfamiliar and abstract ideas that he was developing, but sometimes he wanted to claim that archaeology and psychoanalysis were literally addressing the same issues. Moreover, because he established multiple equivalences and inter-connections between phenomena at different temporal and social scales, he promoted a kind of conflation of different aspects of the depth metaphor. Stratigraphic depth comes to be inextricably connected with the collective, the primordial, the profound, the origin, and the archetypal. To be fair, this is no more than an elaboration on some of the key themes in high modern thought, and these connections were being made in many other areas as well. But Freud's work has contributed to an essentialist conception of archaeology as a discipline that delves into the depths of the past in search of the hidden, originary truths of the human condition.

Conclusion

In recent years, commentators like Donald Spence (1987: 5) have argued that the archaeological metaphor has done more harm than good to psychoanalysis. In particular, it has been suggested that what began as a useful tool for thinking came to be understood as the literal truth: psychoanalysis *was* archaeology, or a superior form of archaeological investigation. The archaeological metaphor promoted the notion that the unconscious is a thing-like, content-rich entity, and that unconscious thoughts must be physically located in some *place*. And just as it upholds a vision of the mind as stratified container of representations, so it reifies clinical symptoms as objects which can be addressed as if they were physical pieces of evidence. Finally, because it supports the image of psychoanalysis as an empirical science, the archaeological metaphor is a keystone in a reactionary rearguard action against a hermeneutic psychology. Such a psychology would be concerned more with breadth than depth, and would address the ways in which people deal with the world rather than the hidden content of their minds (Dreyfus and Wakefield 1988: 278). This might suggest that psychoanalysis would do well to turn its back on archaeology. However, it may be that the archaeological metaphor in psychoanalysis relates to archaeology as it was practiced a century ago, the archaeology of Freud's own time. Many archaeologists would now understand their discipline as a hermeneutic enterprise, which works with evidence that is both theory-laden and context-dependent, just like clinical data in psychology. Rather than alienated objects, archaeologists now conventionally see artefacts as imbricated in social relationships and cultural traditions. Similarly, many of us reject the representational theory of the mind, and seek to identify thought as an activity that is radically embedded in a worldly context and a material embodiment.

Archaeology has yet to fully relinquish its obsessions with cultural and biological universals, with origins and essential truths hidden in the remains of the past. But it is arguable that the time is ripe for a productive re-engagement between archaeology and psychoanalysis. Could we imagine a new series of metaphors that spark some creative re-description in both disciplines? While we might wish to unravel the tangle of ideas that ties depth to essence and universality, there might also be areas of Freud's thinking that would repay some reconsideration by archaeologists. In particular, we might consider the dream-work (Freud 1932), the way in which symbols are connected in dreams. It may be here, rather than in the 'cultural books' that we may find important clues to the way that culture is put together. Freud's concern with 'free association' in analytical practice has long been an inspiration for post-structuralist approaches to language and culture, at least at an implicit level, and involves necessary reliance on depth models. Archaeology and psychoanalysis have a long shared history, and while this has had detrimental effects on both disciplines, it also provides the platform for future developments which may prove enriching for us all. Just as more recent forms of psychoanalysis may be useful for archaeology, it may be that a transformed understanding of archaeology and its practices could help psychoanalysis to re-evaluate its own history.

Bibliography

Bernfeld, S C (1951) 'Freud and archaeology' *American Imago* 8: 107–28.
Bowdler, S (1996) 'Freud and archaeology' *Anthropological Forum* 7: 419–38.
Collingwood, R G (1946) *The Idea of History,* Oxford: Clarendon.
Daniel, G (1950) *A Hundred Years of Archaeology,* London: Duckworth.
Deigh, J (1991) 'Freud's later theory of civilisation: changes and implications', in Neu, J (ed.), *The Cambridge Companion to Freud,* Cambridge: Cambridge University Press, 287–308.
Dreyfus, H and Wakefield, J (1988) 'From depth psychology to breadth psychology: a phenomenological approach to psychopathology', in Masser, S B, Sass, L A and Woodfolk, L L (eds), *Hermeneutics and Psychological Theory,* New Brunswick: Rutgers University Press, 272–88.
Ferris, P (1997) *Dr Freud: A Life,* London: Sinclair-Stevenson.
Flem, L (2003) *Freud the Man,* New York: Other Press.
Foucault, M (1970) *The Order of Things: An Archaeology of the Human Sciences,* London: Tavistock.

Foucault, M (1978) *The History of Sexuality, Volume 1: An Introduction,* Harmondsworth: Penguin.
Foucault, M (1979) 'Cuvier's position in the history of biology' *Critique of Anthropology* 13/14: 125–30.
Freud, S (1896) [1953] 'The aetiology of hysteria', in Jones, E (ed.), *Collected Papers of Sigmund Freud, Vol. I,* London: Hogarth Press, 183–219.
Freud, S (1918) *Totem and Taboo: Resemblances Between the Psychic Lives of Savages and Neurotics,* Harmondsworth: Penguin.
Freud, S (1930) *Civilisation and its Discontents,* London: Hogarth Press.
Freud, S (1932) *The Interpretation of Dreams,* London: George Allen and Unwin.
Freud, S (1936) [1953] 'A disturbance of memory on the Acropolis', in Jones, E (ed.), *Collected Papers of Sigmund Freud, Vol V,* London: Hogarth Press, 302–12.
Freud, S (1937) [1953] 'Constructions in analysis', in Jones, E (ed.), *Collected Papers of Sigmund Freud, Vol V,* London: Hogarth Press, 358–71.
Freud, S (1950) *Aus den Anfängen der Psychoanalyse,* London: Imago.
Freud, S (1993) *Dream and Delusion in Wilhelm Jensen's* Gradiva, Los Angeles: Sun and Moon Press.
Gamwell, L (1989) 'The origins of Freud's antiquities collection', in Gamwell, L and Wells R (eds), *Sigmund Freud and Art: His Personal Collection of Antiquities,* London: Freud Museum, 21–32.
Gay, P (1988) *Freud: A Life for Our Time,* New York: W W Norton.
Harris, E (1989) *Principles of Archaeological Stratigraphy,* San Diego: Academic Press.
Hutton, J (1788) [1795] *Theory of the Earth,* Edinburgh: Cadell and Davies.
Jameson, F (1984) 'Post-modernism or the cultural logic of late-capitalism' *New Left Review* 146: 53–93.
Kuspit, D (1989) 'A mighty metaphor: the analogy of archaeology and psychoanalysis', in Gamwell, L and Wells, R (eds), *Sigmund Freud and Art: His Personal Collection of Antiquities,* London: Freud Museum, 133–51.
Lucas, G (2001) *Critical Approaches to Fieldwork: Contemporary and Historical Archaeological Practice,* London: Routledge.
Lyell, C (1830) *Principles of Geology,* London: John Murray.
MacCannell, J F (1996) 'Signs of the fathers: Freud's collection of antiquities', in Barker, S (ed.), *Excavations and Their Objects: Freud's Collection of Antiquity,* Albany: State University of New York Press, 33–56.
Morgan, L H (1877) *Ancient Society, or Researches in the Lines of Human Progress from Savagery through Barbarism to Civilization,* Chicago: Charles H Kerr.
Paul, R A (1991) 'Freud's anthropology: a reading of the "cultural books"', in Neu, J (ed.), *The Cambridge Companion to Freud,* Cambridge: Cambridge University Press, 267–86.
Saussure, F (1959) *Course in General Linguistics,* New York: The Philosophical Library.

Schorske, C E (1991) 'Freud: the psychoarchaeology of civilisations', in Neu, J (ed.), *The Cambridge Companion to Freud*, Cambridge: Cambridge University Press, 8–24.

Schuhmann, K (2004) 'Brentano's impact on twentieth-century philosophy', in Jacquette, D (ed.), *The Cambridge Companion to Brentano*, Cambridge: Cambridge University Press, 277–97.

Smith, W (1816) *Strata Identified by Organised Fossils,* London: W Arding.

Spence, D P (1987) *The Freudian Metaphor: Toward Paradigm Change in Psychoanalysis,* New York: Norton.

Taylor, C (1985) *Human Agency and Language: Philosophical Papers I,* Cambridge: Cambridge University Press.

Taylor, C (1989) *Sources of the Self: The Making of the Modern Identity,* Cambridge: Cambridge University Press.

Taylor, C (2000) 'What's wrong with foundationalism? Knowledge, agency and world', in Wrathall, M and Malpas, J (eds), *Heidegger, Coping, and Cognitive Science,* Cambridge, Mass: MIT Press, 115–34.

Thomas, J S (2004) *Archaeology and Modernity,* London: Routledge.

Trigger, B G (1989) *A History of Archaeological Thought,* Cambridge: Cambridge University Press.

Ucko, P J (2001) 'Unprovenanced material culture and Freud's collection of antiquities' *Journal of Material Culture* 6: 269–322.

Wallace, J (2004) *Digging the Dirt: The Archaeological Imagination,* London: Duckworth.

Imagine This: Archaeology in the Experience Society

Cornelius Holtorf

The end of archaeology?

The end of archaeology. Imagine this — I stop and wave a hand to take in the books on my desk.

> 'Imagine this' — Jake stopped, and waved a hand to take in the beach. '[The envisaged themepark] Ravensworld opens to a marching band of costumed Indians and archaeologists. The main attractions light up in giant flashing signs. Raiders of the Lost Petroglyphs. Indiana Jones and the Temple of the Coast Salish. Indiana Jones and the Last Shell Midden. Get your tickets here for the wildest ride of your life. A park to rival Disney World... I can see it now, Harrison Ford swinging through the trees, a giant stone ball rolling over his head and landing smack on top of ours. It's sacrilege, Angeline'.' (Cannon 2004: 32)

In the novel *The Raven's Pool*, by Deborah Cannon, the construction of a theme park is portrayed as a threat to archaeologists and their ambition to promote archaeological heritage and an understanding of the past. A similar sentiment is apparent in Julian Barnes' satirical novel *England, England* (1999). Here the theme park developer instructs the project's historian in the following way:

> Let me put it this way. You are our Official Historian. You are responsible, how can I put it, for our history. [...] Well, the point of *our* history — and I stress the our — will be to make our guests, those buying what is for the moment referred to as Quality Leisure, *feel better*. [...] We want them to *feel* less ignorant. Whether they *are* or not is quite another maker, even outside our jurisdiction. (Barnes 1999: 70)

Both stories describe what is a common nightmare and apocalyptic vision among archaeologists and historians: when academics are portrayed as movie characters, when the past is presented like a Disney theme park, when knowledge and insight become secondary to entertainment and commerce then archaeology and history are thought to have reached their end (cf. Urry 1990: 92).

The mind boggles

In fact, when all this happens, archaeology and history are reaching their fulfilment: their fulfilment as subjects that are not marginal — confined to museums, universities and specialist libraries — but that lie at the heart of popular culture (see Holtorf 2005; 2007). Their fulfilment as part of the culture people choose for themselves, proving, in the words of British historian Raphael Samuel, that 'history is not the prerogative of the historian, nor even ... a historian's "invention". It is, rather, a social form of knowledge;

the work, in any given instance, of a thousand different hands' (1994: 8). It is mind-boggling to me how academics, precisely at the point when their disciplines enjoy significant popular appeal, can lament a decline of serious interest in their fields — as they often do (cf. Korff 1994; Hjemdahl 2002).

This paper has a double purpose. On the one hand, I will consider the meaning and social relevance of archaeology in our own culture (in the so-called Western world), based on an analysis of how archaeology is presented in contemporary theme parks and other themed environments. On the other hand, I will discuss what, if anything, archaeological themes that loom large in some such parks and environments, in turn, have to offer to our society.

Las Vegas

Caesars Palace opened in 1966 as the first Las Vegas resort to embody consistently an archaeological or historical theme (Malamud 1998; McCombie 2001). It signifies the popular myth of a decadent and opulent Rome associated with excess and indulgence as it is depicted in movies like *Ben Hur* (1959), *Cleopatra* (1963), or *Gladiator* (2000). Arguably, Caesars Palace creates a museum for the mass audience, a museum free of admission fees, velvet ropes and Plexiglas panels and (falsely) appearing to be free even of security guards. Its architecture and design bear the signs of historicity but lack the

Figure 2.1 The buffet restaurant Pharaoh's Pheast in the Luxor hotel/casino, Las Vegas. Photograph: Cornelius Holtorf, 2001.

tedious labels. The hotel-casino is thus a carrier of culture without many of the explicit behavioural constraints and class implications still found in many ordinary museums. It invites the visitor-customer to experience the past — preferably while taking a break from gambling.

Completed in 1993 in the shape of the world's largest pyramid and with a gigantic sphinx in front of it, the Luxor is another Las Vegas resort. Unlike Caesars Palace, it embraces the clichés of ancient Egypt, incorporating the pyramids, pharaohs, mummies, occult mysteries, fabulous wealth and archaeological excavations (figure 2.1). An authentic reproduction of Tutankhamun's tomb, as it looked when Howard Carter opened it in 1922, lets the common tourist slip into the role of the privileged archaeologist discovering wonderful things (Malamud 2001: 35). The main lobbies of the building are filled with full-scale Egyptian architecture, and in each room walls, wardrobes and bed linen are adorned with Egyptian-style murals and hieroglyphics. The local *What's on* journal even proclaims that the Luxor is 'as much a museum as it is a hotel and casino'. A fact sheet that I picked up in the hotel in 2001 stated not only that 'all ornamentation and hieroglyphs are authentic reproductions of originals' but also that 'our ten story tall Sphinx is taller than the original Sphinx.' [1]

Some economic trends

The success of both resorts — like all the others along the Vegas Strip — are indicative of some economic trends in late twentieth- and early twenty-first-century Western societies, as they have been discussed by the British sociologist Alan Bryman (1999).

One trend is towards emotional labour. Employers are increasingly seeking to control their workers' emotions. The insistence that workers have to exhibit cheerfulness and carry friendly smiles towards customers at all times is as common in Las Vegas as it is in Disneyland or in McDonald's restaurants around the world. Counted are the days of the brusque and territorial sales assistant (a common breed when I lived in Germany).

Another trend is the dedifferentiation of consumption: much of the distinction between hotels, shops, themed amusement parks, tourist attractions and museums is fast disappearing. After all, the more you can do at the same location, the more reason you have to come, the longer you stay, the more you spend... As Caesars Palace and the Luxor in Las Vegas illustrate, casinos incorporate hotels, shops, and museums, and have become major tourist attractions. By the same token, museums and other tourist attractions have been upgrading their shops and cafes. Entire shopping malls, individual shops and restaurants, in turn, increasingly provide amusement that transforms them into themed tourist attractions (Urry 1990: 85, 147–53; Crawford 1992; Beardsworth and Bryman 1999; Gottdiener 1997: 76–91; Hopkins 2000).

---

1   The Luxor announced in 2007 that the Luxor is to be thoroughly renovated and much of the Egyptian scenery will be removed.

This development is helped by a trend towards branding and merchandising drawing on closely protected names, images and logos. Successful marketing increasingly uses brands that can reappear in any field of consumption (Klein 2001).

Finally, there is a trend for themes to be at the heart of consumption. Themes are sets of imagery to which people can easily relate and which immerse them in a world different from the normal routines and restrictions of everyday life (Köck 1990; Gottdiener 1997). The Romans in Caesars Palace and the Egyptians in the Luxor create an atmosphere of exotic luxury metaphorically transporting customer-guests into another world. That world is removed from daily life and its conventional responsibilities and controls, encouraging fantasy — and of course spending, which is what these resorts are all about. Even entire countries are now theming themselves in their attempts to attract tourists, transforming travel from an encounter with other places and cultures to an experience of familiar attractive metaphors. See for example the recent advertising campaigns *Malaysia. Truly Asia,* playing on Orientalism, and *Live your myth in Greece,* playing on the ancient origins of European civilization and perhaps also on philhellenism.

Consuming collective fantasies

In our age, people are commonly consuming products by consuming stories and experiences. Consumption is increasingly linked to signification, life style and identity (Crawford 1992; Gottdiener 1997: 126–28, 153–54; Hopkins 2000). We are buying products as potent signifiers of who (we think) we are and who we would like to be. People consume what brings them in touch with stories they tell about themselves, with their own collective imaginations and fantasies. This trend is helped by theming.

Theming is so effective because it often draws on the virtual capital that consumers have acquired from mass media such as cinema and especially television (Hennig 1999: 94–101; Beardsworth and Bryman 1999: 252; Hall and Bombardella 2005: 9). Popular culture has accordingly been described as 'a form of dialogue which a society has with itself' (Maltby 1989: 14). For example, Disneyland's most famous ride, the Jungle Cruise, was based on the film *The African Queen* (1951) and is meant to create a cinematic experience. Similarly, the *Indiana Jones Adventure*, Disneyland's most popular ride at the moment, is based on the blockbuster movies featuring Harrison Ford (Marling 1997: 105, 111–19). This corresponds to an increasing intertextuality across a wide range of media: books refer to other books ('as argued in...'), newspapers to other newspapers ('As The Guardian reported...'), and TV programmes to other TV programmes (TV presenters appearing in TV talk shows). In each case, the primary reference point is not reality but other popular cultural form.

Theme parks and other themed environments are generally seeking to evoke cultural ideas that are widely shared and appreciated, including all sorts of clichés and stereotypes. In Las Vegas, it is possible to observe from a single vantage point many representations that we can all relate to, for example from *Discovery Channel* and *National*

Geographic magazine. Among them may be a giant Easter Island sculpted head, an immense lion, a huge medieval castle, and a giant Sphinx in front of a pyramid (Gottdiener 1997: 106). As this short list already indicates, many popular cultural ideas draw on historical or archaeological themes. Archaeology embodies and evokes motifs that are in particular demand in Western popular culture (see also Sorensen 1989; Boyer 1992; Barrowclough 2004; Dawid 2005; Hall and Bombardella 2005). They are closely related to major themes of which the fantasies of Hollywood, Las Vegas and many theme parks are made (Gottdiener 1997: 151–52; see figure 2.2). Archaeology has therefore much to offer to contemporary popular culture:

- dramatic adventures in exotic locations,
- treasures discovered,
- science progressing through technological wizardry,
- big mysteries solved, and
- ancient worlds nostalgically remembered.

Figure 2.2 Tomb Blaster — an archaeological attraction in the English theme park Chessington World of Adventures. Photograph: Cornelius Holtorf, 2002.

In the spirit of the dialogue society has with itself through popular culture, the historian in *England, England* is told that 'we don't threaten people. We don't insult their ignorance. We deal in what they already understand. ... The Historian is there to advise us on how much History people already know' (Barnes 1999: 71). This may have been meant satirically in the novel, but Fred Beckenstein, a senior Euro Disneyland manager, actually stated in an interview that 'we're not trying to design what really existed in

51

1900, we're trying to design what people think they remember about what existed' (cited in Bryman 1995: 137).

Yet, who of us is to keep strictly distinct what really existed at one point in time from what we are all used to seeing represent that time? Is not the degree of experienced pastness rather than that of recreated accuracy the appropriate unit for measuring the significance of the past in the present (Holtorf 2005: chapter 7)? These are not purely intellectual quibbles about abstract concepts. Large-scale themed attractions and branded entertainment at Las Vegas and Disney indicate major trends in the entire Western world. At least 200 million people visit theme and amusement parks every year. The Spanish Costa Brava and the Italian Adriatic, both major beach holiday regions of the Mediterranean, each do not receive even half of the 30 million visitors the single site of Disney World attracts every year (Hennig 1999: 165). Similarly, Euro Disney attracted in its first year more visitors (11 million) than the two classical travel destinations of the Eiffel tower and the Louvres in nearby Paris taken together (Korff 1994: 211). It is not for nothing that sociologists have been writing about 'The Disneyization of society' (Bryman 1999).

Quite rightly anthropologists have begun wondering why phenomena like Disneyland and Euro Disney have not been studied more carefully. They are not only visited by so many but these places also reveal the principles and practices of contemporary mass culture particularly clearly (Korff 1994: 207).

The Experience Society

Over a decade ago, the German sociologist Gerhard Schulze (1993) published an influential study describing *Die Erlebnisgesellschaft* (The Experience Society). Schulze argued that *Erlebniswert* (experience value) is quickly replacing use and monetary values in significance. As people in affluent Western societies have become economically secure and possess all the tools they require, they are orientating their lives more and more towards experiences: to live and to experience have nearly come to mean the same thing. Customers express who they would like to be, how they would like to live and what they would like to experience by buying products that appear to confer those properties. Although this is not an entirely new trend, the market for experiences is expanding particularly fast. From travel agencies to shopping centres, from TV stations to universities, and from swimming pools to theme parks, all are offering 'experiences' to their customers (see also Köck 1990: 77–82; Pine and Gilmore 1999; Schmitt 1999; O'Dell 2002).

When the German leisure expert Horst Opaschowski (2000) recently reviewed these developments, he found that the Experience industry was still expanding. According to his analysis the experience industry is essentially telling fairytales and selling dreams rather than products. What matters more than the veracity and authenticity of these tales and dreams is that they create the right sensual experiences and thus customer satisfaction (see also Dawid 2005). More generally, the American economists Joseph Pine and

James Gilmore argued in their book *The Experience Economy* (1999: 25) that those 'businesses that relegate themselves to the diminishing world of goods and services will be rendered irrelevant'. Instead, businesses now need to offer experiences to people. These experiences consist of more than entertainment and are first and foremost about *engaging* people sensually, cognitively, socially, culturally, and emotionally. How to do just that is developed with examples in the economist Bernd H. Schmitt's account of *Experiential Marketing* (1999).

Also revealing has been a book entitled *The Dream Society* by the Danish marketing consultant Rolf Jensen (1999). Jensen argued that consumers are increasingly buying stories along with products. For example, when we buy eggs we are willing to pay a little more in order to hear a story about free-ranging chicken. Likewise, we are prepared to donate money to Amnesty International or Greenpeace because (besides everything else they do) they tell us stories about rescuing human beings or natural environments that we respond to very passionately. By the same token, advertising is becoming more emotional, appealing to our hearts rather than our brains.

Archaeological themes

Archaeologists are good at studying material culture, or so one thinks. Theme parks are among the clearest material manifestations of the Experience Society, the Experience Economy and the Dream Society. This is where some very significant consumer preferences and economic changes of our age are manifesting themselves in *things*.

Disneyland	Anaheim, California, USA	*Indiana Jones Adventure* ride	disneyland.disney.go.com
Caesars Palace	Las Vegas, Nevada, USA	Roman themed casino and resort	www.caesars.com/Caesars/LasVegas
Luxor	Las Vegas, Nevada, USA	Egyptian themed casino and resort	www.luxor.com
Chessington World of Adventures	London, U.K.	*Forbidden Kingdom, Tomb Blaster* ride	www.chessington.co.uk
Blackpool Pleasure Beach	Blackpool, U.K.	*Valhalla* ride	www.blackpoolpleasurebeach.com
Europa-Park Rust	Freiburg, Germany	Greek village featuring Troy, Mycenae and Knossos, *Poseidon* ride	www.europapark.de
Playmobil FunPark	Nürnberg, Germany	*Jungleworld* featuring Maya ruins	www.playmobil-funpark.de
Mystery Park	Interlaken, Switzerland	Erich von Däniken's take on megaliths, Egyptian pyramids, Maya calendar, Nazca lines	www.mysterypark.ch
Furuvik Parken	Gävle, Sweden	*Barnen Hedenhös* ride for children and archaeological museum	www.furuvik.se
Sun City	Pilanesberg, South Africa	*The Palace of the Lost City* resort	www.suninternational.com

Table 2.1 Some major family destinations incorporating archaeological themes.

In Arkansas, USA, for instance, the remains can be found of a theme park called *Dogpatch USA*. Operational between 1968 and 1993, all of monetary value has now been removed and sold. But the bulk of the structures of the park still exist due to the fact that the defunct park is located in a commercially unattractive and undeveloped rural area. What is left of the park would provide a great opportunity for contemporary archaeologists to study the material culture of the emerging Experience Society. Instead, urban explorers have taken to investigating the remains, although recently others have begun cleaning up the site (Wikipedia 2007).

As mentioned earlier, theme parks are also places that have explicitly adopted archaeological themes themselves — thus indicating one significant role the subject plays in contemporary society (see table 2.1). In addition to themed amusement parks, archaeological themes appear, among other places, in zoos, restaurants, hotels, shopping malls, and on golf courses (figure 2.3). We are all different individuals but we share some of our imagination and enjoy collective fantasies such as those evoked by archaeology.

Figure 2.3 Lost Treasure Golf with Professor Hacker leading an expedition to search for ancient gold and diamonds. Seen in Branson, Missouri. See also http://www.losttreasuregolf.com/. Photograph: Marcia-Anne Dobres 2001, reproduced by permission.

Ever since the nineteenth century, maybe even before that, discovering wonderful treasures, solving the mysteries of ancient civilisations, appealing reconstructions of past ways of life, and dramatic stories about fieldwork in remote places have been the most important dimensions of archaeology in popular culture. They are arguably at their

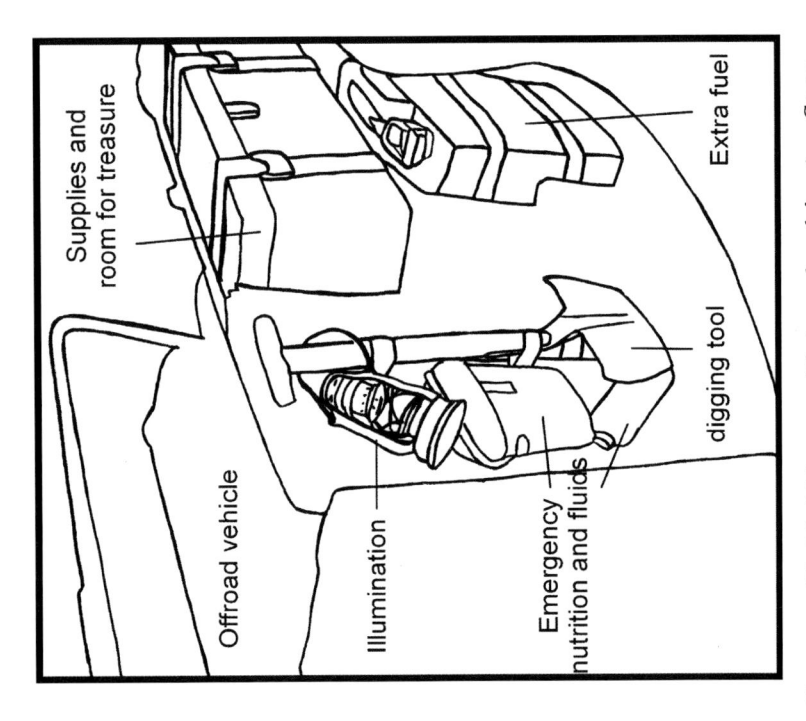

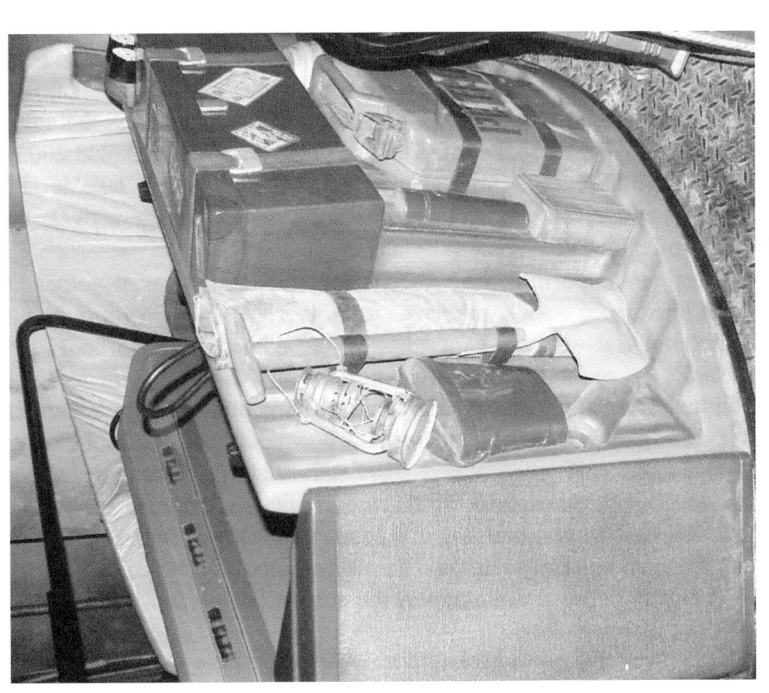

Figure 2.4 The material culture of the archaeologist as hero, as seen in Chessington World of Adventures. Photograph and drawing: Cornelius Holtorf, 2002/2005.

The fascination with both the past and archaeology evidently lies, however, on a different level than professional archaeologists — pleased by the interest in their work — tend to assume. Many of the popular stories archaeology tells and many of the engaging experiences it offers draw more on the exciting process of doing archaeology than on any particularly desirable insights about a past that really once existed. It is the tomb *raiding*, the treasure *hunting*, the *solving* of mysteries and the *revealing* of truths that moves millions (Holtorf 2007), and not the latest addition to ceramic typology or settlement distribution patterns. By the same token, it is not the historicity as such of ancient sites and monuments that is meaningful to the majority of tourists of our time but the value they have as leisure destinations and appealing stage sets evoking cultural capital (Urry 1990; Svensson 1997; Hennig 1999; Gruffudd et al 1999). It appears thus that the meaning of history and archaeology in our society is more to do with metaphors and stereotypes than with factual truths about the past. Academics may not all agree with this impression but they are compelled to digest it.

The British archaeologist Julian Thomas argued in his book *Archaeology and Modernity* (2004) that the discipline of archaeology has been intrinsically linked to a modernist worldview. It could only have been generated in the specific context of the modern world and is firmly tied to the conditions of modernity as they developed over the past few centuries in the Western world. Swedish archaeologist Björn Magnusson Staaf (2000) made a similar argument regarding the defining influence of modernism on archaeological heritage management and research design. As the modern world and its conditions have changed beyond recognition, both Thomas (2004: 223) and Staaf (2000: 192) have been wondering whether that means that scientific archaeology and heritage management, too, will need to change in order to remain relevant.

A new archaeology for a new society

What, then is the lesson of the Experience Society for archaeology? The German journalist and archaeological author Dieter Kapff (2004: 130) recently stated that

Archaeology appeals to a large number of people. But members of the contemporary fun-society are not actually interested in increasing their knowledge, in education, information or intellectual stimuli. The educated classes [Bildungsbürgertum] of the nineteenth and early twentieth centuries no longer exist. Today, people want entertainment. (my translation)

In other words, asking what archaeology means to people today is asking what kind of experiences it can offer. But does a new type of society really require a new profile for archaeology? Have the links between archaeology and traditional values of education irreparably been cut? Is the popular portrayal of archaeology indicating the subject's only future? It is impossible at this point to give confident answers to any of these questions.

As I have discussed earlier, already now popular archaeology contributes to some of the themes and stories that are enjoyed by very large sections of the population and valued because they ultimately improve their quality of life. Computer game manufacturers, Hollywood studios and entrepreneurs like von Däniken have been benefiting considerably from the currency of archaeological themes. As society continues to transform itself, archaeologists need to ask themselves with increasing urgency where they wish to position their own discipline and profession, and the fields of activity of their institutions, in relation to the existing appeal of the subject of archaeology. In the light of a number of particular significant themes that have come to define the subject of archaeology in the popular domain, the entire field may need to be rethought — and certainly the way archaeologists themselves have been relating to their popular representations (Holtorf 2007).

The issue is, however, most definitely not how archaeologists can make those people who love Indiana Jones, treasure hunting and revelations about ancient mysteries more interested in the professional's own version of archaeology. The issue is rather what these popular concepts can tell the professionals about popular themes and interests they need to address themselves. As a major report of the Economic & Social Research Council in the UK recently stated, the problem is not one of a lack of 'public understanding of science' but increasingly it is one of a lack of scientific understanding of the public (Hargreaves & Ferguson 2000).

Archaeology as storytelling

At the end of the day, most professional archaeology today is not in the education but in the storytelling business. That is not to say that archaeology is any less important, quite the opposite. As many have argued, storytelling and the foregrounding of experience have become central to the society in which we live. Appropriate stories and experiences contribute to peoples' social identities and can give inspiration, meaning, and happiness to their lives (Schulze 1993; Jensen 1999; Pine and Gilmore 1999; O'Dell 2002; Gruffudd et al 1999). Arguably, society at large benefits from citizens who occasionally fulfil their dreams by taking part in (imaginary) adventures. Many are dreaming about being somebody else. Making such dreams temporarily come true can later let the familiar routines appear desirable again (Maltby 1989: 14; Hennig 1999: 89–93).

Moreover, popular culture forms relating to entertainment, leisure and recreation have an important role to play in helping us to recognise the roles we are playing ourselves: at work, as citizens, and in our families. The popular media, especially TV, supply not simply information (or occasionally misinformation) and entertainment but also 'images and impressions which instruct us in the conduct of our lives' (Maltby 1989: 7). They define not only what (and who) we are but also what we desire to do and who we desire to be. For better or worse, they encourage us to copy the ideals of behaviour which they depict, and they thus have an important function of orientation.

But travelling through time and space as evoked by archaeological themes can also quite simply be fun. As Horst Opaschowski (2000: 49) put it, it is the satisfaction gained from experiencing happiness by consuming familiar themes that makes people visit themed environments. Insofar as archaeologists contribute to that happiness, they can directly improve peoples' lives. In the Experience Society and its Experience Economy the bottom line for archaeologists has got to be the same as the bottom line for managers: 'you have to somehow enrich people's lives and provide enjoyment for your customers... The ultimate — if you will humanistic — goal of marketing is providing customers with valuable (i.e. optimal) experiences' (Schmitt 1999: 60).

Disneyfied history

But wait — how heretical has this argument become? Am I forgetting that imaginative storytelling and dreams-come-true in theme parks can fool people? Fool them into consuming things they do not need, thereby generating profits for a few clever entrepreneurs? Fool them into false ideologies by providing opportunities for compensating the deficiencies of modernisation, or by conveying a historical consciousness referring to a past that never happened? Of course the comprehensive critique of Disney's legacy (e.g. Fjellman 1992) must be acknowledged by all. So must be the critique of that critique. Some outspoken critics, like Julian Halevy, have dismissed Disneyland as 'a sickening blend of cheap formulas packaged to sell.' But others, like Greil Marcus, dismissed in turn that critique as 'polemical, ideological, or merely self-congratulatory, smug' (Marcus 1997: 203).

Disney theme parks are in parts about escapism from a daily reality rather than about engagement with that reality. But at the same time they allow and encourage people to engage with their surroundings to a far greater extent than most other parts of reality. The American geographer Yi-Fu Tuan argued that essentially all culture is, 'in a fundamental sense, a mechanism of escape' (Tuan 1998: 27). Culture, in his sense, is the result of an unwillingness 'to accept "what is the case" (reality)' when it seems either 'unjust or too severely constraining' (ibid.). Might Disneyland accordingly be described as the realisation of an ideal culture that removes unnecessary constraints of our reality? Disneyfied history improves the past and represents what history should have been like; it celebrates America, technological progress and nostalgic memory; it hides wars, political and social conflicts, and human misery (Wallace 1985; Fjellman 1992: chapter 4; Bryman 1995: chapter 6).

Arguably, such history is false in as much as it is highly selective and simplistic rather than balanced and suitably complex, celebratory rather than critical, playful rather than serious, and profit-orientated rather than educational. But traditionally taught history is false too. False in that all history is to some extent invented (Samuel 1994: 430–37). False in that historical curricula are always selective and carry politically motivated agendas. False in that commercial factors, among others, influence what and indeed whose history reaches millions. False in that much historical education makes us more knowledgeable about the past while at the same time more ignorant about the future (Fuld 2005: 261–67). There is no need at all to be defensive about ignoring traditional, academic histories.

Emotional realism

The Australian Richard Maltby suggested that 'if it is the crime of popular culture that it has taken our dreams and packaged them and sold them back to us, it is also the achievement of popular culture that it has brought us more and more varied dreams than we could otherwise have known' (1989: 14). And dreams can shape reality!

Popular theme parks may be fabricated but they are nevertheless real, maybe more real than some museums. After all, those visiting themed environments do not follow imaginary but real desires (Maltby 1989: 15–16). Themed experiences are not alternatives to an abstract reality but very much part of lived realities (Holtorf 2005: 139–44). Their realism may not be that of a once-lost but now-revived past or of any genuine objects associated with that past. Their realism rather takes the form of the visitors' active engagement with the past, evoking authentic experiences that turn into what might be termed an 'existential authenticity', a special state of Being in which one is true to oneself (Wang 1999). That bodily engagement, typically facilitated by rides or other strong experiences, is activity-related and involves sensual impressions that engender feelings and emotions which people connect with their authentic selves, and treasure.

According to Gaynor Bagnall (1996), this kind of emotional realism is underpinned by a desire for the experience to be genuine and based in fact. But in fact many people neither seek historical veracity in themed environments nor mind its absence. Whether adults or children, they simply enjoy the sensual stimuli and playful experiences of imaginary spaces (Hennig 1999; Hjemdahl 2002). Contrary to Bagnall's conclusions, I have thus argued elsewhere that a superficial appearance of factuality that is not actually believed can be sufficient to ensure full emotional satisfaction (Holtorf 2005: chapter 7).

It is intriguing to ask at this point whether themed rides and theme parks could in the future be replacing historic sites, exhibitions or entire museums. Even Disneyland conveys some accurate historical information after all. The American public historian Mike Wallace (1985: 33) speculated in a now classic essay that Walt Disney, through his theme parks, may have taught people more history, in a more memorable way, than they ever learned in school. Gottfried Korff (1994: 223–26), a German anthropologist, suggested accordingly that Disneyland can serve as a model for successful museum didactics — precisely because (and not despite) it informs visitors only discreetly, casually, and in an entertaining way. Can, or rather must, archaeological museums learn from that? Some already have.

JORVIK, the Viking age attraction in York in northern England[4], has attracted more than 14 million visitors since it opened in 1984 (although it is not cheap!). What is the secret? JORVIK does not present itself as a museum, but instead offers a themed ride during which visitors can experience a fully reconstructed Viking town at the very site where it once stood. On the way to and from the ride, visitors encounter displays about the underlying archaeological methods and techniques so that, as a result of the visit, they feel decisively less ignorant. There is no need to imagine this.

---

4   www.jorvik-viking-centre.co.uk (accessed 11 October 2007)

Acknowledgements

I presented earlier versions of this paper to audiences at the Annual Conference of the Royal Geographical Society in London, the Interdisziplinäres Altertumswissenschaftliches Kolloquium at the University of Basel, the Annual Meeting of the European Association of Archaeologists in Cork, and the Swedish National Heritage Board in Stockholm. I am extremely grateful to Bodil Petersson and Angela Piccini for carefully reading and critically commenting on an earlier draft of this paper, giving me many useful suggestions which improved this paper. Special thanks for help with literature to Anka Dawid, for permission to use one of her images to Marcia-Anne Dobres. A different, shorter version was published in *The SAA Archaeological Record* 7 (3), 2007.

Bibliography

Bagnall, G (1996) 'Consuming the Past', in Edgell, S, Hetherington, K and Wade, A (eds), *Consumption Matters: the Production and Experience of Consumption*, Oxford: Blackwell, 227–47.

Barnes, J (1999) *England, England*, London: Picador.

Barrowclough, D A (2004) 'Pleasure presented: a rollercoaster ride through Valhalla', in Barrowclough, D A (ed.), *Our Precious Past: Sharing Responsibility for Our Archaeological Heritage*, Cambridge: Red Dagger, 31–48.

Beardsworth, A and Bryman, A (1999) 'Late modernity and the dynamics of quasification: the case of the themed restaurant' *The Sociological Review* 47: 228–57.

Boyer, M C (1992) 'Cities for sale: merchandising history at South Street Seaport', in Sorkin, M (ed.), *Variations on a Theme Park: The New American City and the End of Public Space,* New York: Hill and Wang, 181–204.

Bryman, A (1995) *Disney and His Worlds*, London and New York: Routledge.

Bryman, A (1999) 'The Disneyization of society' *The Sociological Review* 47: 25–47.

Cannon, D (2004) *The Raven's Pool,* Victoria, BC: Trafford.

Crawford, M (1992) 'The world in a shopping mall', in Sorkin, M (ed.), *Variations on a Theme Park: The New American City and the End of Public Space*, New York: Hill and Wang, 3–30.

Dawid, A (2005) 'Poseidon, Pommes und Piraten — zum Unterhaltungswert der Archäologie im Europa-Park Rust' *Museumsblatt (Mitteilungen aus dem Museumswesen Baden-Württembergs)* 38: 26–30.

Fjellman, S (1992) *Vinyl Leaves: Walt Disney World and America*. Boulder etc: Westview.

Fuld, W (2005) *Die Bildungslüge. Warum wir weniger wissen und mehr verstehen müssen*, Frankfurt/M.: Fischer Taschenbuch.

Gottdiener, M (1997) *The Theming of America: Dreams, Visions and Commercial Spaces,* Boulder: Westview Press.

Gruffudd, P, Herbert, D T and Piccini, A (1999) '"Good to think": social constructions of Celtic heritage in Wales' *Environment and Planning D: Society and Space* 17: 705–21.

Hall, M and Bombardella, P (2005) 'Las Vegas in Africa' *Journal of Social Archaeology* 5: 5–24.

Hargreaves, I and Ferguson, G (2000) *Who's Misunderstanding Whom? Bridging the Gulf of Understanding Between the Public, the Media and Science*, Report published on behalf of the Economic and Social Research Council.

Hennig, C (1999) *Reiselust. Touristen, Tourismus und Urlaubskultur,* Frankfurt/M.: Suhrkamp

Hjemdahl, K M (2002) 'History as a Cultural Playground' *Ethnologia Europaea* 32: 105–24.

Holtorf, C (2005) *From Stonehenge to Las Vegas: Archaeology as Popular Culture*, Walnut Creek: Altamira.

Holtorf, C (2007) *Archaeology is a Brand! The Meaning of Archaeology in Contemporary Popular Culture*, Oxford: Archaeopress and Walnut Creek: Left Coast Press.

Hopkins, J (1990) 'West Edmonton Mall: landscape of myths and elsewhereness' *The Canadian Geographer* 34: 2–17.

Jensen, I and Wieczorek, A (eds) (2002) *Dino, Zeus und Asterix. Zeitzeuge Archäologie in Werbung, Kunst und Alltag heute*, Mannheim: Reiss-Engelhorn-Museen and Langenweißbach: Beier & Beran.

Jensen, R (1999) *The Dream Society. How the Coming Shift from Information to Imagination Will Transform your Business,* New York: McGraw-Hill.

Kirchner, H (1964) 'Die Archäologie im Geschichtsbild der Gegenwart. Gedanken zu repräsentativen Stimmen der Zeit' *Jahrbuch des Römisch-Germanischen Zentralmuseums Mainz* 11: 1–14.

Klein, N (2001) *No Logo,* London: Flamingo.

Köck, C (1990) *Sehnsucht Abenteuer. Auf den Spuren der Erlebnisgesellschaft,* Berlin: Transit.

Korff, G (1994) 'Euro Disney und Disney-Diskurse' *Schweizerisches Archiv für Volkskunde* 90: 207–32.

Kulik, K (2003) 'Same story, different spin? British national press coverage of the 1998 hominid discovery in Sterkfontein, South Africa, unpublished manuscript.

Maase, K (2003) 'Selbstfeier und Kompensation. Zum Studium der Unterhaltung', in Maase, K and Warneken, B J (eds), *Unterwelten der Kultur: Themen und Theorien der volkskundlichen Kulturwissenschaft,* Köln etc.: Böhlau, 219–42.

Mahler, D L, Paludan-Müller, C, Stummann Hansen, S (1983) *Om Arkæologi. Forskning, formidling, forvaltning – for hvem?,* Copenhagen: Hans Reitzels Forlag.

Malamud, M (1998) 'As the Romans did? Theming Ancient Rome in contemporary Las Vegas *Arion* 3rd Series 6 (2): 11–39.

Malamud, M (2001) 'Pyramids in Las Vegas and in outer space: Ancient Egypt in twentieth-century American architecture and film' *Journal of Popular Culture* 34: 31–47.

Maltby, R (1989) 'Introduction', in Maltby, R (ed.), *Dreams for Sale: Popular Culture in the 20th Century*, London: Harrap, 8–19.

Marcus, G (1997) 'Forty years of overstatement: criticism and the Disney theme parks', in Marling, K A (ed.), *Designing Disney's Theme Parks: The Architecture of Reassurance*, Paris and New York: Flammarion, 201–07.

Marling, K A (1997) 'Imagineering the Disney theme parks', in Marling, K A (ed.), *Designing Disney's Theme Parks: The Architecture of Reassurance*, Paris and New York: Flammarion, 29–177.

McCombie, M (2001) 'Art Appreciation at Caesar's Palace', in Harrington, C and Bielby, D (eds), *Popular Culture: Production and Consumption*, Oxford: Blackwell, 53–63.

O'Dell, T (ed.) (2002) *Upplevelsens Materialitet*, Lund: Studentlitteratur.

Opaschowski, H (2000) *Kathedralen des 21. Jahrhunderts. Erlebniswelten im Zeitalter der Eventkultur*, Hamburg: B.A.T. Freizeit-Forschungsinstitut.

Pine, J, II, and Gilmore, J (1999) *The Experience Economy: Work is Theatre & Every Business a Stage*, Boston, MA: Harvard Business School Press.

Samuel, R (1994) *Theatres of Memory Volume 1: Past and Present in Contemporary Culture*, London and New York: Verso.

Schmitt, B (1999) *Experiential Marketing: How to Get Customers to Sense, Feel, Think, Act, and Relate to Your Company and Brands*, New York: The Free Press.

Schulze, G (1993) *Die Erlebnis-Gesellschaft. Kultursoziologie der Gegenwart*, 3rd edition, Frankfurt and New York: Campus.

Sorensen, C (1989) 'Theme parks and time machines', in Vergo, P (ed.), *The New Museology*, London: Reaktion, 60–73.

Staaf, B M (2000) 'The Rise and Decline(?) of the Modern in Sweden' *Current Swedish Archaeology* 8: 179–94.

Svensson, B (1997) 'Vardagsmiljöer och söndagskulisser', in Saltzman, K and Svensson, B (eds), *Moderna Landskap*, Stockholm: Natur och Kultur, 21–44.

Thomas, J (2004) *Archaeology and Modernity*, London and New York: Routledge.

Tuan, Y-F (1998) *Escapism*, Baltimore and London: Johns Hopkins University Press.

Urry, J (1990) *The Tourist Gaze: Leisure and Travel in Contemporary Societies*, London: Sage.

Wallace, M (1985) 'Mickey Mouse history: portraying the past at Disney World' *Radical History Review* 32: 33–57.

Wang, N (1999) 'Rethinking authenticity in tourism experience' *Annals of Tourism Research* 26: 349–70.

Wikipedia (2007) Dogpatch USA, http://en.wikipedia.org/wiki/Dogpatch_usa (11.10.2007).

Then Tyger Fierce Took Life Away: The Contemporary Material Culture of Tigers

Sarah May

An eighteenth-century tiger

There is a gravestone in Wiltshire with the following epitaph:

HANNAH TWYNNEY

Who died October 23rd 1703
Aged 33 Years

In bloom of Life,
She ???? from ????,
She had not room,
To make defence,
For Tyger fierce,
Took Life away,
And here she lies,
In a bed of Clay,
Until the Resurrection Day

The gravestone is unusual in a number of ways, not least that it appears Hannah Twynney was a barmaid, so we would not expect her to have such an elaborate headstone. Perhaps this is partly due to the odd nature of her death. I was certainly surprised when I saw the headstone to find that there were tigers in Wiltshire in 1703. There is some argument as to whether the Tyger in the poem could have been a stranger rather than a big cat as the term was used in this way in the early eighteenth century. But the local story is that the tiger was part of a travelling menagerie that was stopping at the pub where Hannah worked. In either case, the headstone shows that tigers were seen as fierce and dangerous beasts, outsiders to be kept under control. Although we don't know much about the material culture of this particular tiger, these concepts are potentially associated with chains, cages and other instruments of control.

Twenty-first-century tigers

This contrasts sharply with a more recent portrayal of tigers taken from the 2003 Iraq war. The Baghdad Zoo was a well-visited public space before the invasion. Similar in structure to 1950s zoos in Western Europe and America it had a large collection of exotic animals. During the invasion it was the site of major battles and after the fall of Saddam Hussein it was subject to extensive looting. There was substantial media coverage focused on the plight of the animals. The Americans decided at this point to make the rehabilitation of the zoo a metaphor for the reconstruction of Iraq. Substantial resources were made available and an international task force was brought in (Mayell 2003).

The zoo became a popular place for off-duty soldiers and parties were held there outside opening hours. At one of these parties a drunken soldier put his arm in a tiger's cage and was bitten. A colleague proceeded to shoot the tiger. Public sympathy and press coverage focused on the outrage against the tiger and the zoo dropped out of sight as a 'good news' story (AFP 2003; for a summary of the military involvement with the zoo see *www.globalsecurity.org/military/world/iraq/baghdad-zoo.htm*)

The next twenty-first-century tiger to hit the news was a performer in the magic show, 'Siegfried and Roy'. Most cases where trainers and keepers are attacked by performing cats are out of the public eye. So it was all the more shocking when magician Roy Horn was attacked by one of the white tigers that form a central part of his act, in front of a Las Vegas audience of 500. Las Vegas is known for its creation of alternate realities, so the intrusion of the predatory reality of the tiger was particularly disturbing. 'There were a couple of gasps, and people thought it was part of the act, and then it was real quiet', said audience member Paul D'Antonio (quoted in Weatherford 2003).

Much press coverage interpreted the event as an indication that tigers can never be domesticated. 'The big cats are always a wild animal, even with all the gentle training and habit-forming techniques', said Dirk Arthur, one of several illusionists who works with exotic cats (ibid).

This insistence that wildness is genetic flies in the face of common archaeological understandings of domestication, in which a domesticated animal is '…one that has been bred in captivity, for purposes of subsistence or profit, in a human community that maintains complete mastery over its breeding, organization of territory, and food supply' (Clutton-Brock 1994: 26). The management of captive tigers displays these indicators of domestication clearly.

The Species Protection Plan (SPP) for tigers is an agreement between zoos for the management of captive tiger populations. It mostly covers American zoos but it is working more closely with other regional plans (Tilson, Traylor-Holzer and Brady 1994). The biggest concern of the plan is breeding, including specialised 'stud book' software, and the identification of 'surplus animals' whose breeding will not enhance the genetic profile of the population (Seal et al 1994). But it also concerns itself with exhibit design (organisation of territory), and feeding (Tilson, Traylor-Holzer, Brady and Armstrong 1994). This satisfies all the conditions of the Clutton-Brock definition above. The only element which remains uncertain is profit.

The specialist breeding of white tigers by Horn and his partner Fischbacher clearly relates to profit. What is more, the animals are not simply trained, they are socialised in the manner of pets as this description of the birthing facility shows:

When a White Lion or White Tiger is pregnant she is cared for in special birthing facilities and Roy begins meditating with her, creating serenity in the giant cats. Roy is there at the time of birth, comforting the mother and introducing himself to the squalling cubs. 'The first voice they hear is mine, the first touch they feel is mine, the first human face they see is mine', he says.

On many deliveries, the mother has blocked Roy's path as he tried to go for help when the cubs began arriving. The mother would clean the babies as they were born, then drop them in Roy's lap in an amazing show of trust. (*www.siegfriedandroy.com/conservation/nursery.php*)

Obviously, this text relates to the image the magicians wish to project, and the evidence of the attack undermines this image. But it is a far cry from the whip and the chair taming the savage beast. Of course, while Siegfried and Roy may treat tigers as part of the family, they are still performers. There are, however, a large and increasing number of tigers kept solely as pets.

Pet tigers came into the news at the same time as the attack on Horn, due to the dramatic capture of a tiger being kept as a pet in a Harlem apartment building (Polgreen and George 2003). The cat, named Ming, had been the pet of Antoine Yates for three years when it mauled him. When he sought treatment for the wounds, hospital staff notified police who rappelled down the wall of the building and shot Ming with a tranquiliser gun. The cat was taken to a sanctuary that specialises in big cats that have been kept as pets.

The outcry surrounding this case tended to focus on the fact that the apartment was five floors from the ground, with a subsidiary concern that the tiger was always indoors, and indeed that Yates was a tenant in public housing. The message seemed to be that Yates was not wealthy enough to have a tiger as a pet. The case also sparked a general campaign to outlaw tigers as pets in U.S. states where it is currently legal, and to stop the trading and of tigers across state lines (API 2004) And there was a similar discussion to those in the Siegfried and Roy case centring on the essential nature of the tiger as wild (and therefore dangerous) beast.

However, there were also those who saw the erosion of the human / animal boundary as a positive thing. Yates himself stated in the press and at his trial (for criminal endangerment) that his intention had been to create a kind of paradise where all animals could live together. This was a vision he shared with his neighbours: 'I walked in the door and (the tiger) was standing there looking at me', Mrs Domingo, 49, recalled. But eventually, 'we all became family' (quoted in *The Age* 2003).

Dominance and affection

Between the eighteenth century and the twenty-first century tigers have moved from dangerous outsiders, from which humans need to be protected, to endangered insiders in need of protection themselves. They have been reduced in number through habitat loss and hunting so that two of the subspecies are extinct and the remaining six are critically endangered. They have been moved from their areas of natural habitat and now exist in greater numbers in towns and cities than in forests and jungles. This change in habitat has been accompanied by a change in the cultural position of tigers.

This is immediately apparent in the way tigers find expression in our material culture. Even in the early twentieth century people had photos taken while proudly standing over the tiger they had killed (Quamen 2003: 38). Up to the 1960s the GI Joe 'white tiger hunt' toy showed what popular expectations were for our relationship with these animals. Today we are more likely to be photographed with plush tiger toys, or with tiger cubs held as infants (see figure 3.1).

Figure 3.1 Live cubs have replaced dead trophies in late twentieth-century family portraits. Photograph courtesy Christina Wessely.

The keeping of tigers as pets is seen by many as a direct challenge to the human-animal divide, as a political statement about the nature of civilisation. In both cases mentioned above there are people who argue that the divide is unbreachable: 'wild animals will always be wild'. There are also people who see a utopia in the breach.

Yi-Fu Tuan argues that the keeping of pets does indeed indicate that 'wild' animals can be brought into the human world. But this is a relationship of 'dominance and affection' (Tuan 1984: 88–114). Certainly humans care for their pets, but the rules of the relationship are established by humans, for humans. Historically speaking, keeping animals as part of a human household has demonstrated the power of the keeper to other humans and is part of a range of activities such as gardening or irrigation which glorify control over nature (Tuan 1984: 18–36).

If we view pets in this light then tigers as pets are not so different from tigers as performers or tigers as zoo animals. In all cases humans have established a relationship with the animal in which the human is dominant and is seen to care for the animal in return for specific behaviour. What differs is how the animal is required to perform the relationship and what message is to be communicated to other humans. These performances are both managed and augmented by material culture.

There is a whole set of material culture which has been developed for tigers, so that we recognise appropriate and inappropriate spaces and objects to associate with the animals. For example, we 'know' that an apartment is an inappropriate place for a tiger, but an apartment-sized space in a zoo is socially acceptable. This development of social norms challenges the 'wild' status of the animal. Indeed tigers now live in four major circumstances, each with its own material culture; firstly in zoos; secondly as performing animals; thirdly as pets; finally in forests and jungles of eastern Asia. This last category is by far the smallest. In fact there are more Bengal tigers in Texas than there are in the wild (*www.tigerlink.org/5a.html*). So in what sense are tigers 'wild' animals?

Wild tigers

Of course, our notions of the wild are culturally constructed and any space considered wild today is held as such through careful management (Oelschlaeger 1991: 3). In Siberia and Malaysia, where the largest concentrations of non-captive tigers are now found, tiger management is a complex business. The size of the population is monitored through regular censuses — the methodology of which is complex because tigers are solitary and elusive creatures (Gore et al 1993; Basu 2006; Quamen 2003: 337–38). In Malaysia and Bangladesh, where tiger reserves are cheek-by-jowl with areas of intensive agriculture, there are also major management plans for conflict with local populations (Quamen 2003: 385–90). A sizable number of wild tigers have been fitted with radio collars or chips to allow researchers to track their movements (Quamen 2003: 375–78). Finally, there are the laws and law enforcement surrounding the continuing hunt of tigers for their skin and bones. So these animals live in a complex nexus of boundaries, codes, scientific research and surveillance. Since they are still hunted they are both predator and prey. This ambivalent relationship is one of the things that 'humanizes' them. We tend to attribute agency to things that can harm us (Quamen 2003: 5–6).

Material culture of tigers in zoos

Zoos have the greatest investment in this notion of wild tigers and their endangerment since the dominant contemporary model of zoo keeping is conservation. As part of the research undertaken for this study, I systematically searched the Internet over an 18-month period using the 'Google News' service for news stories containing the terms 'tiger and not golf'. Almost every newspaper report I read discussing tigers refers to their status as an endangered species, usually giving (hugely contested) numbers of tigers remaining in the wild. The numbers given vary from five thousand to eight thousand, with some articles referring to the numbers of subspecies separately. Zoos have responded to this through a tightly controlled breeding programme known as the Species Survival Plan (Tilson, Traylor-Holzer and Brady 1994). The plan includes standards for the 'habitat' in which the animals must be kept.

The National Geographic website has an interactive game called 'Cyber Tiger', which explains the foundations of this approach to children (*www.nationalgeo graphic.com/tigers/maina.html*). Enclosures should be designed so that the captivity is hidden from humans — glass or moats rather than bars. Enrichment, toys and other challenges should be offered to the animal. But the animal should not be fed live prey because that would be distressing to human visitors. These restrictions focus on the needs of the visitor, to see the animal, to see it active, to watch it feed without confronting death. While the toys do increase variety in a captive life, they can hardly be said to increase species survival.

Obviously there is more to this approach to tiger keeping than can be presented in a children's game, but zoo life for most tigers remains defined by visibility, activity and docility. There is great variability in tiger enclosures. St Petersburg Zoo has a two-by-four metre raised cage with vertical bars, painted greenery and a bathtub (where the tiger expressed its displeasure with these arrangements by spraying visitors with urine) (see figure 3.2). These conditions are common for roadside and travelling zoos in the United States as well. The Bronx Zoo has recently opened a large exhibit named Tiger Mountain with interior and exterior space, a range of enrichments and considerably more space.

Figure 3.2 Tiger in Leningradskij zoopark, St Petersburg. Photograph: Cornelius Holtorf, 2003

In Britain, the Isle of Wight Tiger Sanctuary is probably typical of the middle range. Twenty tigers of varying sub-species are kept in an arrangement much like a terrace of houses. The animals are kept in fenced enclosures about the size of a suburban garden during the day and small, windowless rooms at night. The straw in the night cage is changed daily and joints of meat are left in with it, to encourage the tigers to return to this smaller space at night. Some of the daytime cages have paths of concrete slabs around their perimeters because the tigers in those cages walk the route so constantly that the soil would wear if not protected. These slabs also keep the animals from digging under the fencing, though the fencing is not bedded into the concrete. Each of the day cages has a platform in it. This serves two functions: it allows the cats to be at different heights from each other so that they are not always in line of sight. Perhaps more importantly, it brings the animals up to a height where visitors can see them easily.

There has been much focus on increasing enclosure sizes for tigers in the last thirty years, but the largest of these enclosures looks tiny beside the Amur tiger in Siberia's recorded range of 400 square miles (*www.tigerhomes.org/siberian_tiger.cfm*), an area the size of greater London. Compare this with the Isle of Wight Tiger Sanctuary, where all the tigers are kept with a range of other animals within the walls of a Victorian fort. Zoologists from Oxford University, Georgia Mason and Ros Clubb, say a range of problems — including high infant mortality and a tendency to pace around in the cage — are directly related to the size of the animal's home range in the wild (Clubb and Mason 2003). A healthy breeding population of tigers would need an area the size of France. These are habitat pressures that will not be solved by breeding books.

None the less, some people are hopeful that captive breeding will maintain genetic diversity and allow for release programmes in the future. With this in mind a number of Chinese zoos are engaging in a 're-wilding' programme with South African zoos (*www.savechinastigers.net*). Under this programme Chinese tigers are sent to South Africa where they are taught how to be wild so they can be released in China. Zookeepers give the tigers instruction in hunting, dominance battles, and then convince them to avoid humans (for a diary of the tiger's experience see *www.savechinastigers.net/articles.php?cat=SART+day2day*). Clearly it is the human definition and construction of wildness that matters. Animals that perform wildness will be deemed suitable for release.

Material culture of performing tigers

Of course the performance of wildness has long been a requirement of tigers in the west. As stars of circuses and other animal shows their performances show the skill of the trainer, and by extension the dominance of humans over the natural world. It is precisely because they are predators that it pleases and thrills audiences to see them commanded — we keep expecting the dominance to break down.

Each performance space is different, but there are some commonalities. Most conform in size to traditional theatrical performance spaces - a thrust stage or the theatre in the round of the circus (Stokes 2004). Again the scale requirements of humans have been accepted for a species with much larger territorial requirements. The performance space also gives cues to the animal and creates expectation amongst spectators. When we see a ring we know that the animal is required to jump through it.

This performance environment can be manipulated in quite complex ways. Until the tiger attack left Horn unable to perform Siegfried and Roy used smooth white surfaces combined with lighting effects to communicate a modern fantasy of wealth and freedom (see figure 3.3). The emphasis on and special breeding of white animals, including the white tiger that attacked Roy, highlights the way in which the animals were both artefact and agent.

Figure 3.3 A tiger in the 'palace' of Siegfried and Roy at the Mirage resort, Las Vegas. Photograph: Cornelius Holtorf, 2001.

It is more common for the performance space of tigers to be fairly stark. There may be pedestals or 'seats' for the tigers, rings and other essential props but little in the way of stage sets. This makes the material culture of this group of tigers much less obvious than that in zoos. This is partly because the social position of the animals is less ambiguous and therefore requires less support from it material culture. The material culture that is important here is the space and infrastructure itself — which holds the tigers' position within a much wider performance context.

It also relates to the fact that performing tigers are the most mobile of the groups discussed here. A zoo tiger may have only a small cage, but they have a stable place in the zoo landscape. The only consistent space for most performing tigers is the cage in which they are transported. The sparse performance space provides a degree of stability in this changing world. There is a growing body of veterinary work on how transport affects tigers (Chenault 2002). This mobility is a longer standing element in the life of captive tigers than the stability of the zoo, but it does seem to resonate strongly with people's hyper mobility in the twenty-first century.

Material culture of tigers as pets

This is the area with perhaps the greatest variability and about which I have the least information. For these animals, their material culture is remarkably similar to that for a large dog, though the leash may be more substantial:

> Basically, anyone can go out and purchase one of these animals. When Parks and Wildlife [regulated wild animals], they would inspect the cages and the animal's care and feeding. When more people find out they don't need a permit, they'll go out and get themselves a big cat and tie it up out back. (Jackson quoted in Barker 1998)

Some people rely on the same fencing as their neighbours to contain the tiger. Occasionally this leads to people being mauled by tigers that escape, or even drag children under the base of a chain link fence (Mitchell 2003). This type of material culture is most common in the U.S. where the laws differ State to State and the importance of individual (human) freedoms is strong.

More people than one might think keep tigers as part of small menageries, with similar arrangements to roadside zoos. We see these described in newspapers when the economic or personal costs become too high and the animals are removed to a 'sanctuary', as in the Yates case. Most of these 'sanctuaries' are very similar in form to the 'home' the pet is being removed from, though better funding and maintenance lead to better welfare for the inhabitants. Rasmussen describes the effort required to avoid this and gives a detailed account of the material culture of her pet tiger (Rasmussen 2004).

Despite the fact that there are approximately 8,000 pet tigers in the U.S. alone (*www.tigerlink.org/7c.html*), it remains a culturally marginal activity. The Yates story discussed above precipitated a long discussion of the issue in the U.S. and many more states have since outlawed the keeping of endangered species as pets. It is interesting that, once again it is the endangerment of the species that calls into question the personal relationship rather than the welfare of the individual or the threat the tiger might pose to a community.

Patterning

These different tiger lifeways present a bewildering array of material culture. What is more, very little of it is documented, or amenable for study through fieldwork since

Burmese zoo when a woman breastfed an orphaned tiger cub. The cub did not thrive on human milk and died (Neighbour 2005).

Dominance and affection in Heritage

My approach to material culture is archaeological and I also find that there are ideas from the work that feed back into archaeology. The most significant of these is the way in which endangerment domesticates dangerous things. Much of the material we deal with as archaeologists is the product of oppression, violence and tragedy; medieval castles providing an example of all three. Yet the public, and indeed the professional, image of these sites, and archaeology as a whole, is more about excitement and romance. In many instances this is a result of ruination, which frees the site from its original context by providing the space for individual fantasy (see Woodward 2001).

Figure 3.4 The commemorative mug on the 200th anniversary of Hannah's death. Photograph: Sarah May, 2004.

The potential for trivialization of past anguish is demonstrated in the recent use of the story of Hannah Tywnney, with which this paper began. In 2003, the bi-centenary of the event was marked with a tourism-related promotion of the story, which included a humorous poem reworking the epitaph and a commemorative mug with a smiling tiger sculpture peeking over the top. Tigers have become something we care for rather than treat with care.

In the last part of the twentieth century the development of heritage management has seen a greater concern with conservation and indeed 'rescue' of archaeological sites. Like zookeepers, professional archaeologists always highlight how rare and vulnerable the material they study is. This shifts the focus from the intellectual and emotional results of our work to the need to protect it. This can neutralise uncomfortable political aspects of argument so that learning from the past becomes less important than 'saving the past for our future'.

Once again media coverage of the 2003 invasion of Iraq provides an example of this process at work. The breakdown of social order, which the invasion precipitated, led to widespread looting. The western illegal antiquities trade had prepared for this and used the opportunity to arrange the theft of vast quantities of artefacts from museums and to step up the unauthorised 'mining' of sites such as Babylon for further lucrative artefacts (see *http://iwa.univie.ac.at/index.html* for a comprehensive listing of articles). In addition American troops used many sites, including Babylon, as military bases, damaging and destabilising buildings and other deposits (Curtis 2004). The effects of the war on the heritage of Iraq are undoubtedly catastrophic and it has been argued that, as in other wars, this destruction was, to some extent, deliberate. In denigrating the heritage of the civilisation, the invading powers denigrate the status of the country as a nation (Bevan 2006)

In addition to this direct damage, the destruction provides an opportunity to domesticate the dangerous past of Iraq. The material in question provides some of the earliest and most startling expressions of imperial power outside of China. Nineteenth-century empires filled their museums with friezes, statues and whole buildings from these empires, constructing the antiquity of their own power. This powerful past is dangerous to the New World Order in two ways. Firstly, acknowledging the age and extent of imperial power in Iraq challenges the image of 'backward savages in need of rescue' that fuelled the invasion. And secondly, the fact that the empires in question fell provides an unwanted *memento mori* for the invading powers.

How much more convenient for archaeologists and the media to focus on the theft and destruction of that past than the messages and indeed threats we could draw from it. There have been outraged articles accusing the occupiers of failing in their duty of care for this fragile past (Deblauwe 2005); teams from the British Museum co-coordinating training for Iraqi conservators (Christensen 2003); and heroic attempts to recover material stolen from Baghdad museums (Handwerk 2003).

All of these activities are worthy and justified but they draw attention away from the material itself and underline the responsibility and the power of the occupiers. This is not an intentional act on the part of archaeologists involved; indeed many are using the opportunity to present more information on the archaeology of Iraq on the Internet. The British Museum, for example, includes excerpts from their catalogue with explanatory material on their website, but the site is still called 'The British Musuem: Iraq Crisis (Christensen 2003). The value that the material is given in these presentations is affectionate. 'They speak to us directly through the centuries. Their beauty, their design, their true-to-life-ness, their slice-of-life quality can be more eloquent than a hundred excavation reports.' *(iwa.univie.ac.at/index.html*: Introduction). This language evokes the same emotions as referring to captive tigers as Ambassadors of Nature. As Hamilakis has pointed out, while giving agency and rights to the artefacts, this response denies the agency and rights of the Iraqi people (Hamilakis 2003: 107).

So we exert dominance over the Iraqi past both by allowing its destruction and demanding its preservation. As our appeals for its value tend to focus on its beauty and rarity we evoke affection for the material. In short we domesticate it, treat it as a pet in the same way that the soldier in Baghdad Zoo treated Mendouh the tiger.

Our colleagues dealing with distant pasts, particularly those which have been extensively looted, may argue that material is genuinely rare and in need of protection — as is the case for tigers (see Holtorf 2001 for an opposing view). The same cannot be said for the material basis of contemporary archaeology. In fact, superabundance of data is a major methodological problem for the discipline. This leaves us with the opportunity and perhaps the responsibility of valuing the material precisely because the intellectual and emotional impact is often both accessible and subversive (Buchli and Lucas 2001: 174). Unencumbered by the endangerment discourse that domesticates much of the heritage field, the material culture of the recent past remains wild, dangerous but powerful.

Acknowledgements

This paper stems from my work with the Archaeology of Zoos network and I am grateful for the support and challenge that group has always brought me. I am particularly thankful to Cornelius Holtorf for sharing figures 2 and 3 with me and to Christina Wessely for figure 1. Angela Piccini and Cornelius Holtorf have been most patient and supportive in helping me develop this paper from the original presentation at TAG 2003.

Bibliography

AFP (2003) 'US military probes tiger killing at Baghdad zoo', 22 September 2003, *www.terradaily.com/2003/030922124751.ubzdg8u6.html* (21.03.2006).

Barker, G (1998) 'Lions and tigers and bears, oh my! Counties aren't wild about animals' *County*, Texas association of counties 10 (1).

Basu, N (2006) 'National Parks implement new Tiger Census' *NDTV*, 22 January 2006, *www.ndtv.com/environment/Wildlife.asp?id=84014&callid=1* (21.03.2006).

BBC News (2006) 'Purr-fume to get tigers turned on' 13 February 2006, *http://news.bbc.co.uk/2/hi/uk_news/england/london/4708042.stm* (21.03.2006).

Berger, J (2003) 'At the zoo, good fences make healthy neighbors' *New York Times*, 18 March 2003, *www.nytimes.com/2003/03/18/nyregion/18PROF.html?ex=1048654800&en=42051462fd038bbd&ei=5062&partner=GOOGLE* (21.03.2006).

Bevan, R (2006) *The Destruction of Memory: Architecture at War*, London: Reaktion.

Buchli, V and Lucas, G (2001) 'Presencing Absence', in Buchli, V and Lucas, G (eds), *Archaeologies of the Contemporary Past,* London and New York: Routledge, 171–74.

Chenault, E A (2002) 'Hold that tiger: research studies circus tigers' behaviour, environment' *AgNews*, Texas A&M University, 2 July 2002 *http://agnews.tamu.edu/dailynews/stories/ANSC/Jul0202a.htm* (21.03.2006).

Christensen, B (2003) 'Conservation programme', 14 July 2003, *www.thebritish museum.ac.uk/iraqcrisis/* (21.03.2006).

Clubb, R and Mason, G (2003) 'Animal welfare: captivity effects on wide-ranging carnivores' *Nature* 425: 473

Clutton-Brock, J (1994) 'The unnatural world: behavioural aspects of humans and animals in the process of domestication', in Manning, A and Serpell, J A (eds), *Animals and Human Society: Changing Perspectives*, London: Routledge, 23–35.

Curtis, J E (2004) Report on Meeting at Babylon 11th–13th December 2004 *www.thebritishmuseum.ac.uk/iraqcrisis/reports/Babylon%20Report04.pdf* (21.03.2006).

Deblauwe, F (2005) 'American Graffiti' *The Guardian,* 15 January 2005 *www.guardian.co.uk/Iraq/Story/0,2763,1391038,00.html* (21.03.2006).

Gore, A P, Paranjpe, S A, Rajgopalan, G, Kharshikar, A V, Joshi, N V, Watve, M G, Gogate, M G (1993) 'Tiger census: role of quantification' *Current Science* 64 (10): 711–14.

Hamilakis, Y (2003) 'Iraq, stewardship and "the record"': an ethical crisis for archaeology' *Public Archaeology* 3: 104–111.

Handwerk, B (2003) 'Hunt for stolen Iraqi antiquities moves to cyberspace' *National Geographic News*, 29 April 2003 *http://news.nationalgeographic.com/news/2003/04/0429_030429_iraqlooting.html* (21.03.2006).

Holtorf, C (2001) 'Is the past a non-renewable resource?', in Layton, R, Stone, P and Thomas, J (eds), *Destruction and Conservation of Cultural Property,* London: Routledge, 286–97.

Hough, R (2003) 'Cat woman' *The Guardian*, 5 April 2003, *http://books.guardian.co.uk/departments/generalfiction/story/0,,929846,00.html* (21.03.2006).

Mayell, H (2003) 'Baghdad Zoo animals to get help from U.S. zoos' *National Geographic News*, 18 April 2003, *http://news.nationalgeographic.com/news/2003/04/0418_030418_baghdadzoo.html* (21.03.2006).

Mitchell, M (2003) 'Boy, 10, killed by tiger in Wilkes County; child was shovelling snow near cage when he was pulled inside' *Winston - Salem Journal* 1, 15 December 2003.

Neighbour, M (2005) 'Cubs breast-fed by woman die in zoo' *The Scotsman*, 13 May 2005, *http://news.scotsman.com/international.cfm?id=517902005* (21.03.2006).

Oelschlaeger, M (1991) *The Idea of Wilderness*, New Haven and London: Yale University Press.

Polgreen and George (2003) 'Adult Tiger evicted from Harlem public housing' *The New York Times*, 6 October 2003, *www.sfgate.com/cgi-bin/article.cgi?file=/c/a/ 2003/10/06/MN172749.DTL* (21.03.2006).

Quamen, D (2003) *Monster of God: The Man Eating Predator in the Jungles of History and the Mind*, New York and London: W W Norton.

Rasmussen, A (2004) 'Raising Tigers in a Changing World' *Feline Conservation Federation Newsletter*, *www.exoticcatz.com/sptigerarrow.html* (21.03.2006)

Roberts, A M (2004) 'Too Close for Comfort' *AWI Quarterly*, 9 October 2004 *www.awionline.org/pubs/Quarterly/05_54_1/541p1011.htm* (21.03.2006).

Seal, U, Wildt, D, Tilson, R, Donoghue, A, Reindl, N, Taylor, R. (1994) 'Reproduction and propagation in tigers', in Tilson, R, Traylor-Holzer, K, Brady, G and Armstrong, D (eds), *Management and Conservation of Captive Tigers, Panthera tigris*, AZA *www.tigerlink.org/husbandry/husman.htm* (21.03.2006)

Stokes, J (2004) '"Lion Griefs": the wild animal act as theatre' New Theatre Quarterly 20: 138–54.

n.a. (2003) 'Tiger country: five floors up in the city' *The Age*, 7 October 2003, *http://www.theage.com.au/articles/2003/10/06/1065292525139.html* (21.03.2006).

Tilson, R, Traylor-Holzer, K and Brady, G (1994) 'Regional and global management of tigers', in Tilson, R, Traylor-Holzer, K, Brady, G and Armstrong, D (eds), *Management and Conservation of Captive Tigers, Panthera tigris*, AZA *www.tigerlink.org/ husbandry/husman.htm* (21.03.2006).

Tilson, R, Traylor-Holzer, K, Brady, G and Armstrong, D (eds) (1994) *Management and Conservation of Captive Tigers, Panthera tigris*, AZA *www.tigerlink.org/hus bandry/husman.htm* (21.03.2006).

Tuan, Y-F (1984) *Dominance and Affection: the Making of Pets*, New Haven, Connecticut and London: Yale University Press.

Weatherford, M (2003) 'Tiger Attack: Roy's injuries "severe"'
Las Vegas Review-Journal, 5 October 2003 *www.reviewjournal.com/lvrj_home/2003/ Oct-05-Sun-2003/news/22305515.html* (21.03.2006).

Woodward, C (2001) *In Ruins*, London: Vintage.

http://animalplanet.co.uk/favourite/feature1.shtml (21.03.2006).

http://iwa.univie.ac.at/index.html (21.03.2006).

www.altpet.net/buddy.html http://www.qadesh.com/your_photo.htm (21.03.2006).

www.dickdale.com/images/ddtiger.jpg (21.03.2006).

www.globalsecurity.org/military/world/iraq/baghdad-zoo.htm (21.03.2006).

www.nationalgeographic.com/tigers/maina.html (21.03.2006).

www.savechinastigers.net (21.03.2006).

www.savechinastigers.net/articles.php?cat=SART+day2day (21.03.2006).

www.siegfriedandroy.com/biography/inspire.php (21.03.2006).

www.siegfriedandroy.com/conservation/nursery.php (21.03.2006).

www.tigerhomes.org/siberian_tiger.cfm (21.03.2006).

www.tigerlink.org/5a.html (21.03.2006).

www.tigerlink.org/7c.html (21.03.2006).

Part 2: Recording and preserving twentieth-century heritage?

'Professor Gregory's Villa' and Piles of Pony Poop: Early Expeditionary Remains in Antarctica

Mike Pearson

On 3 August 1895 delegates at the Sixth International Geographical Congress, held at the Imperial Institute in London, passed a resolution declaring '[T]hat this Congress records its opinion that the exploration of the Antarctic regions is the greatest piece of geographical exploration still to be undertaken' (see Huntford 2000: 49). Thus commenced the so-called 'heroic era' of Antarctic exploration: over the next twenty years ships from Belgium, Germany, Sweden, Scotland, France, Japan and Australia journeyed south. Amongst British parties were those of Carsten Borchgrevink (*Southern Cross*, 1898–1900), the first to over-winter on the continent; Robert Falcon Scott (*Discovery*, 1901–04 and *Terra Nova*, 1910–13); Ernest Shackleton (*Nimrod*, 1907–09 and *Endurance*, 1914–17). With objectives ranging from the winning of new territory to geophysical investigation and biological research to naked adventurism, their successes and 'heroic' failures became foundational narratives of late imperialist endeavour.

Early expeditions arrived ill prepared. After initial sledging escapades in 1902, Scott noted: 'The errors were patent; food, clothing, everything was wrong, the whole system was bad' (Scott 2001: 273). The quest for an effective *system* — a combination of shelter, equipment, nutrition and transport that would ensure survival and the success of exploratory and scientific enterprises in the coldest, driest, windiest environment on earth — came to preoccupy explorers. Some employed the latest technology, with varying success: the 'Primus' stove became a mainstay (Norris n.d.: 48–9), whilst motor vehicles failed. Others favoured approaches based on anthropological models and practices: the use of dogs and fur clothing enhanced Amundsen's chance of success on his Polar attempt. Whether through accident or design, all parties over-wintered, leaving traces: contentiously, Antarctica is one of the few places in the world where the remains and material record of man's first encounter and habitation exist, and in some profusion. The detritus of their presence, the freeze-dried relics of explorers, their animal companions and victims — dwellings, equipment, bodies — still litters the landscape, though some recorded sites have not been visited since desertion and others have disappeared in the dynamic climatic conditions.

In the Ross Dependency, there are thirty-four historic sites: rock shelters, memorial crosses, cairns, field depots, message posts and a grave. Some are ephemeral, though even the temporary campsite at Cape Crozier, immortalised in Cherry-Garrard's *The Worst Journey in the World*, produced 100 artefacts, including test tubes and pencils that — presaging future complexities — were returned to New Zealand; in 1992, a lantern, a sock and an Emperor penguin were still visible at site beneath 100 mm of ice-topped water (Harrowfield 1995: 53). And some are unregarded: piles of faeces mark the place where ponies were temporarily tethered after unloading from *Nimrod*.

More substantial are five wooden huts, at four locations accessible by ship: the expeditionary bases of Borchgrevink, Scott and Shackleton, with many of the provisions of the inhabitants still intact. The *Terra Nova* hut alone contains 8,000 inventoried items — clothing, food, utensils, scientific apparatus, furniture, animal carcasses: ordinary objects in extraordinary settings, in deposits that extend across the immediate terrain. Although these prefabricated buildings were temporary structures intended for habitation over one or two polar winters at most, they have survived in the exceptional circumstances of isolation, and of preservation: unvisited for forty years, the *Terra Nova* hut gradually filled with ice. They represent the vestiges of particular densities of human experience: they are 'genuine "time capsules"' (Discovery 2004: 12). The New Zealand based Antarctic Heritage Trust (AHT) is currently engaged in a project to survey, stabilise, conserve, restore and reconstruct these surviving, and powerfully evocative, sites, and their contents; it is further responsible for displaying and interpreting them for growing numbers of tourists.

As archaeological contexts and assemblages, the formational processes here are complex, resulting from both environmental and human agency, in historical and modern periods. The salt-laden atmosphere bleaches wood; high winds disperse loose objects, and blast scoria against outer surfaces. Higher temperatures and humidity, occasioned by visitors, increase rates of biological decay and metal corrosion. Tourists' boots abrade the floor; at the *Nimrod* hut, it is Adèlie penguins that trample the site and coat it with guano. Levels of ultra-violet light cause defibration and the fading of printed labels. Objects are decaying differentially, though all rates have accelerated following the removal of ice from the huts in the 1960s; some rotting stores — oil and paraffin containers — are ecologically threatening.

What survives, why and in what state, and how these unique sites and artefacts might be interpreted performatively are the subject of this chapter.

All here is not what it seems; the locations have been subject to repeated incursion. During the 'heroic era', hut sites were visited and inhabited by each successive expedition: they raked over, scavenged and reused materials, reordered internal layouts, and moved stores from one site to another. All three huts were occupied by the Ross Sea Party, (RSP, my abbreviation), of Shackleton's 'Imperial Trans-Antarctic (*Endurance*) Expedition'. Charged with laying depots to support Shackleton's putative retreat from the Pole, they were stranded from 1915–17 with few supplies, after their ship *Aurora* was driven offshore. The attribution and provenance of artefacts is thus difficult; multi-occupancy leads to uncertainties of sequence and chronology.

More recently the huts have been entered, with varying degrees of appreciation and acknowledgment of their historical significance and integrity. In 1947 crewmen of US ice-breaker *Burton Island* visited the *Discovery* hut. Scattered outside they found pony snowshoes, skis, sledges, mutton carcasses, a hitching rail and cases; they removed one sledge (Harrowfield 1995: 35). The *Nimrod* hut was first reencountered by the US icebreaker *Edisto* in 1948: the crew sampled foodstuffs — still in excellent condition — and collected maize kernels that later germinated (ibid. 38). The site was irretrievably altered in 1956 by the unauthorised entry of men from USS *Glacier*, enticed by photographs of an abandoned meal taken through a window and published in the *National*

Geographic magazine in the previous year. Many items were subsequently stolen. It was not until the late 1950s that planned excavation, recording and conservation of the sites commenced, initially by the New Zealand Antarctic Society.

Each expedition took a finite amount of equipment, listed in its ship's manifest, along with the personal belongings of crew members: a range of the expected and the surprising, these constitute *closed assemblages*. On *Discovery*, there were sufficient provisions for forty-eight men for three years, as well as two observation balloons, and a windmill to generate electric light; the stores listed for *Nimrod* include an 'Albion' printing press, a roulette wheel, a 'Remington' typewriter, a 'Singer' sewing machine, a full set of the Encyclopaedia Britannica. On *Terra Nova* there were forty-five tons of pony fodder and three 'Wolseley' motor tractors, as well as a 'Broadwood' pianola, an 'HMV' gramophone with records by Nellie Melba and Harry Lauder, and 'mystery bags which contained material for *The South Polar Times*, toys and frivolous presents to liven us up at the midwinter and other festivities' (Evans n.d.: 101). The *dramatis personae* was also *closed*; everything that was done was achieved by particular groups of known individuals, with no random presences. Explorers wrote about themselves and their companions, both human and animal, in diaries, published accounts and scientific papers. Men were filmed and photographed at work and play by official photographers such as Herbert Ponting on *Terra Nova*; less formally, they recorded each other. Surviving objects are pictured *in situ*, and men and animals stand in places still discernible, despite the ravages of time and weather. Text and image allude to and illustrate objects and events that are observable in both museum collections and in the on-site archaeological record: documents and artefacts mutually reference each other. In museological reconstitutions, there is an exceptional opportunity to draw together people, places and things.

Figure 4.1 Herbert Ponting in his darkroom, Cape Evans (By permission of the Scott Polar Research Institute, University of Cambridge)

Expeditions were inventive, creating and customising new equipment from their own stores, and from recovered materials: 'However well equipped an expedition may be, there are always special arrangements and adaptions [*sic*] necessary to further the labour-saving contrivances and extend the radius of action' (ibid. 129). The given repertoire, augmented by elements drawn from local faunal sources, had to be used and reused, and refashioned to fulfil expeditionary imperatives, or more expedient matters of survival, or pleasure. On *Terra Nova* Edgar Evans made ski boots, and pony shoes based 'on vague ideas of our remembrance of the shoes worn for lawn mowing' (Scott 2003: 296). When their tobacco ran out, the RSP resorted to 'Wild's Hut Point Mixture', a combination of tea, coffee, sawdust and dried herbs (Norris n.d.: 59–60). In Antarctica, men also employed objects for purposes that were never intended: the RSP used oars from the *Discovery* dinghy to stun seals (McElrea 2004: 146). They built others that become an ambiguous presence, problematising notions of an archaeological record based solely upon functionality: a ship's tarpaulin becomes a theatre curtain becomes a sledge sail (see Pearson 2004). In this extreme milieu, objects began to circulate, no longer confined to their ascribed identity. In improvised responses to an environment of limited resources, as a way of making sense with the tools to hand, in forms of *bricolage*, their employment was *ad hoc* and provisional. A pea tin turns into a blubber lamp, a cornflower crate into the binding of a book, a hank of hawser into a theatrical wig. Any object might be *functional, decorative, representational, fictive* and/or *cognitive*, both from time to time and concurrently (see Pearson 2004: 56). There is an inherent instability in the nature and meaning of things that poses a museological challenge.

What survives at the huts is partial: that which was *not* consumed; that surplus to requirements, or having served its purpose; that deemed of neither further use nor value, not worth bringing back, even as far as New Zealand where much was deposited in the Canterbury Museum basement, eventually providing an extraordinary resource for the Antarctic Gallery. There was an ostensible aspect of altruism to abandonment. At the *Nimrod* hut, Shackleton left stores for fifteen men for one year: 'The vicissitudes of life in the Antarctic are such that such a supply might prove of the greatest value to some future expedition' (Shackleton 2000: 378). At their own hut, the *Terra Nova* expedition left 'what equipment we could spare' (Norris n.d. 57–8), and at the *Discovery* hut 'the necessities of life to any less fortunate party who may follow in our footsteps and be forced to search for food and shelter' (Scott 2001: 350).

Much material was left purposefully in the field. Expeditionary practice was to cache supplies at regular intervals, in snow-cairns surmounted by flags, to replenish the return leg of long-distance treks: a process of measuring, burying, marking, seeking, uncovering. Scott notoriously perished within eleven miles of his 'One Ton Depot'. Most have long since disappeared, under accumulations of ice and snow, or into the sea, through the movement of the ice-shelf. Other equipment was lost accidentally: from ill-packed sledges, or more dangerously down crevasses. During unloading from *Terra Nova*, one of the motor tractors crashed through the sea ice. Much was simply left: in 1915 members of the Ross Sea Party found a failed 'Wolseley' tractor at Scott's 'Safety Camp', completely buried in drifted snow. Or deposited provocatively, symbolically. At the South Pole Amundsen left his tent, a letter to be forwarded to King Haakon, and a note for Scott: 'If you can use any of the articles left in the tent please do not hesitate to do so' (Evans n.d.: 232). Scott's own body would be interred under his collapsed tent, and a snow-cairn topped by a cross made from a pair of skis. Occasionally stores disappeared, mysteriously: the coal and oil deposited on the beach at the *Terra Nova* hut by the RSP vanished. Other material was just jettisoned: 'We dumped Griffith Taylor's bed and a couple of tons of rubbish into the Ross Sea' (Harrowfield 1995: 48).

Expeditions first visited existing huts from curiosity, only later of necessity. For some members, this was a return to old haunts; others were struck by the uncanny atmospheres of these deserted places. Of the *Nimrod* hut Cherry-Garrard wrote 'The whole place is very eerie'; 'I could have sworn that I heard people shouting to each other' (Cherry-Garrard 1994: 101–2). They left graffiti: the RSP wrote their names on the wall of the *Discovery* hut. And then they began to forage, to appropriate, and to transfer materials: the RSP moved caribou sleeping bags left at the *Nimrod* hut by *Terra Nova* men whilst surveying back to the *Terra Nova* hut.

In the fabric of the huts are marks occasioned by human presence, and passing: the names of mules are written on the wall in the *Discovery* stable. Less formally, in certain places, there are signs of regular and habitual contact, the prints of bodies: stains, smears, the hoof marks of ponies. In others, the marks of singular actions: the unintentional, the random, the intimate, unplanned touch of history's passing — scuffs, scratches, axe cuts from chopping seal meat. At the *Nimrod* hut the steel hawser to which the ponies were tethered survives; there is a groove in the exterior wall that it wore when eventually affixed there. It is possible then to observe traces of the moments of which men write. An artefact too wears in its use (see Shanks in Pearson & Shanks 2001: 90–101). Marks upon it attest to events it has witnessed, things that have happened to it: marks of origin and individuality; marks of ageing and time, of processes referred to in documentary accounts.

Scott's *Discovery* hut — 'Professor Gregory's Villa' — at the eponymous Hut Point is a prefabricated structure purchased in Australia, hence its incongruous sun veranda; assembly marks are visible on the outer wall. It was always cold, and used by Scott only as a storeroom, workshop, laboratory and, in 1902, as the 'Royal Terror Theatre' (see Pearson 2004). A partition to separate men from officers was never built, though a makeshift division was rigged from boxes and heavy sacking (Discovery 2004: 52). The hut was inhabited by all subsequent expeditions: each modified the disposition, and introduced its own items. A party from *Nimrod* entered through a window and found it free of snow: 'It was very interesting to me to revisit the old scenes' (Shackleton 2000: 151). Outside, the marks of picks and shovels used to collect ice on *Discovery* were still visible; Shackleton noticed too an old case in the ice, recalling the day it was thrown away. Eventually, they would use cases of biscuit and tinned meat to build a 'hut inside a hut', even sweeping it with an old broom from *Discovery*. In the hope of attracting *Nimrod*, Shackleton would later attempt to burn Scott's smaller magnetic observation hut (Chaplin n.d.: 15).

On his return in 1911, Scott was incensed to find the hut full of ice: Shackleton had left the window open. 'I had had so much interest in seeing all the old landmarks and the huts apparently intact' (Scott 2003: 94–5); 'There is something depressing about finding the old hut in such a desolate condition' (Discovery 2004: 26). But they retrieved copies of *Contemporary Review, Girl's Own Paper*, and Stanley Weyman's *My Lady Rotha* which was 'thawed out and read by everyone, and the excitement was increased by the fact that the end of the book was missing' (Cherry-Garrard 1994: 167). In preparation for the attempt on the South Pole, the interior was eventually cleared, and Oates and Meares built a blubber-stove from oil cans, scrap metal and bricks from the 'debris heap outside the hut' (Evans n.d.: 85). Awnings were rigged around the sleeping and cooking space, and the veranda converted into a dog and pony shelter, though in bad weather the animals were taken inside; hut inhabitants drank cocoa from *Discovery* and ate tins of peas and butter from *Nimrod*.

The Ross Sea Party broke a window to enter. From *Terra Nova* they found cigars, bottles of crème de menthe, Bower's stores' tally book and Oates' 'Wolsey' jersey, which was taken as a gift for their expeditionary colleague Reverend Arnold Spencer-Smith (McElrea 2004: 50). They later made extensive use of the hut; Captain Mackintosh repeatedly issued instructions to tidy and clean the building. Returning from depot-laying in 1916, RSP members lived primarily on seal meat; bones and rubbish accumulated in a pile outside one window. They were unaware of stores heaped in an ice filled corner; they chopped up Scott's observation huts for fuel, though mainly they burned blubber in the *Terra Nova* stove, turning themselves and the hut interior black.

Shackleton's *Nimrod* hut at Cape Royds was also prefabricated. Although the expedition took enough provisions for two years, a seven light carbide acetylene generator, a cooking range and a motorcar, the stables and garage were built from fodder bales and timber off-cuts. Each man had to make his own bed from packing cases; tables, chairs and shelves were also constructed. Individual cubicles were partitioned with curtains: artist George Marston decorated his with images of Joan of Arc, Napoleon and a fire burning in a grate (Shackleton 2000: 96).

Expeditions were financially precarious undertakings; in 1909 many valuable stores were repatriated on the returned *Nimrod*. In January 1911 the *Terra Nova* crew found evidence of rapid departure: a meal on the table including rolls with impressions of bites given them in 1909, boots scattered on the floor, socks hanging on a line. Griff Taylor found the roulette wheel, and paper used to produce the book *Aurora Australis*, of which over sixty copies were printed and bound in packaging plywood for future sale; on Marston's bunk was a sixpenny copy of *Bessie Costrell*, left open. They lit the range, and found Shackleton's supplies a useful reserve to fall back should need arise. Scott removed five hymnbooks: 'this increase will improve our Sunday Services' (Scott 2003: 224). The RSP sought here for matches, tobacco and soap; they found the hut 'an oasis of Edwardian civilisation', complete with portrait of Edward VII and Queen Alexandra (McElrea 2004: 235). They too lit the range, above which was an exhortation from a *Terra Nova* party to leave the dishes clean; Joyce used printing ink to daub 'Joyce's

Skining Academy Free' [*sic*] on the wall. They recovered old clothing, 'which could be mended and made serviceable' (Shackleton 1999: 297).

Scott's *Terra Nova* hut at Cape Evans was best equipped, with acetylene generators, heating stoves, and full darkroom and laboratory facilities. But again the stables were constructed from timber off-cuts, coal briquettes and fodder bales; the latrine was the upturned packing case of a motor tractor. The Ross Sea Party was struck by the neatness of the place: 'little compact heaps of store cases surrounded the hut itself' (Harrowfield 1995: 44). At first, they collected keepsakes: Ninnis found Oates' pipe, Atkinson's tobacco pouch and boots marked RFS (ibid.); Larkman took Oates' belt (McElrea 2004: 49). They landed little of their own equipment, and no clothing. Once marooned they were forced to salvage and repair Scott's equipment, not only to provide for themselves but also to support Shackleton; they amassed 4,000 lbs of stores. They overhauled old 'Primus' stoves; tents, sleeping bags and pony rugs were fashioned into trousers and jackets. Fortuitously they found a sledge load of old boots. And they occupied places familiar from Antarctic common knowledge: Spencer-Smith used Ponting's darkroom as a chapel.

Modern engagement with the sites has ranged from opportunist pilfering to planned archaeological investigation; certainly, 'various interventions have added to the confusion' (Nimrod 2003: 67). Some objects have been permanently removed: a copper cylinder from the *Aurora* memorial was presented to the National Maritime Museum in 1947; in the late 1950s Edmund Hilary sought Cherry-Garrard's permission to present a thermos flask from Cape Crozier to Canterbury Museum. Before regular access to Antarctica and the onset of tourism, artefacts were regarded as better viewed in museum collections than at site. More recently, objects have been temporarily withdrawn for safekeeping and conservation, though even recovered items have been misplaced and lost (Harrowfield 1995: 31). At site, materials found outside have been temporarily stored indoors. And visitors have regularly repositioned artefacts to dramatise the locations, or to make them most closely resemble original documentary photographs; the Emperor penguins on Scott's desk at the *Terra Nova* hut, as if ready for examination, are from the Ross Sea Party.

In January 1956, ninety artefacts including provisions, a sledge, sleeping bag, thermometer and harpoon were removed from the *Discovery* hut, and elsewhere, and shipped to England (ibid. 35–6); increasing numbers of American servicemen stationed at the McMurdo base were forbidden to enter, but many took souvenirs. In January 1958, the crew of HMNZS Endeavour cleared 'rubbish' from around the hut, and this was 'bulldozed into the sea' (Discovery 2004: 32); in January 1964, a US Navy bulldozer clearing debris inadvertently eradicated the foundations of Scott's observation huts (ibid.). In 1964 members of the New Zealand Antarctic Society began to chip out ice, revealing the RSP's improvised sleeping platforms, finding chessmen carved from a broom handle and, from behind the blubber stove, scones (Harrowfield 1995: 36). Outside, in the rubbish heap, was part of the script of 'Ticket-of-Leave', performed in the 'Royal Terror Theatre' in 1902 (see Pearson 2004). The first tourists arrived in 1967–68; the memorial cross to Scott was at some point vandalised.

At the *Nimrod* hut some objects have been moved more than once: 'There is no historic significance to the current location of many of the artefacts' (Nimrod 2003: 72). From 1957 onwards, New Zealand parties have cleared, cleaned, tidied and rearranged material. Outside, stores have been restacked, restrapped and removed, 'with the disgarding of nonessential material' (Harrowfield 1995: 42); 'the Heritage Management Plan sets guidelines and defines what is considered rubbish' (ibid.). Certain dispersed stores are regarded as threatening the cohesion and visual unity of the site (Nimrod 2003: 67), an attitude somewhat belied by period photographs of the chaotic site and interior (Huntford *et al* 2002: 126–33).

Figure 4.2 Sir Charles Wright and L.B. Quartermain in Ponting's darkroom, Cape Evans, December 1960 (By permission of Canterbury Museum, New Zealand)

At the *Terra Nova* hut — where 95% of the items are Scott's and only 5% from the Ross Sea Party — 20% are deemed beyond preservation; the environs are regarded as a 'complex cultural landscape' (Terra Nova 2004: 47). In 1957 crewmen of MMNZ Endeavour burned 'rubbish' and generally tidied the site. In the late 1950s/early 1960s objects were removed by pick and shovel — resulting in some damage, particularly to glass items — and thawed outside; Ponting's darkroom and Wilson's laboratory were in remarkable condition, though black with soot from the blubber stove of the RSP. No plan was made of where objects were found: many were placed back on rebuilt shelves, from where they were assumed to have fallen, or 'in locations considered to be most appropriate' (ibid. 76); others have since been repositioned (ibid. 36–7). In the early 1970s, a rubbish heap outside the entrance poignantly revealed Oates' jersey, Spencer-Smith's keepsake (Harrowfield 1995: 46).

The Antarctic Heritage Trust grades period artefacts from A — iconic, of high cultural heritage value — to C, where multiple similar artefacts exist. Iconic objects from *Terra Nova* held off-site include Ponting's projection screen and Scott's pipe holder, and from the Ross Sea Party, Spencer-Smith's rosary beads and an improvised man/dog sledge hauling harness. On-site objects, of special value, range from dog skeletons to Scott's cubicle. AHT policy proposes that an artefact may be disposed of if it has decayed to a point where it endangers other artefacts, or brings no benefit to interpretation; where it is a threat to environment or wildlife. Or when it is impossible to conserve (Discovery 2004: 90). Or when 'it does not contribute in any significant way to our understanding of the hut, its occupants or the history of Antarctica; it does not contribute to the visual qualities of the site or the hut; when it is not a unique or a relatively rare item' (ibid. 91).

The *Discovery* hut now stands alone: bulldozing has removed all surrounding material. Inside, objects are currently displayed approximately where they were found at the time of clearing in 1963–64; the arrangement of blubber stove and sleeping platforms is that as left by the Ross Sea Party. But the setting has a contrived feel, like a museum or 'set for tourist photographs' (ibid. 59). Although there are only 350 items, the paucity ostensibly echoing the hardships experienced by the RSP — though 'the whereabouts of many other artefacts is a mystery' (Harrowfield 1995: 37) — specific attribution is difficult. But the site does encapsulate the history of exploration; all parties left their mark here, from the bentwood chair and seal carcass of *Discovery*, to the graffiti of *Nimrod*, to the wooden stool and pony hoof marks of *Terra Nova*, to the handmade mitts, boots and canvas trousers of the RSP. It is a *palimpsest* of the 'heroic era'.

At the *Nimrod* hut, the shelves are stacked with Edwardian provisions, though the partition curtains and roulette wheel have gone. Many artefacts are beyond restoration, and regarded as 'rubbish' (Nimrod 2003: 34). Iconic objects include a wheel from the car, dog kennels, the cooking range and Shackleton's room (ibid. 57). As part of the Antarctic Heritage Trust strategy for restoration, the stables, garage and latrine are to be rebuilt, despite their original *ad hoc* nature. Inside, the policy is to reposition artefacts if there is photographic or written documentation of their original location, when wear and tear or other witness marks indicate that location, or when there is strong cause for conjecture (Nimrod 2003: 72). The ambition is to give the impression that the original occupants have just exited. At the *Terra Nova* hut there will be extensive rearrangement, given the plethora of original descriptions by Cherry-Garrard et al and photographic images, and wealth of artefacts: here questions may centre on how adequately to reflect the presence of the Ross Sea Party. At the *Discovery* hut one proposal is to evince the occupancy of all four expeditions through a dispersal of relevant artefacts to four different areas in the hut (Discovery 2004: 97).

Figure 4.3 Recent view of northside shelves, Ponting's darkroom, Cape Evans (Photograph: Michael Morrison. By permission of the Antarctic Heritage Trust, New Zealand)

Close scrutiny of the material record, in combination with the recovery of the day-to-day experiences of explorers from text and photograph, might inform the standing arrangement and display of an interior, in the recreation of a particular 'historical moment'. But such restaging risks the construction of a *simulacrum*, a perfect replica — including replicated objects — of something that never existed in the first place. These were always cluttered and ever-changing places, untidy beyond what the provisos of current health and safety regulations, and the operational exigencies of museum convention might allow. Further, they are now characterised by *absence* — as much by that consumed, removed, left elsewhere, lost or stolen — as by what survives. Any strategy must surely acknowledge circulation, and shifts in the nature and meaning of things; the role of improvisation and contingency; the distinctions made between 'icon' and 'rubbish', and ascriptions of value. It should demonstrate fluidity and movement, both physical and semiotic. And in this the performative — of its nature transitory, yet recurrently generative of meaning — may provide valuable agency.

Contemporary art practices might inspire alternative interpretative approaches: the on-site exhibition could resemble an installation as much as a theatrical setting without the players, drawing together objects into contiguities and discordances of type, function and appearance that confound simple attributions of period and provenance; Peter Greenaway's long-term project to reorder museum collections might be indicative (see Greenaway 1991). We might envisage the realignment of projections of original photographs upon the extant architecture — as Shimon Attie achieved with photographs of pre-war Jewish buildings and population on the walls of post-war Berlin (Young 2000: 62–73) — regularly changing to illustrate different occupations.

But contemporary performance itself — integrations of site, body, and technology — has a particular facility. As a *time-based* genre, it provides an opportunity for meanings to be successively presented, challenged, confounded, inverted, and reinvented, in both sequence and parallel: it can say and do 'this' *then* 'that', or 'this' *and* 'that' at the same time. As an essentially *post-dramatic* practice — no longer predicated in form by concerns for character and plot — it can juxtapose, superimpose and elide various kinds of narrative — data, poetics, fiction, reminiscence, genealogy — in ways of telling that can address the complexities of experience present in the huts. As an ephemeral medium, it can avoid ascribing permanent value, attending equally to 'Professor Gregory's Villa' and the pony poop. And in the rhetorical devices of its dramaturgy, it can reveal itself as a work of transitory reconstitution rather than historical reconstruction: it knows its own subjectivity, and shows that it knows.

Performance is, however, unlikely to be manifest live, in *real time*; performers could hardly reside at the huts waiting for tourists to arrive. If they did, then they might stage events as much indifferent to, or in conflict with, the sites as congruent with them, revealing them obliquely — enabling them to 'speak for themselves' — rather than through direct denotation as the setting for historical reenactment (see Pearson & Shanks 2001: 23–4). The use of recorded media might make present 'absent' performers; multiple audio guides employing different, synchronised tape sequences might instruct various audiences to visit dispersed, though marked, locations where certain kinds of conflicting or contradictory historical and topographical information is made available, and in so doing choreograph the visitors themselves. Recent work on combinations of GPS, locative media, web-casting and mobile telephony might make available performance being created at locales *remote* from the sites themselves (see Giannachi 2004). And elsewhere, we might conflate period documents and modern records such as 360 degree digital modelling, to create *virtual* tours of places that few of us are likely to visit, and where physical visitation itself may be damaging.

The attention of performance might focus upon particular objects, both iconic and mundane — from Oates' jersey, the *Discovery* dingy oar and a binding of *Aurora Australis*, to oil cans and fodder bales — tracking their *life-histories* to detail expeditionary practice, demonstrating how constituents of material culture exist within overlapping frames and trajectories of time. Certain artefacts might illuminate shortfalls in the account, that not spoken of — that non-discursive, inarticulate, delinquent, disregarded — providing, for instance, evidence of prolonged engagement in play and leisure activity. Rather than seeking to enhance *aura*, performance might also work with *trace*, favouring a renewed sensitivity to the details of dwelling, to the marks and patinas of activities and multiple occupancy — of long term evolution and unconnected short term ruptures and singularities, small acts of vernacular defiance — that reveal difference and distinctiveness: from hut assembly instructions to graffiti, from axe cuts to fatty stains. It might address the genesis and history of existing marks within the locale, using them as a mnemonic for the events that caused them: discerning in them the movements, moments and encounters involved in their making — maps of practices and behaviours; using them to evoke the transient and evanescent; enhancing public perceptions of everyday life at the historic sites, and providing alternatives to pervasive narratives of courage, endurance and survival.

Bibliography

Chaplin, P (n.d.) *The Historic Huts of the Ross Sea Region*, Christchurch, New Zealand: Antarctic Heritage Trust .
Cherry-Garrard, A (1994) [1922] *The Worst Journey in the World*, London: Picador.
Evans, E (n.d.) *South with Scott*, London: Collins.
Giannachi, G (2004) *Virtual Theatres*, London: Routledge.
Greenaway, P (1991) *The Physical Self*, Rotterdam, Netherlands: Museum Boymans van Beuningen.
Harrowfield, D (1995) *Icy Heritage: Historic Sites of the Ross Sea Region*, Christchurch, New Zealand: Antarctic Heritage Trust.
Huntford, R (2000) *The Last Place on Earth*, London: Abacus.
Huntford, R, Summers, J, and Rowley, D (2002) *The Shackleton Voyages*, London: Weidenfeld & Nicolson.
McElrea, R. and Harrowfield, D (2004) *Polar Castaways*, Christchurch, New Zealand: Canterbury University Press
Norris, B (n.d.) *Antarctic Reflections*, Christchurch, New Zealand: New Zealand Antarctic Society.
Pearson, M (2004) '"No joke in petticoats": British polar expeditions and their theatrical presentations' *The Drama Review* T181 Spring 2004: 44–59.
Scott, R F (2001) [1905] *The Voyage of the Discovery, Volume I*, New York: Cooper Square Press.
Scott, R F (2003) [1923] *Scott's Last Expedition*, London: Pan Macmillan.
Shackleton, E (2000) [1909] *The Heart of the Antarctic*, London: Penguin.
Shackleton, E (1999) [1919] *South*, London: Penguin.
Young, J E (2000) *At Memory's Edge*, New Haven, US: Yale University Press.
(2003) *Conservation Report: Shackleton's Hut* Christchurch, New Zealand: Antarctic Heritage Trust (Nimrod 2003 in text).
(2004) *Conservation Plan: Discovery Hut, Hut Point* Christchurch, New Zealand: Antarctic Heritage Trust (Discovery 2004 in text).
(2004) *Conservation Plan: Scott's Hut, Cape Evans* Christchurch, New Zealand: Antarctic Heritage Trust (Terra Nova 2004 in text).

Archaeologists, Activists, and a Contemporary Peace Camp

Colleen M. Beck, John Schofield, and Harold Drollinger

Introduction

Along a lonely stretch of highway, 100 kilometres northwest of Las Vegas, Nevada in the far western United States is an undefined space of land in the desert where anti-war groups, anti-nuclear coalitions, environmentalists, and Western Shoshone Indians have gathered over the last five decades to protest against activities at the Nevada Test Site, the United States government's continental nuclear weapons testing ground. This particular locale, commonly referred to as the Peace Camp, is a place where more than 200 national and international groups have congregated to support and participate in the protests for hours, days and weeks at a time. The protesters are generally a combination of marginalised special interest groups who convene at the camp to express their views and feelings, forming a loosely organised community of short duration. No two protests had the same constituency. The Peace Camp is the only location in the United States recognised and used repeatedly by so many groups to express their objections to national and world trends in nuclear testing, nuclear waste storage, various wars, devastation of the earth, and other like issues. As such, it is an important place to the protesters and to those who support their causes.

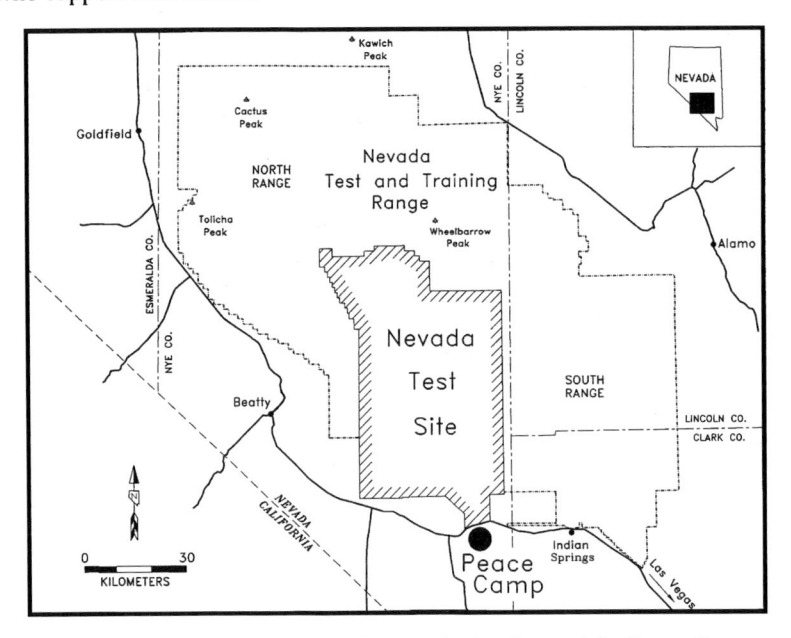

Figure 5.1 Map showing the relationship of the Nevada Test Site and the Peace Camp

Across from the Peace Camp is the fenced Test Site where nuclear tests and experiments have been conducted since 1951 (figure 5.1). Craters, tunnels and buildings designed to withstand a nuclear explosion are visible on this landscape as well as the infrastructure and facilities to support this scientific endeavour. The presence of this testing area is the reason for the existence of the Peace Camp and thus their histories are intertwined as the protesters' demonstrations seek to remind the Test Site workers that not all are in favour of the government activities there.

Over the past fifteen years, several facilities and testing locales at the Nevada Test Site have been surveyed, recorded and recognised for their historical importance at a national level (Beck 2002), while the counterpart to these testing-related structures (figure 5.2), the Peace Camp, received no attention. To document the other side of the story, the authors have conducted archaeological research at the camp. Ironically, this research effort faced its own political challenges due to the various entities and persons we encountered on our archaeological journey there. In this chapter, we discuss the challenges of working on a contemporary archaeological site steeped in controversy and still in use today.

Figure 5.2 Portable tower that is placed over a nuclear test hole for assembly of equipment and the placement of a nuclear device in the test bed. Photograph: authors.

The protests and protesters

The Peace Camp is the base of operations for the protestors, where they gather together and share in activities in support of their political positions. This is a stark landscape, a desert of xeric vegetation with rocks scattered throughout an undulating surface that is cut by shallow drainages. All water, food and shelter have to be transported to the camp.

According to Futrell and Brents (2003), the protest movement at the Test Site consisted of three phases. The first of these, the Early Years (1957–84), was very sporadic, loosely organised and non-violent. It comprised small numbers of people, ranging from religious groups to a women's movement for peace. The anti-nuclear protests at the Test Site increased significantly in the Peak Years (1985–94), when the professional and better-organised activist groups, such as Greenpeace, the American Peace Test (figure 5.3) and the Nevada Desert Experience, became involved. The protest events still remained relatively peaceful and non-violent given the number of them and the large numbers of people involved. The last phase, Post-Testing, began shortly after the nuclear testing moratorium was enacted in 1992. The number of protests and people significantly decreased, almost to the level of the initial phase, and currently the larger protest events generally correspond to specific days, such as New Years and Mothers' Day.

The first documented protest at the Test Site was in 1957 on the eve of a nuclear test. It consisted of a small, diverse group of thirty-five people belonging to the newly formed Non-Violent Action Against Nuclear Weapons organisation (Bigelow 1959: 24; Wittner 1997: 54–55). This small group stationed themselves at the main entrance and after a prayer vigil about a third of them lined themselves in rows and marched toward the facility, crossed the line, were arrested and transported to the nearest town for arraignment. They were given suspended sentences for trespassing and released, whereupon they returned to the Test Site and once again took up their prayer vigil. Protests continue at Peace Camp, with the occasional presence of vehicles, tents and campers signalling the protesters' re-appearance to those travelling on the adjacent highway. The actual protest events occasionally take place on the adjacent highway and always at the entrance to the Nevada Test Site. The protesters organise themselves at the camp and, armed with printed and hand-written signs conveying their points of view, they march and congregate along the road, praying and chanting and at times obstructing the flow of traffic. During some protests, they have blocked the entrance to the Test Site and a number of protesters have crossed the boundary line of the restricted facility with full knowledge that this act would cause their arrest (figure 5.4). One protester told us of the day he and his wife crossed the boundary with their 13-year-old daughter. It was important to him that their daughter understood the importance of political activism and results of the commitment to such actions. This story also reflects the general view of the protesters that crossing the boundary line in defiance of the authorities and the willingness to step foot on the Nevada Test Site demonstrates one's dedication to the cause and, like a rite of passage, the protesters who have not crossed the line are a different constituency from those who have engaged in this act of civil disobedience.

Figure 5.3 American Peace Test gathering at the Peace Camp 1988. Photograph: Gary Thompson, courtesy of the Las Vegas Review Journal.

Figure 5.4 Mothers' Day Protest at the Nevada Test Site 1987. Photograph: Gary Thompson, courtesy of the Las Vegas Review Journal.

As mentioned earlier, the frequency of protests and the number of protesters have declined over the last decade following the moratorium on nuclear testing. From 1986 to 1994, however, over 500 demonstrations took place involving more than 37,000 participants, 15,740 of whom were arrested (Rogers 2002). During this era, the Peace Camp was reflective of the expanding international, worldwide nuclear protest movement of the '80s, involving large numbers of people and highly organised protest groups that greatly influenced governments and politics (Wittner 2003). In 1988 it was estimated that 8,800 participants were involved in a single protest event at the Nevada Test Site, with 2,067 being arrested. Protests do continue today, with most opposing the current activities at the Nevada Test Site as well as an on-going government proposal for the Yucca Mountain nuclear waste disposal facility at the western edge of the Test Site.

Research

Why did archaeologists from the University of Nevada and English Heritage decide to undertake an archaeological study of this Peace Camp? Archaeologists do not study every site they encounter. Rather, they make choices regarding which sites they will invest their time in, whether the sites are ancient or recent, simple or complex; whether the site or landscape presents challenges or the potential to address research questions that excite or interest the researchers; whether the project will provide answers, or further more probing questions and insight that move the subject forward. This process reflects professional and personal interests, backgrounds, beliefs, and opportunities and this decision-making affects an archaeological undertaking from its inception. All of these issues shaped our involvement with Peace Camp.

In the case of the Nevada Peace Camp, several lines of inquiry and interest coalesced in this project. All the authors had previously worked in prehistoric and historic archaeology and at recent military-related locations. Broadening our research to address anti-military locations was due to the realisation that documenting military sites told only one side of the story and the study of protest sites would be a logical corollary to our other work by bringing another viewpoint to military history as well as to the history of social movements. As a prehistorian originally, John became interested in protest activities at Greenham Common Air Base in the United Kingdom as an extension of his earlier work on the transient occupation of landscapes, and reconstructing settlement from often subtle surface traces. He has conducted a preliminary archaeological study of the protest occupation at Greenham Common (Schofield and Anderton 2000), a piece of work which one colleague said could 'only have been written by a prehistorian'! Colleen and Harold, while conducting archaeological work on the Nevada Test Site, including nuclear testing sites, would begin and end some days witnessing groups of anti-nuclear activists camping and protesting at the facility's entrance. Questions often asked were: Who are these people? What do they do at the camp? How is the camp organised? What does their occupation leave behind? Definitely, curiosity played a role in generating this research. Eventually our interests came together with the shared belief that there is value in recording this archaeology of social dissidence and documenting a material culture view of the activists' actions. Given the uniqueness of the Peace Camp in importance and longevity, it was easily agreed that it would be the best place to conduct an archaeological study of the culture of protesters.

The heritage at the Peace Camp represents the time and effort expended by large numbers of people to have their voices of protest to government actions listened to by those in power in the United States and around the world. Protest movements have risen throughout history in the desire to alter an existing set of policies with some even resulting in new leaders and new countries (see Goodwin and Jaspar 2003; McAdam et al 2001). While not all protest actions are successful, they are a long-standing tradition when there is intense opposition to a situation and an important cultural phenomenon. The archaeological record of protesters at the Peace Camp and its attendant importance as a place to those who have spent time there form its cultural legacy.

Prior to our research, objectives established for the research design were to document the cultural features and objects on the landscape, analyse the data to address research questions, and conduct interviews with camp residents to augment the archaeological data and to understand their views of this land. The basic research question for the study revolved around the use of the landscape and of space with the goal to establish what makes a protest camp distinctive as a settlement type and to determine what it has in common with other types of settlement. Also, did changes in the philosophy or actions of protesters over the years result in a changing material record that today leaves an archaeological trace? And, what other ways has the opposition to nuclear testing been represented?

It was hoped that interviews with Peace Camp protesters would reveal how they see the landscape and if their perceptions of space and use when compared to the archaeological record and its interpretation coincide. Of most interest is how they perceive the function of the camp. Is it just a staging area? Is it ceremonial? Are activities group-oriented? Are camp activities as important to them as the actual protests at the perimeter of the Nevada Test Site?

Another research interest came from experience with prehistoric and historic archaeology in the region. Some sites were occupied by large groups of surrounding indigenous people for short periods of time at annual festivities, often referred to as fandangos. The intermittent use of the Peace Camp is similar, but of more recent vintage. The regional archaeology that includes prehistoric and historic American Indian campsites and the Peace Camp can therefore provide data for a comparative study on the organisations of special purpose campsites in the region, showing general over-arching trends and differences in how people organise themselves at such locales. To further complicate the picture, the active presence of Western Shoshone at the Peace Camp may have created a situation where the indigenous camp model overlaps the modern Peace Camp organisation.

The design for our study was based on one brief visit to the site and predictions of the types of remains that would exist at a camp of this type. In developing our approach to the site, we acknowledged that while the site is representative of an aspect of our modern culture, we, the archaeologists, lack familiarity with the subculture of protest actions. We are not part of this movement and do not really know what has gone on at the camp itself. So to us, the camp is like studying an archaeological site where we are investigating activities in which we have no direct personal experience. We did have expectations because of our initial awareness of the site as a camping area where we would encounter hearths, tent pads, rubbish, sweat lodges, a few peace symbols and other artistic items related to the protest activities.

The fieldwork was formulated according to traditional archaeological practices with site survey, mapping, and the recording of all cultural remains. Attempting to be objective about objects that are closely familiar to us (rock piles, wooden artefacts, stone arrangements etc) we made no value judgments regarding what was important or not important to record. We made a conscious effort to treat the site as we would one from another culture or time, and recorded all that we encountered. In terms of compiling a map of occupation, and to recognise ultimately zones of activity within it, we understood the need to record fully everything we encountered that might have its origin in the occupation of Peace Camp, however obvious, ephemeral or potentially natural it may be. Discarded bottles received the same treatment as elaborate rock symbols on the landscape. What would be called graffiti in modern terms, and usually disregarded, were recorded as personal and often intimate expressions. All materials were considered significant to the study regardless of our own views and beliefs. Our challenge was to understand the importance of these items to the people who use the camp.

One issue we faced that is not common to archaeological projects, but recognised as part of the archaeological record, is the continuing re-use of the Peace Camp. There was the possibility that parts of the landscape might change between field visits and possibly even if protesters camped and utilized the area over weekends when we were away from the site. Therefore, we accepted the situation that the recording of a particular site area would reflect the material culture of that portion of the site as it existed on the days we worked there. Re-use would exhibit continuity in the patterns of use. The realisation that a place recorded several months earlier was now different in some ways was disconcerting, but it was an acknowledgement of the changing nature of the camp.

Two field sessions were conducted in 2002 at the Peace Camp, one in March and one in November. The actual fieldwork effort itself went smoothly. When we began the archaeological research at the Peace Camp, we estimated the size of the camp to be 400 by 200 meters or so, about eight hectares, with fifty to sixty features. With the entire camp recorded, we now know we greatly underestimated its size because we had not realised the protesters utilised a much greater landscape than just the camping areas and land immediately adjacent. The survey revealed the Peace Camp covers about 240 hectares, stretching some 2,000 meters along the highway and about 1,000 meters away from it. Initially, the archaeologists systematically walked in all directions to determine the extent of the distribution of the Peace Camp cultural materials and the boundaries were drawn to encompass all the identified cultural materials with this perimeter determination confirmed during the recording of the site.

The site is complex, with 765 features identified and recorded to date (figure 5.5). Features include rock cairns, caches, rock circles, foundations for statuary or sculptures, geoglyphs (landscape symbols created out of stone alignments), fencing, flagpoles, flagpole holes, nature gardens (plants circumscribed with rocks), graffiti, hearths, dirt paths, dirt roads, rock lines, stacked rocks, sculptures, sweat lodges, sweat lodge centre holes, tent pads and sleeping areas, wickiups, wood piles and a single porta-potty donated by the federal agency for the Test Site. There are artefacts purposefully placed at certain features. These include crystals, a dream catcher, knives, shells and a watch. One result of the involvement of the American Indians at the site is the cleaning of surface trash in keeping with the notion of helping and respecting mother earth. As a result, discarded or lost items are rare, distributed across the landscape, with only a bottle or two and some small items, such as nails, a cigarette lighter and a child's toy. The toy was found near a parking area and possibly left behind unintentionally by a child when preparing to leave the camp.

Figure 5.5 Stylised stone peace symbol. Photograph: authors

Controversy and reactions

We had suspected that by conducting an archaeological study of a politicised landscape that our work might create some interest from different groups. But some things that happened were completely unexpected and we were not prepared for our research to create its own political milieu. While discussions of conducting this research had been on-going for several years, our field effort was instigated by a Nevada Department of Transportation interest in reviving two gravel pits at the Peace Camp for road construction. Materials-testing holes and markers outlining the proposed area of removal indicated pending work that would destroy a portion of the camp. Prior to these activities, archaeologists conducted a survey and concluded that no archaeological or historical remains were present. Their work was conducted under the jurisdiction of a federal agency that is responsible for much public land in the western United States, including the Peace Camp.

Our inquiry into these results, with an explanation of the potential importance of the Peace Camp location, resulted in strong statements by the archaeologist for this land agency. Verbal comments were 'the Peace Camp is too recent to be considered significant' and 'the protest site had no legal historical importance'. In fact, we were told the first archaeologists at the Peace Camp were encouraged to pick up modern trash and clean up areas in the course of their work, and that this may have happened at the Peace Camp. Our arguments to the contrary, regarding the precedence of the recognised significance of testing remains at the Nevada Test Site of the same age and the relationship between the two locations, fell upon deaf ears; but permission to conduct a field study of the Peace Camp was granted to us even though we were told that we really did not need it because we were not doing archaeology.

Figure 5.6 American Indians drumming as they cross the cattle guard onto the Nevada Test Site 1991. Photograph: James Kenney, courtesy of the Las Vegas Review Journal

On the other hand, due to Western Shoshone Indian involvement in the Peace Camp, we had discussions with their Spiritual Leader, Corbin Harney, and his staff regarding the planned archaeological work. They expressed support for our research and offered ideas and assistance for the effort because of the importance of the location to them. The Western Shoshone hold to the idea that the Test Site land belongs to them, according to the 1863 Ruby Valley treaty agreement between the tribe and the United States government. Furthermore, because of the perceived environmental degradation of the land and other resources from nuclear testing, Western Shoshone and members from other tribes have become increasingly aware and involved in the protest movements at the Test Site (figure 5.6) (Futrell and Brents 2003: 758; Harney 1995: 15). They, like the other protestors, want nuclear testing to cease, but, specifically, for the land, mother earth, to be free of the pollution, here and around the world. Harney (1995: 19–21) states:

> As I see it all around me, the trees are dying out, our water is contaminated, and our air is not good to breathe. ... This contamination that we're putting into Mother Earth is not the way. ... We know there's contamination on the land today. We know it's in the water, and that it's spreading throughout the world. ...We're trying to do something about this by stopping nuclear development. We're trying to put a stop to this thing that we don't understand but which creates enormous problems for us.

On the first day of the fieldwork, it was only hours before we began to face the politics of our endeavour. A deputy sheriff for Nye County, the regional jurisdiction within which the Peace Camp is located, came to see what we were doing there. We learned that his interest did not just stem from his work in the county, but because he is one of the deputy sheriffs assigned to law enforcement work at the Nevada Test Site. This Peace Camp is under varying degrees of surveillance and he probably came to find out if a protest or other actions were going to occur. We explained to him that we were not protesters but archaeologists conducting a study of the Peace Camp. His response to this was positive and to share stories about the protest activities and to recommend persons to whom we might want to talk about past protest actions at the camp. In fact, this deputy sheriff was involved from the law enforcement side in several protests, especially during the 1980s when the protests were at their height. As a result of his experiences, he was very interested in our research and knew the history and importance of the events that took place.

Several days later, a visitor was not nearly as cordial. A truck zoomed up to our work area and a very angry Shoshone Indian, known as a strong activist for Western Shoshone interests, exited the vehicle. He demanded to know why we were there and what right we had doing our work. Although we explained the purpose and extent of our research and the contacts we had made prior to initiating the work, our attempts to communicate with him failed because he did not want to hear what we were saying and he left as angrily as he arrived. It was unfortunate there was no way to reach some accord with him.

A week after this, Corbin Harney, the Western Shoshone spiritual leader, came to the Peace Camp to conduct a morning sunrise service to which we were invited. In attendance were some of his followers, peace activists, a group of Zen Buddhists, and John and Colleen. Corbin conducted the service. During prayer time John entered the circle to thank Corbin and the Western Shoshone for supporting our work and our presence at Peace Camp. Corbin then spoke to the group regarding his feelings about the land, the activities at the Nevada Test Site and the Western Shoshone Indians. After the ceremony, over breakfast, we first spoke to people who have stayed at the Peace Camp and protested at the entrance. It quickly became apparent the protesters interpreted our interest in the Peace Camp and presence at the ceremony as our personal support for their cause and began telling us stories about the Peace Camp and their actions against the Test Site. Some of the stories might not have been told if some had known we were also involved in conducting archaeological research on the Test Site. Usually, anyone who works there is considered untrustworthy to the protesters, and this is somewhat borne out based on the political history and past animosities from both sides during a protest event. Consequently, this was a particularly uncomfortable experience for us because of the dichotomy of our situation. Corbin Harney was familiar with our work both at the Peace Camp and on the Nevada Test Site and understood that we were conducting our research in good faith and that we would handle the information appropriately.

Before our first field season ended, a reporter from the Las Vegas Review Journal came out to do a story on our research at the Peace Camp. He had written multiple stories on the protests at the Test Site and was very interested in our work. This article ran as a feature story in a Sunday edition and included the fact that Colleen and Harold also conduct archaeological work on the Test Site (Rogers 2002). Subsequent to this article, we received telephone calls and emails from protesters and other reporters. Some understood that we were not the enemy, but others were suspicious of the reasons for the research and of us for our interest in the Peace Camp. It was as if we might be spies for the government. Nevertheless, a few protesters' web sites offered readers the link to this article and we have even discovered it listed on web sites as far away as Russia.

Response to the article from the federal agency managing the Nevada Test Site was mixed. Several individuals who worked for the government offered to talk to us about their experiences during the protests, but management expressed concern regarding our work. The greatest issue was the highlighting of protest activities by persons also working on the Nevada Test Site. So, Colleen and Harold found themselves in a situation where the protesters did not trust them, neither of the government agencies managing the Test Site and the land for the Peace Camp were pleased with their extra-curricular activities and, ironically, the most support came from the Western Shoshone Indian community. Colleen and Harold have worked with the Western Shoshone on their historical and traditional interests in the land at the Nevada Test Site for more than a decade. The work has involved participating in government consultations with the tribes regarding issues of importance to them, conducting field studies with tribal elders to determine which places and sites retain importance to them and reviewing archaeological collections with tribal members in order to identify items and human remains that belong to a group and need to be repatriated to the tribes for re-use and reburial. This continued personal contact with some of the tribal members has created a climate of trust and they were supportive of our activities, in spite of one or two individuals' anger over it all.

The awkwardness of the situation was apparent to John and he realised that to conduct other aspects of our research, such as interviews and participating in the camp activities during a protest event, the work would largely fall upon him. As a foreigner from the UK with no apparent political agenda, he may be able to extend the research into areas Colleen and Harold cannot access. We do expect, however, that some within the protest community will be willing to work with all of us in spite of our association with the Test Site. Due to these political issues, our original interview objectives, particularly those related to the protesters' view of the camp could not be achieved in conjunction with the fieldwork. It is hoped that as time passes, we will be able to obtain the relevant interviews.

When we returned for our second field season, eight months later, we were dismayed to discover that some graffiti recorded during our first season of work had been obliterated by the application of grey paint to entire sections of the writings and art and a number of these writings and art had been there for more than two decades. It is likely that the pictures of the graffiti in the newspaper article on our work drew attention to its existence and it was subsequently destroyed, possibly by the transportation agency responsible for the highway drainage tunnels used for the graffiti. This was a totally unanticipated and unfortunate impact of our research.

Furthermore, the area we designated during our time at the site in 2002 as the current ceremonial centre, with sweat lodges and associated features and artefacts, was cleared of all such features and cultural material in 2004. This unfortunate occurrence was due to a cross-country motorcycle event that staged its main operations at this place, a location approved by the managing federal agency. In order to set up their operations, the remains of the previous group, the users of the Peace Camp, were removed. However, one large hearth feature in front of the lodges was kept and used by the motorcycle race participants. The ceremonial centre was the focal point for the Western Shoshone and it was there that the indigenous camp model could be tested. Interestingly, most indigenous camps do not have sweat lodges, but where they do occur, they are in proximity to a hearth area, similar to the Peace arrangement, as heated rocks are integral to the sweat-house ceremonies.

In terms of the future of the Peace Camp material culture, during the recording phase of our work, the cultural richness of the site astounded us and has presented its own dilemma. Now that we have this information, we want to utilise it in a way that does not endanger the site. An article in the newspaper ended up destroying graffiti. Greater exposure of the site could have even more dire consequences. The Peace Camp is isolated and the land is open to the public with easy access and no protection for the cultural heritage there. Almost no one outside the protest groups realises the enormity of the site and there is the potential for a government entity to decide that such cultural features on the landscape are an unacceptable environmental degradation and use this as an excuse to take a course of action that could destroy them. In addition, many of the items could be of interest to collectors, a thought that creates an image of people scouring the landscape searching for the artefacts based on our descriptions. Likewise, there are those with a personal agenda, political or otherwise, bent on destruction. This is a major issue with which we continue to grapple in hopes of finding a solution that will allow us to share our research in the same fashion as other archaeological studies. That said, this is always an issue with archaeological research of all periods. The point here is that the swift and thorough destruction of ephemeral (and for some sacred) remains by those with a particular political wish is not given wider publicity and attention. We do not want to be the unintentional agent for the loss of cultural materials at the Peace Camp, and the source of disquiet and discontent amongst the sites' traditional owners.

Conclusion

Archaeologists working on contemporary archaeology are rare in the United States and there is conflict over the value of the research. While archaeologists involved in such research see modern society as part of the historical continuum and contributing to the study of archaeology and society, others see contemporary archaeology as unimportant to the discipline and society as a whole. Unlike traditional archaeological topics, coverage of the archaeology of movie sets, hippie communes, and moon landings appear sensational and are considered irrelevant. The situation with the Peace Camp, where an archaeological team initially discounted the Peace Camp material culture and we have argued for its importance, highlights this dichotomy within the discipline. Recently, when the federal archaeologist responsible for archaeology on the land where the camp resides was offered a tour, he said he would not go because there would be nothing to interest him there and chided Colleen for saying our work was archaeology.

The archaeological study of the Peace Camp also exemplifies an issue that confronts contemporary archaeology: the value of the research to those who hold interest in a contemporary site. In this case, some of the Western Shoshone Indians welcomed the research, recognising that a study of the site could produce information that would substantiate the area's importance and possibly protect it from governmental actions. Others were glad to hear of the study because it would bring attention to the camp, the activities, and their cause. And one protester mentioned that it was good to see that people outside of their community recognised the importance of the Peace Camp. Nevertheless, other protesters, marginalised in the greater society by their beliefs and actions, mistrusted us and our research motives, creating a situation where we, the archaeologists, were the political concern due to our personal experiences and backgrounds.

Our efforts at conducting the research have created a variety of cultural responses, some to the detriment of the Peace Camp remains and the fact that we have conducted research at the Peace Camp has raised the issue of how archaeologists should report on cultural manifestations of cultural groups who may not want this information made public. At the Peace Camp, there are personal offerings, messages to Mother Earth and other expressions of personal beliefs. So, we need to ask ourselves if it is within our purview to make the decision, with our own biases and relatively limited interpretations, to publicise what another group of people are doing when they express their beliefs.

These are tough issues — the archaeologists as political figures, the effects of our research on a site, and the interests of those who created and use the site. While not all aspects of these issues are confined to contemporary archaeology, they are brought to the fore because we are working on locations where there are people still alive who have attachments, memories and emotions about these places. Some protesters believe their protest efforts at the Nevada Test Site contributed to the nuclear moratorium, one of their primary goals. While proud of their accomplishments, the protesters we did talk to all had stories, many poignant, about their experiences at the camp and during the protests. Their relationship with the camp was related to the activities with friends, family and the other protesters and their spiritual experiences there. There is a strong sense of ownership as they see the camp as their place. And conversely, the archaeologists themselves have also developed attachments, memories and emotions, albeit different from the original inhabitants. The weeks of long days spent exploring and documenting the Peace Camp resulted in numerous fascinating finds and provided the archaeologists a unique opportunity to see the protesters' way of life with its formerly unrecognised complexities, including the artistic and personal expressions scattered throughout the desert. This overall experience combined with the personal interactions that occurred during the fieldwork has generated a strong connection between us and this piece of land.

These experiences highlight the often hidden politics of archaeology due to the contemporary setting of the research, and in this case at times it appeared there was a behind-the-scenes struggle over who controls archaeological research. The archaeologists have their research goals and commitment to communicating the results of their efforts; the local community and other persons with involvement in the site have a strong interest in whether or not archaeological work should be conducted at a location, how the work is done, and the manner in which the information is disseminated; and government entities have their own agendas about the places in which they wish to invest time, not to mention their weighty opinions regarding the importance and validity of the study of specific sites and research topics. In the case of the Peace Camp, the politics escalated because of the strong feelings by various groups 'for and against' the protest activities and the distrust engendered over the years between the protesters and the government. For some people the archaeological research became attached to the protest camp as an activity in support of the protesters' actions with the researchers themselves interpreted as proponents of activism. Some protesters viewed the archaeology endeavour as more governmental interference. However, a number of people including the news reporter understood the goal of the research, which is the documentation and interpretation of an important and unknown contemporary archaeological landscape. These types of complexities in contemporary archaeology are some of the reasons that the work at the Peace Camp and at other contemporary sites can be so challenging and also such a rewarding experience.

Although the government is no longer engaged in full-scale nuclear tests, other research is conducted at the Nevada Test Site. Protesters object to some of these experiments, but most importantly, they protest the continued existence of the Nevada Test Site. As time passes, the Peace Camp will evolve as new protesters are introduced to the site and the issues change. The politics of archaeological work at the camp probably will endure, but over time we expect to have the opportunity to document and report on the landscape of this political and social group's changing culture.

Acknowledgements

The authors thank the Desert Research Institute and English Heritage for their support of this project. They also express their gratitude to Corbin Harney and his staff for their assistance, to the protesters who talked to them about their experiences, to Keith Rogers for his lasting interest in their research, and to Wayne Cocroft for participating in the second season of fieldwork. In addition, the *Las Vegas Review Journal* graciously allowed the authors access to and use of the newspaper's photographic archive.

Bibliography

Beck, C M (2002) 'The archaeology of scientific experiments at a nuclear testing ground', in Schofield J, Johnson W G and Beck C M (eds), *Matériel Culture: the Archaeology of Twentieth Century Conflict*, London: Routledge, 65–79.

Bigelow, A (1959) *The Voyage of the Golden Rule: An Experiment with Truth*, Garden City, New York: Doubleday and Company.

Futrell, R and Bents, B (2003) 'Protest as Terrorism? The Potential for Violent Anti-Nuclear Activism' *American Behavioral Scientist* 46 (6): 745–65.

Goodwin, J and Jaspar, J (2003) *The Social Movements Reader: Cases and Concepts*, Malden, Massachusetts: Blackwell Publishers.

Harney C (1995) *The Way It Is: One Water...One Air...One Mother Earth*, Nevada City, California: Blue Dolphin Publishing.

McAdam, D, Tarrow, S and Tilly, C (2001) *Dynamics of Contention*, Cambridge: Cambridge University Press.

Rogers K (2002) 'Pleading for Peace' *Las Vegas Review Journal*, 24 March 2002 www.reviewjournal.com/lvrj_home/2002/Mar-24-Sun-2002/news/18354606.html (21.03.2006).

Schofield J and Anderton M (2000) 'The queer archaeology of Green Gate: interpreting contested space at Greenham Common Airbase' *World Archaeology* 32 (2): 236–51.

Wittner L (1997) *Resisting the Bomb: A History of the World Nuclear Disarmament Movement, 1954–1970, The Struggle Against the Bomb, Volume Two*, Stanford: Stanford University Press.

Wittner, L (2003) *Toward Nuclear Abolition: A History of the World Nuclear Disarmament Movement, 1971 to the Present, The Struggle Against the Bomb, Volume Three*, Stanford: Stanford University Press.

Notes on a Record of Fear: On the Threshold of the Audible

Louise K Wilson

For the project *Contemporary Art in Historic Places* in 2005, three artists were invited to create new work inspired by historic properties in the 'East of England'. This shared initiative among the National Trust, English Heritage and Commissions East, was developed to 'attract new visitors to heritage sites or to engage existing visitors in new ways' (www.commissionseast.org.uk/cstudy/NT_EH.html). The properties were varied, with the seventeenth-century country house of Fellbrigg Hall (Norfolk), the linked locations of Dunstable Downs and De Grey Mausoleum (Bedfordshire) and the ex-military history site, now nature reserve, of Orford Ness (Suffolk) chosen for artists' intervention.

For the artists ultimately selected – Richard Wentworth, Imogen Stidworthy and I — the brief was to produce temporary site-specific projects by working closely with property staff, volunteers, visitors and nearby communities, 'taking inspiration from the unique character, culture, heritage and environment' of the site (www.commissionseast.org.uk/cstudy/NT_EH.html).

At that time I was starting to generate a body of work looking at the cultural and physical legacy of the Cold War, exploring the role of art in addressing the heritage issues of sites with politically 'difficult' histories. The starting point was a desire to play with beliefs around the apparent 'transportability' of the past (and present) through sound. There was, I discovered, something timely about exploring ideas of embodied experience of place in relation to Cold War sites in Britain. English Heritage was starting to record sites in England and planning a national assessment to determine the most significant ones for conservation and preservation. They were also initiating a project examining oral histories and the wider (cultural and social) impact of the Cold War.

I became interested in concepts of heritage in this context and intrigued by the particular philosophical difficulties that such attention can give rise to.

Over three years I made repeat visits to Spadeadam, a remote ex-rocket test site in Cumbria, producing a number of artworks including a film called, simply, *Spadeadam* (2003), which centred on my observation of an English Heritage archaeological survey of the Blue Streak rocket launch site. The chance to observe and document the archaeologists at work offered a useful opportunity to comment on Spadeadam at a remove. I did not want simply to edit together shots of the empty and desolate launch site ruins but attempted to provide scale and perspective (both architectural and contextual) through the documenting of this process of mapping. The knowledge that these Cold War structures (with a complex history within living memory) were to be scheduled as Ancient Monuments added a paradoxical captioning.

The film was principally about investigating space, taking temporary visual ownership by flying over RAF Spadeadam in a light aircraft on a weekend when the airspace nerability' trials in the 1940s and 1950s. Wainwright recalled the arrival one day of thirty to forty bottles on the same stretch of beach, sent from a school in Holland, due east. Balloons also touch down en masse: 'I think they're all from fairs and for some reason they must blow across the country and descend when they get to Orford Ness and end up inside the buildings — sometimes drifting round in the eddies'. He recalled the shock of first encountering a 'Mr Blobby' balloon (a regular intruder) floating around like some live being in a little dark room off Lab 3.

(A month or so after our conversation I found a message in a plastic bottle sent from an aquarium in Belgium in 2003 and lodged in the entrance to Lab 2, but the name and address inside was bleached and too indistinct to read.)

During a preliminary site visit in January, I was struck by the conspicuous range of sounds and prevalence of anecdotes involving sound. Grant Lohoar told numerous stories from the enormous reservoir of information he has gathered over the years. He spoke about the extraordinary reverberation inside the relatively small Control Room built in 1955/6 that suggested a space many times bigger. In fact the National Trust employees said when painting the room, it was almost unpleasant to remain inside and attempt any conversation because of the ricocheting acoustic.

Angus Wainwright recalled how in the early days of work on the Ness to assess its suitability for preservation there were no weatherproof buildings for the surveyors to stay in; but it was possible (and actually pleasant) to sleep out in a bomb hole on a warm night. Wainwright observed in conversation that there is a very interesting acoustic down in a hole — a slight wind and the rattle of the grass whereas above it there is deafening wind-blowing noise. The shingle holds the warmth and gets quite comfortable as it moulds into one's back shape. He also noted from these experiences spending solitary spells on the Ness that it was important to take time to concentrate on the surprisingly subtle soundscape that already exists beneath the ever-present and familiar noise. He remembered how

in the evening it was really nice to just sit and stare and listen, and suddenly you'd just start hearing the birds and interesting little tiny noises that you wouldn't normally hear because you're crunching on the shingle. After a while you're aware that all you're hearing is your footsteps in the shingle going 'crunch crunch crunch' and the wind and the seagulls. It's a kind of monotonous soundscape and it was good just to sit and be aware of the quietness and these little noises. (recorded interview, 13 October 2005)

I started to listen in on these extra-ordinary sounds that travel around the now-derelict military buildings. The wind animates the site, producing noises like oddly tuned musical or percussive instruments. Flute-like harmonics on top of the Bomb Ballistic building hit me first — a breathy presence in the steel railings of the external staircase that provides a soundtrack to a landscape that encourages just standing and staring. Elsewhere, in the Control Room, the wind intermittently enters the building through discrete wall holes to produce symphonic 'voices'. This structure functioned firstly as the control centre for Lab 1, where Britain's first (operational) atomic bomb, Blue Danube, was vibration-tested. In the absence of the heavy machinery and monitoring equipment in these spaces, a number of the ex-AWRE (Atomic Weapon Research Establishment) buildings such as the Control Room have become exceptionally reverberant.

Animals, especially resident and migratory birds, occupy these buildings and broadcast their (seasonal) presence: pigeons and doves audibly nest and are sometimes trapped in the air-conditioning ducts. On approaching the Labs, there is an auditory 'explosion' of exiting pigeons. Some downy white feathers on the grimy floor of Lab 5 are the sole residue of a duck that had become ensnared in the razor wire defence. But mainly bird and other animal tracks are more life affirming: for example, hares create trails over the sides of the shingle-topped buildings constructed to test weapon parts.

This atmosphere of secrecy, strangeness and renewed 'occupation' became the starting point for a series of audio and video works I produced in autumn 2005, which sought to explore aspects of transmission and reflection on this extraordinary site. The wish to incorporate audio and ideas of 'aurality' was key since fictions, anecdotes and stories readily circulate around Orford Ness. Aside from the sonic 'fallout' from its military testing past, there are numerous tales of ghost sightings (such as the apparition that appeared in one of the pagodas during a guided tour, apparently angry that the National Trust was giving away Britain's military secrets); unexplained nocturnal noises; and stories linking the Ness to its proximity with the infamous UFO incident at Rendlesham Forest in the 1980s (viewed in certain circles as Britain's 'Roswell'). Other stories of electrical disturbances, malfunctioning compasses, computers and camera monitors are commonplace.

Figure 6.1 Bird in duct. Photograph: Louise K Wilson.

The ideas behind my series of temporary audio (and video) installations ultimately made for the Ness, collectively entitled *A Record of Fear*, were in response to both the site's raw history and the current rich soundscape.

There was a desire to make audible what is absent or intangible or cannot be said. The resulting artworks were installed temporarily on the Ness and in Ipswich in late August to the beginning of October 2005. In addition, for one day only in late September, visitors had the unique opportunity to enter a number of the normally inaccessible test laboratories on a self-guided walk. In certain buildings, sound works were specially installed for this occasion. It was intended that this series of pieces, heard over time and foregrounding human and mechanical voices, would prompt a moment of reflection on the past and the continuation of the military project.

Black Beacon: visibility and audibility

The unrelenting flatness of Orford Ness is notably broken by the presence of the AWRE labs, the Lighthouse and by a black timbered building called Black Beacon. This curious structure was built in 1928 for the Royal Aircraft Establishment, Farnborough, to house an experimental 'rotating loop' navigation beacon. The top floor of this octagonal building (one of just a few on the Ness open to visitors) provides an elevated viewing area through seven viewing slots, akin to a bird hide. The viewing gallery presented

Figure 6.2 Black Beacon Receiver (ie, object on shelf). Photograph: Richard Davies, Courtesy Commissions East.

itself as the obvious location for a temporary audio artwork that might suggest a new listening station. The piece — called *Black Beacon Receiver* — drew on manipulated field recordings I had made with other sound recordists over some months on the Ness.

The audio system for *Black Beacon Receiver* comprised seven custom-built earpieces connected to a central 'transmitter' unit, housing a bank of MP3 players triggered by a motion sensor.

Looped soundscapes could be heard through a series of earpiece sculptures that looked both peculiar and oddly utilitarian, evoking the mysterious objects found washed up or half-buried on the Ness. Despite the decontamination of the site, the intermittent appearance of the bomb disposal squad affirms that this is not a place where the visitor should casually pick up strange objects. People sometimes do, however, and there is an *ad hoc* 'museum' of identifiable and alien rusted artefacts near the Warden's Office and in storage elsewhere. Angus Wainwright had earlier emailed me a picture of an object he had unearthed on the Ness looking like 'a rusty iron vase about twenty-five centimetres high with a "wasp waist" and flaring to each end. Quite an elegant artefact with a wonderful iron oxide patina' (email, 5 August 2005). The earpiece and playback systems were produced by the Glasgow-based design company Pavillion, stimulated by an email exchange of images of archaic weaponry, shell speakers, the aforementioned 'iron vase', ear trumpets and so on. Bands of colour across the finished objects suggested electrical wiring or the colour-coded signifiers across bombs. The casing for the weapon WE177A, for instance, housed in the nearby Control Room, has rings of orange and yellow paintwork around the nose cone to denote the explosive chain reaction.

Figure 6.3 ON Detritus (ie Orford Ness Detritus). Photograph: Louise K Wilson

Each earpiece 'broadcasted' edited sounds gathered from a visible stretch of land specific to the view from that window. There was an interest in exploring how viewpoint may or may not appear to correspond with the likely source of sound. To quote artist Bill Fontana:

> In visual perception, there is usually simultaneity between the viewer and the object of perception. With sound there is often a time lag, since we can often hear a sound source before or after we see it. In aural perception, we sometimes do not see what we are actually hearing. (n.d.)

In *Black Beacon Receiver*, the sound (source) *was* largely still present, but may not necessarily have been visible or (perceptibly) audible. Visitors were invited to listen carefully to both what is already capable of being heard in the landscape and what is generally inaudible to the human ear. An array of contact mics, hydrophones, ultrasonic recorders and regular microphones had been used to capture the subtle ambient sounds of the site. Timeless natural processes were heard knitted together with those suggesting transitory manmade dereliction. These sounds, gathered largely from the natural world, became more sinister and difficult to contextualise when recorded and played back in this fashion. As Judith Palmer notes of *Receiver* 'these soundscapes tap into the site's acoustic signature — the Splash of waves on the shore; the screech of a startled barn owl; the creak of dislodged iron-sheeting; the doomed clattering of a pigeon trapped in a vent-shaft... Insects click, the mudbanks sigh, and bats echolocate, as the sub-audible and subliminal are made to materialize' (2006).

Madrigal Rooms

London-based choir the Exmoor Singers use the Base Camp barracks at Orford Ness as a weekend rehearsal site once a year before playing concerts in local Suffolk churches and castles. I became very excited on hearing this information from Dave Cormack, the resident Orford Ness warden. He also told me he had once taken the Singers on a guided tour of the disused labs. In one of the pagoda buildings, they felt impelled to start singing a Russian song they were rehearsing at the time. Stephen Hall, from the Singers, acknowledged in conversation that this was done in the spirit of cheeky defiance (toward the lingering 'Allied' presence on the old Cold War divide).

I met the choir on the Ness during their annual stay in May 2005. We travelled out to Lab 6 and to the Control Room and choir director James Jarvis selected extracts from the repertoire to 'test out' the acoustics. I wanted to hear male and then female voices, single then multiple, to consider how these sounded in the different reverberant spaces. The meaning of the words of songs was less crucial: witness the choir clustered around the WE177A nuclear bomb singing 'The Bare Necessities' (from Disney's *The Jungle Book*) in order to foreground baritone voices.

For *A Record of Fear* the Singers agreed to perform selected madrigals in some of the empty military buildings, in solo and choral arrangements. The vibrant human presence singing songs of love, yearning and an awareness of the passing of time would provide an affecting counterpoint to the stark and disturbing interiors. Two of these buildings in particular provided powerfully resonant visual and aural locations for the recorded singing.

Figure 6.4 Exmoor Singers in Pagoda 4. Photograph: Louise K Wilson

Lab 6 was a combined centrifuge and vibration facility built in 1966 and operated by EMI to subject electronic missile components, possibly from Polaris, to 'G' forces and (random) vibration tests. The disordered interior is dark and hazardous, and perilous access for the choir dictated a vault over a bricked-up entrance before reaching the staircase down into the 'pit'. The acoustics in the centre of the bare centrifuge space were demonstrated to act as a remarkable performance space. According to Jarvis:

> The most striking impression when singing John Bennet's madrigal 'Weep, O mine eyes' in the centrifuge pit was sonic. Though hardly designed as a performance space, the room's cylindrical shape and reflective walls formed an extraordinary acoustical environment when the singers arranged themselves in a coaxial circle facing into the centre: the sheer volume of sound that could be driven within this resonator by a few voices was overwhelming; the harmonic possibilities of the common chords could be exploited to the nth degree; and the dissonant suspensions had a searing effect. The physical symmetry of the situation meant that there was no room for passive listeners other than the central microphone, so that performers and audience became one entity; which made this, incongruously, the ideal madrigal room and added to the poignancy of the experience. (email, 11 November 2005)

The choir was recorded both on video and hard disc recorder, to enable the layering of different sung 'takes'. The video camera was positioned in the centre of the singers and panned round each in turn, individually matching sung voice with recognisable performer to intensify further the idea of warm human presence (in such an unlikely place).

Figure 6.5 Solo Exmoor singer in Lab 6. Photograph: Louise K Wilson

In another of the subsequent video works, a solo female singer performs 'Weep, O mine eyes'. Two recordings made on opposite sides of the 'pit' at separate times were edited together to prompt thoughts of subjective interpretation over time. Her (purificatory) recitation of 'Weep, O mine eyes, and cease not...that I may drown me in you...' was strangely fitting in the pool-like recess of the centrifuge with its pale aquamarine-painted brickwork.

In retrospect this solo and ensemble singing has come to be seen as transubstantive. It is perhaps less a speaking back (to the ghostly past work of the AWRE engineers and scientists), than a quieter more reparative gesture.

The visual presence of the choir in the Control Room singing 'Come, sable night', arranged around the solitary exhibit, the WE177A nuclear bomb, was perhaps more obviously strongly emotive in considering the disparity between meaning and performance context. Jarvis had written:

All Elizabethan madrigals, especially the slow ones, seem to mourn the passing of a golden age. In the control room, singing it in the gathering dusk clustered around the casing of an nuclear bomb, the words of John Ward's 'Come, sable night' were transformed into a lament for an age of pre-nuclear innocence. Images out of Doctor Strangelove came vividly to the mind's eye and a striking spiritual, if scarcely formal, relationship between Ward's music and Penderecki's 'Threnody for the victims of Hiroshima' hardly seemed fanciful at that time and place. 'Behold, the sun hath shut his golden eye, the day is spent' conjured images of the light of a thousand suns followed by nuclear winter; 'All things in sweet repose their labours close' acquired a bitter irony; and, in an age when nuclear proliferation seems to have begun again and the despoilation of the planet by deforestation, carbon emissions and wind turbines seems unstoppable, the last line: 'all... hopes do faint, and life is failing' aptly summed up the exquisite melancholy of the moment. (email, 11 November 2005)

In audio editing 'Come, sable night' sound engineer, Gareth Jones, and I took tiny sung moments of the madrigal and added a convolved reverb of the room's acoustic. This reverb effect works by taking an impulse response (taken in the real space of the Control Room) and convolving it with a new sound. This recreates the acoustic of the original. So in essence the new sound is combined with the original recording and has the properties of the original imposed on it. In short, the recording of the choir singing in the Control Room was temporally extended with the reverberation of this same space added again.

I then wondered how far one can 'archive' atmosphere. In looking to make sense of resonance and reverberation, I see the convolved reverb as adding materiality to the transience of sound. I consider it as a kind of archaeological artefact stored in the audio software. These sound 'splinters' were on the edge of legibility, when installed on speakers underneath the nuclear bomb in the Control Room. A visitor to *A Record of Fear* said these punctuating sonic bursts reminded her of sound effects in *The Wizard of Oz* (1938) suggesting something magical and transformative.

Figure 6.6 Bell ringer playing on Bomb Ballistic building. Photograph: Louise K Wilson

The soundpiece *Airborne Trial* also sought to use imported music to draw attention to the acoustics of these abandoned spaces. It was made for installation in the porch of St Mary-at-the Quay Church in Ipswich as part of the *Regeneration* exhibition. This piece had its origins in the knowledge that Benjamin's Britten's *Noye's Fludde* (the adapted Chester miracle play) was originally performed in nearby Orford Church and featured a set of hand bells to represent the rainbow (all twelve bells in E flat).

Airborne Trial was made with John Levack Drever and merged discordant and harmonic sounds produced by a set of 100-year-old hand bells. These were rung by Brian Whiting from the Suffolk Guild of Ringers on the roof of the Bomb Ballistic building and in the Control Room and Lab 6. While the recording of the bells was an experiment with resonance, the final mix and installation of these subtle sounds gave rise to the suggestion of changes being rung out.

U

... instead of being constructed to defend against aggressors and repel ballistics, the AWRE buildings function is to contain destruction. They may superficially resemble bunkers but they are in fact laboratories in the truest sense, designed, as far as is humanly possible, to contain the effects of particular experiments and any errors that may occur during the processes. The grand enemy in this case may be the Soviet Union, but the more immediate enemy is the error within, something which must be contained or minimised at all costs. (Flintham 2003)

It felt very important for *A Record of Fear* that a piece of music be specially written to take on the more recent history of Orford Ness and, in a sense, challenge the solidity of the architecture. I approached composer Yannis Kyriakides to consider this: I knew the context and its history would be of great interest. A previous work by Kyriakides called *Spi*, an electronic cantata, juxtaposed two forms of cryptic message communication: 'the clandestine world of spy number transmissions on the shortwave radio, and the enigmatic uttering of the ancient oracle of Delphi. Both media were/are used as forms of political machination' (*www.circadian.net/pages/spi.html*). Although premiered in Holland, *Spi* was later performed in England at the disused Suffolk airbase RAF Bentwaters.

Kyriakides' subsequent piece, *U (amplified choir.sine oscillator)*, was recorded by the Exmoor Singers in a sound studio but consequently installed as a 4.1 surround sound piece in Lab 5 for the one-day walking tour. Lab 5, one of the two 'pagoda' buildings at Orford Ness, was built in 1961/2 to perform vibration, thermal and altitude/vacuum tests and temperature tests on rocket and bomb parts. Kyriakides writes how 'the concept for the piece was one long stream of sound, very quietly sung, on the edge of where the voice speaks. The recording combined very soft singing with extremely close miking (*sic*), to suggest a molecular form of lots of tiny voice-particles and waves which come together into some kind of shape then disperse' (email, 17 July 2005).

When installed, the unearthly quality of these voices heard escaping from the building presented an extraordinary (sound) image. The choir was in fact singing a quotation by French essayist and novelist Georges Perec: 'Space melts like sand running through one's fingers. Time bears it away and leaves me only shapeless shreds' (1999: 91). Kyriakides structured this singing so that

there are about seventeen phrases of ten to thirty seconds which are bordered by silence, so the acoustic and magic of the space can really come to the fore. The text is stretched out as if time was literally stretching over the duration of the piece. Consonants are as important as sung vowels, and this has the effect of a slowly transforming and changing resonance that echoes in the space. (pers. comm.)

Figure 6.7 Jim Drane. Photograph: Louise K Wilson

The sung Perec quotation (a meditation of the passing of time) was combined musically with a sine wave sweep, a reference to an account of an 'aural epiphany', by Jim Drane. Ex-AWRE employee Drane had recalled an incident that occurred when he was working in Lab 1 during one of the 1000-hour trials. There was a defective camera in the Lab and Drane volunteered to correct it. He went in on his own and as he approached the two vibrating units (working four-and-a-half shake so they were in opposite frequency) the noise was quite horrendous. But when he reached the camera which was dead centre, he suddenly realised there was no noise. He took his earpiece off and he described 'virtually absolute silence. The noise was cancelling itself out, dead centre, something I knew in theory should happen but something I've never experienced before' (pers. comm., Orford Ness, June 2005).

Figure 6.8 Gull colony. Photograph: Louise K Wilson

Most of what is now known to the National Trust guardians about the Cold War history of AWRE Orfordness has been garnered through oral testimony from ex-employees. Many facts are still not known because of the Official Secrets Act but anecdotes (with personal and specific memories of the Ness, the sounds and sights) are often told. Jim Drane mentioned for example the foghorn that used relentlessly to sound, its booming radar-esque sweep similar to the dominion assumed by the lighthouse beam.

The pulse of the centrifuge

Lab 2, one of the most dilapidated buildings, is also one of the noisiest buildings with the wind persistently activating loose metal sheeting. The final element of the one-day installation was the temporarily installed sound of a centrifuge back inside the building. Lab 2's centrifuge machinery had been transferred to AWE Aldermaston in 1971, where it is still in use. The historian at AWE Aldermaston was quizzical about my request to make a sound recording of the centrifuge. In an early phone conversation, she made a 'whoosh, whoosh' noise that she said would be the sound I would get and wondered how interesting that would be. After much negotiation I arranged to visit Aldermaston to record this machine in motion. During a site visit I met three engineers involved in environmental testing. They explained the byzantine system of klaxon alarms and exchange of Castell keys to ensure that nobody is left in the building when the centrifuge is in motion. A CCTV camera relays mute images of the working machine to a control room. The sound of the centrifuge had never been heard before.

For the recording boundary microphones were placed on the walls and floor, on opposite sides of the circular chamber, and numerous trials were run. The mixed-down sound was installed for one day in the original centrifuge pit with a high-end speaker set-up (coordinated by ARUP Acoustics). The physical impact was palpable:

the hangover throb of machinery vibrates through the body, as two enormous infrabass subwoofer speakers blast out the memory of air being forced around a giant drum at 100rpm. There's an insistent heavy rhythm, like pterodactyl wingbeats, the fee-fi-fo-fum thump of some monstrous force hurtling faster, menacing, and unbearably loud... Wilson's installation eliminates the witness's physical distance from the sound of the centrifuge, but establishes a new set of dislocations. Was the nuclear era really another age? (Palmer 2006)

This mechanised 'soundtrack' for the site prompted very intense reactions. A number of visitors commented that it was a powerful and emotional experience. One visitor said that it was particularly relevant in the context of what is happening in Iraq and another said it felt like 'an exorcism of the past'. Aldermaston's technical historian wrote:

I must admit that when you first contacted me about recording the centrifuge operation, I was a bit nonplussed about the purpose. However, having actually experienced the recording in the wrecked centrifuge facility at Orfordness, I can only say that the combined visual and audio effect was absolutely stunning (email, 28 September 2005).

In his analysis of a 1976 BBC audiotape *Vanishing Sounds of Britain,* anthropologist David Tomas wondered whether objects 'speak a 'common' language or multiple dialects? What exotic discursive spaces are invisible to the eye but not to the ear, and what aural histories do they speak of?' (1999: 129).

The potential for machine voices to travel (outside the site of their origin) is very revealing. The irony about the visits to Aldermaston for me was about what I could and could not take away. Cameras (whether video, still or camera phone) are strictly prohibited. Sketching or making drawings is not allowed. Evidently sound is considered less dangerous or problematic and can be removed. At the same time, the nature of experimental work at AWE Aldermaston is changing. There is a shift from actual physical testing to computer simulation. Yet the centrifuge, the drop test tower, vibration testing with sine wave sweeps and other facilities that I viewed are still in use. There are clearly heritage issues here about what may be lost (undocumented) and what else has never been heard.

To conclude, this ongoing project will develop to ask further questions of comparative analysis, principally whether some Cold War test sites sound the same, or whether there are at least common denominators. I will continue to look at sound montage as providing an interesting, and sometimes provocative, representation of militarised landscapes with 'the silence representing time before military occupation, and then these bizarre and totally unnatural sounds (some of which will reflect continuing use, and some decay and abandonment) that came after' (pers. comm., John Schofield, English Heritage, 2003). Ultimately I am curious as to how artists' responses can be used to make sense of the Cold War, a period of fear and dangerous technological advance, and its ramifications today — to ask how can we respond to an historical era within living memory that continues to touch lives in profound and complex ways.

Bibliography

Flintham, M (2003) *The Closed Territory: A Spatial Analysis of Domestic Militarised Sites*, unpublished MRes, London Consortium.
Fontana, B 'Sound as Virtual Image', *www.resoundings.org/Pages/sound%20As%20 Virtual%20Image.html* (15.04.2006).
Palmer, J (2006) *A Record of Fear,* Commissions East.
Perec, G (1998) *Species of Spaces and Other Pieces*, London: Penguin.
Sebald, W G (1999) *Rings of Saturn*, London: The Harvill Press.
Tomas, D (1990) 'Collapsing walls or puffing, smoking sea monsters? Ambient sonic spaces, aural cultures, marginal histories' *Public Access Collective* 4/5.
Wilson, L K (2003) *Spadeadam.*
www.circadian.net/pages/spi.html (15.04.2006).
www.commissionseast.org.uk/cstudy/NT_EH.html (15.04.2006).

Part 3: New dimensions of materiality

Garbage or Heritage: The Existential Dimension of a Car Cemetery

Mats Burström

In the very last years of the second millennium AD a small bog in southern Sweden suddenly became the subject of antiquarian dispute. The question was whether the remains of an old junkyard with car wrecks were to be considered garbage and cleared away or protected as cultural heritage. The matter received a lot of media cover and soon large numbers of visitors from near and far found their way to the site.

The visitors were fascinated by the state of ongoing decay they encountered at the site. They saw car wrecks eaten away by rust, with empty, gaping headlights, and with trees forcing their way through the sheet iron. The visitors' impressions were enhanced even more since the cars that decayed before their eyes were not older than people's memories. In fact many could remember when these models were new or still common on the roads. The site seemed to materialise the passage of time and function as a reminder of the lifecycle shared by people and things, as well as the vanity of all worldly goods. What once were not just modern means of transportation but also potent symbols of social position and status have now become bog bodies sinking deeper underground with each passing day. Many visitors experienced the old junkyard in sacral terms and to them the site was a car cemetery, which, like all other cemeteries, should be treated with respect.

It turned out, however, to be a difficult case for the antiquarian authorities to handle a site the foremost quality of which is its gradual disintegration. The case revealed basic differences in opinion concerning our present and future relation to the past and its remains. Within heritage management as well as within archaeology there is a tradition of a rather narrow-minded view on material remains focusing on them just as potential sources of information about the past. Inherent in the material past there is, however, also a strong power to affect people and to evoke reflections concerning eternal human questions. These questions treat issues such as the passage of time, the perishability of the material world, and the conditions of the human existence. We will, of course, never find any definite or final answers to these kinds of questions, but raising them constitutes an important aspect of what it means to be a human. It would seem that this existential dimension is a vital but neglected aspect of the material past as well as of archaeology.

The site

The old car dump is situated on a small bog known as Kyrkö Mosse, close to Tingsryd in the province of Småland in southern Sweden. Here we find about 150 car wrecks dating from the 1930s to the 1970s, all in various stages of breaking down.

The site is very closely associated with the life story of a single man, Åke Danielsson. He was born in poor conditions in 1914 as one of six brothers and sisters. His father, as most others in the region at the time, earned his living by combining several kinds of work. He worked as a woodman, stone worker and tailor; he also had a couple of cows. Åke's mother died when he was six years old and from the age of ten he helped his father in the woods. Later he served as a farmhand with one Sunday off a month (Bergman 1999: 11).

In the late 1930s Åke Danielsson took courage and bought a part of the bog called Kyrkö Mosse (Bergman 1999: 11). In any case that is what he has told, although there is no known contract of sale or legal confirmation of his acquisition (Samuelsson 2001: 12). He started peat-digging the bog with a spade. The peat was grated and sold in bales as litter to local farmers. He constructed a grating machine from parts from an old Chevrolet and some threshing-mills and placed it in a new built peat-barn. To carry the peat he laid trunks of young spruces on the ground and used them as rails for a wagon, with car rims as wheels. Later he built a proper rail and a wagon that was driven by an old car engine (Bergman 1999: 11; Samuelsson 2001: 8). Danielsson was a self-taught man, obviously of great technical talent (Krantz and Jönsson 1999: 4).

Figure 7.1 Åke Danielsson at the house that was his home for more than four decades. Photograph: Åsa Nyhlén.

Danielsson also built himself a small dwelling house. It was about fifteen square metres, made draught proof with peat, and the one window faced the country road passing close by. In this house, with no electricity, water or drainage, he lived alone during all his working life and many years after his retirement in the middle of the 1970s (Krantz and Jönsson 1999: 3). Locally he was known as 'Åke on the bog' (*Sw.* 'Åke på myren'). It is said that he preferred to keep to himself with a dog as his sole company. He stayed on his bog until the early 1990s; his last years were spent in a home designed for the elderly in nearby Ryd (*Ystads Allehanda* 2003).

In the late 1940s and early '50s the profitability from peat-digging went down. At the same time Danielsson's back was stricken by injury from all the hard work in the bog. So he stopped digging and started a small firm doing business in junk instead. He built a workshop behind the dwelling house and took care of old cars that had served their time. He dismantled parts that could be reused and sold, while the rest were left lying around. An old bus served as a stock of spare parts. He could not move the cars himself but he managed to tip them over with the help of a machine he had built from the frame of an old Opel and a discarded jack from the Swedish State Railways. The junk left over first filled the pits in the peat bog, and then gradually more and more of the area around. In the early 1960s, the country road was moved a short distance and then Danielsson started to use the old road as a parking lot for the junk cars (Krantz and Jönsson 1999: 3; Samuelsson 2001: 8–9).

When asked in 1999 if he managed to support himself as a scrap dealer Åke Danielsson replied: '— Live and live. It didn't cost much to live. I've at least not needed to beg my way' (after Bergman 1999: 9, my translation). Danielsson lived in very modest circumstances indeed. Although he was working with cars almost his entire life, he never got a driver's licence. The firm did not give much money so the driver's licence was, and remained, a dream (Bergman 1999: 11). Today it is incomprehensible to most Swedes that someone just a few years ago was living in these conditions. Åke Danielsson passed away in 2000.

The dispute

A couple of years after Åke Danielsson left his home on the bog the formal land owner became worried about the junkyard and the future troubles it might cause. So, in 1997 he notified the local authorities in Tingsryd's municipality about hazardous waste at the site. An inspection revealed a leaking barrel with tar and several barrels with waste oil, all of which were cleared. The landowner also required the authorities to see that the car wrecks and all the other junk that Danielsson had left be removed from his land. He considered all of this to be worthless junk and was afraid that he himself would be burdened with the costs of getting rid of it in future.

The head of environment at the municipality made an investigation. His conclusion was that in accordance with the Swedish Nature Conservation Act the junkyard must be considered as littering, and that a considerable environmental inconvenience could arise if the junk was not removed. In his opinion the junk was in conflict with a number of health and safety rules and regulations. After several turnabouts Danielsson was ordered to remove the car wrecks and all junk before the end of November 1998, otherwise punishable by a fine.

Up to this point the case had been dealt with by the municipality's environment and building department (*Sw.* miljö- och byggnämnden). But in early November 1998 a private individual, Marianna Agetorp, who resided near the junkyard, wrote a letter to this department as well as to the culture, leisure and recreation department (*Sw.* fritids- och kulturnämnden). She requested that the authorities reverse their decision to have the car wrecks removed. She wrote:

> The 'fairy cars' outside Ryd have for a long time been hidden and forgotten, but now they want to have attention. Under no circumstances may they be removed from their cemetery. That would be a desecration!!! People in the area may not yet have had their eyes opened to them, but be sure that the will 'see them' if we let tourists pass to them. Every new tourist attraction in Tingsryd will be an asset to the district. (Agetorp 1998, after Samuelsson 2001, my translation).

Agetorp's arguments included the sacral dimension of the site as well as its potential for tourism and thereby herald many of the discussions that were to follow. The culture, leisure and recreation department rejected her request to save the site without any more profound considerations. They regarded the junkyard as a form of littering and claimed that the law had to be followed. The landowner, however, sent the message that he was willing to give up some of his land and let the junkyard be, on the condition that the local authorities take all future responsibility. The environment and building department sent Agetorp's request forward to the municipal executive board (*Sw.* kommunstyrelsen). They decided that they had nothing to add to the pronouncement made by the culture, leisure and recreation department. So, in December 1998 it was decided that the car wrecks were junk and should be removed.

During autumn 1998 a local newspaper, *Smålandsposten*, contacted Dr Karl Johan Krantz, the director of the county Smålands museum, and asked his opinion about the old junkyard at Kyrkö Mosse. At that time he had not visited the site so he answered in general terms that a junkyard could very well be worth protecting as a part of the recent past. When, later that autumn, he visited Danielsson's old junkyard he was deeply touched by what he saw (Samuelsson 2001: 24).

In January 1999, Krantz sent a petition to the county administrative board (*Sw.* länsstyrelsen) and requested that the junkyard be given legal protection, either by declaring the dwelling house and the workshop as historical buildings, or by making the whole site a culture reserve. He explained his request:

> The buildings with junk as well as the surrounding ground with vehicle wrecks, rims, tyres, sheet metal, and all sorts of junk are a monument to some intensive twentieth-century decades, characterised by an old-time view of the handling of the 'worn out'. At the same time Danielsson's junkyard is also a document of the history of ideas concerning reusing as a philosophy. (Krantz and Jönsson 1999: 6, my translation)

During the spring of 1999 Åke Danielsson's old junkyard got a lot of attention in the media, not only locally but nationwide, by the largest daily newspapers, radio and television. A local government commissioner (*Sw.* kommunalråd), Arne Karlsson, said in an interview in a local newspaper:

— Yes, I think it is very positive with all the attention that the junk site has got. We need also this kind of attractions in our district. (*Smålandsposten* 07.04.1999, my translation).

The petition from the museum director made the municipal executive board ask their culture, leisure and recreation department, as well as the environment and building department to make a pronouncement on his request. The latter declared that they were positive about preserving the junkyard. It posed no acute threat to the environment and they pointed to the great interest media has showed it. They declared that: 'The district is put on the map in a positive way by the junkyard' (Tingsryd kommun 15.04.1999, after Samuelsson 2001: 16, my translation).

The culture, leisure and recreation department chose to visit the junkyard to see it with their own eyes. It is obvious from some of their comments that it was the first time several of the members visited the site, although they had already once before decided that the junkyard was littering. Their reactions were negative: 'this is the worst I've seen'; 'clear this, this is no culture!'; and 'this must be cleared, this is no culture to me' were some of their comments (*Smålandsposten* 31.05.1999, my translation). The members agreed that the junkyard was not a cultural monument; it had to be considered littering and should be cleared away. It is worth noting that the department responsible for environmental issues was positive about preserving the junkyard and referred to the public opinion, while the members of the department responsible for cultural issues were negative and referred to their own ideas of the character of 'real' culture.

The local government commissioner Arne Karlsson invited representatives from both departments as well as from the county administrative board and the county museum to a meeting in August 1999 to discuss the future of Danielsson's old junkyard. Prior to the meeting he declared in an interview in a local newspaper (*Smålandsposten* 08.07.1999, my translation):

— It isn't interesting to discuss what culture is or isn't; it is people's interest and feelings for the phenomenon we shall talk about.
— Every time I pass the side road to the bog there is one or more cars parked there. I'm of the opinion that it is an attraction that we shall take care of.

Karlsson's consideration for the interest expressed by the public should of course be a natural element of heritage management, but by tradition that kind of dialogue between the public and the state authorities has been all too rare (cf. Burström et al 2004). Karlsson suggested that the site should get a temporary building permit for a period of ten years, and then — when the interest from the public had vanished — what was left of it could be cleared.

A most interesting aspect of the formal handling of the case is the difference in opinion expressed by on the one hand the director of the county museum, Karl Johan Krantz, and on the other by the head antiquarian at the county administrative board (*Sw.* länsantikvarie), Margit Forsström. Krantz formulated a number of arguments about why the junkyard should be preserved. He referred to (Krantz and Jönsson 1999: 4, my translation):

- the socio-historical dimension which is expressed by the dwelling house and what we today look on as its poverty,
- the workshop as a symbol of the multiplicity of occupation in Danielsson's strategy for survival,
- the accumulation of junk as a general symbol of the technical geniuses that used to exist in every district and the values they represented in the time their were living,
- the unique character of the junkyard as one of the few still remaining establishments of its kind and in addition in a unique stage of uninfluenced decay.

He added the great interest that media and the general public had shown in the site. Almost every daily paper had, according to Krantz, reported in positive terms the heritage management's interest in remains of the industrial society of the recent past. A great number of people have also contacted the museum and expressed their interest and support for preserving the junkyard. Krantz writes (Krantz and Jönsson 1999: 6, my translation):

It has turned out that the junkyard touches the public in a special way, and it seems the relation to the ongoing degradation process is strong and experienced in well-nigh sacral terms.

Figure 7.2 What once was the most modern is now being recaptured by nature. Photograph: Mats Burström.

This important aspect was also a recurring theme in the media reports. In *Dagens Nyheter*, Sweden's largest newspaper, the site was described as 'the glade with the rusting remains of the welfare state' (Säverman 1999, my translation).

The head antiquarian at the county administrative board, Margit Forsström, was unable to see how that special quality of Danielsson's old junkyard that triggers existential reflections could be handled within the system of state heritage management. In an interview in *Tidevarv*, a news magazine published by the Swedish National Heritage Board (*Sw.* Riksantikvarieämbetet), she declares:

— Our task is of course to stop the decay, to rescue the site from transience. If the junkyard is to be preserved, then it is self-evident that the decay must be locked. (Bergman 1999: 10, my translation).

This standpoint seems to be a true paradox indeed: the condition suggested for preserving the junkyard is to stop just that process — the ongoing decay — that characterises the site and fascinates people so much that they go there almost on pilgrimage! This reveals, as Krantz has remarked (*Smålandsposten* 28.06.1999), a belief in a kind of eternal perspective that frequently occurs within heritage management: a state should be frozen or reconstructed, the passage of time and decay is not supposed to be seen, although it stands to reason that everything ages and no material lasts forever (cf. Shanks 1998). The head antiquarian does not express any concern at all for the great interest people have shown for the car cemetery when she rejects the idea to protect it. This is not a very convincing example of a heritage management serving the public (cf. Burström et al 2004).

In August 1999, the county administrative board decided to reject the petition to protect and preserve the junkyard. They justified their decision on the grounds that they did not see how the decay could be stopped, and that means that the junkyard cannot be preserved in a long-term perspective. As a consequence they see no possibility of protecting the site by the laws they have to practice (Länsstyrelsen i Kronobergs län, Dnr 231-616-99, after Samuelsson 2001: 18). Judging from this it would seem that cultural heritage is forever or not at all.

The decision to reject the proposal to make a culture reserve of the junkyard was appealed to the Swedish Government by the director of Smålands museum. He claimed, as a comparison, that the Cultural Monuments Act (*Sw.* Kulturminneslagen) accepts natural decay since ancient monuments including ruins are generally protected without any demand on measures taken to stop their decay. He saw no reason why the condition of a site should influence its cultural-historical value (Regeringskansliet, Dnr Ku1999/2681/Ka, after Samuelsson 2001: 19). It could be added that in this particular case the specific condition of the junkyard — its stage of decay — is actually crucial for its power to touch and affect people.

While the Government handled the appeal the municipal's environment and building department visited the junkyard once more. They noted that the great attention in local and national media had resulted in a very large number of visitors. More than 5,000 people were estimated to have visited the junkyard during the summer of 1999. Considering this interest, most of the members of the department were positive about preserving the site (Samuelsson 2001: 19).

After more than a year and a number of turnabouts in December 2000 the Government decided to leave the appeal from the director of Smålands museum without consideration. They had reached the conclusion that according to the law the county museum had no formal right to appeal the decision made by the county administrative board (Miljödepartementet, Dnr M1999/4334/Na, after Samuelsson 2001: 20).

At this point, however, the public interest in the junkyard was evident to everyone. Thanks to it the district had got more media attention than ever before and obviously had a new and valuable tourist attraction. So the municipality made a deal with the private landowners to lease the junkyard until the year 2050 for a symbolic sum. The municipality took on responsibility for maintaining order and security, to display information and to build a parking ground. The municipal executive board — eager to do everything by the book — applied to its own environment and building department for permission to build a parking place and for changing the use of the land from junkyard to a 'veteran-car-body facility.' (*Sw.* veterankarossanläggning). The permission was granted in June 2001 and with it the more than three-year-long process on the official handling of Åke Danielsson's old junkyard finally ended.

Resting in peace

Now that the antiquarian dispute is over, the car cemetery at Kyrkö Mosse once again rests in peace. It still attracts many visitors: there are no exact numbers but it is estimated that there are 5,000–15,000 visitors per year (Samuelsson 2001: 30). On the official webpage of Tingsryd Municipality (www.tingsryd.se, read in July 2005) Kyrkö Mosse is presented in Swedish, English and German as a place of interest for tourists:

> This is a cemetery for vintage cars, sited deep in the forest, where nature and machine become intricately, and almost implausibly, entwined. It's a must for those of you who are simply nostalgic for the old motoring days as much as the keen photographer of site-specific art. Join the many thousands of visitors to this one-off art exhibition.

The site has certainly made an impressive career; it has transformed from junkyard and littering to 'cemetery for vintage cars' and 'art exhibition' in just a few years time. A search for 'Kyrkö Mosse' on Google gives more than 370 hits on the Internet (July 2005). Besides road descriptions and comments from motor enthusiasts a large number of the sites are photographers who present their pictures. The rusting car wrecks are a most popular motive; several of the photographers have been awarded prizes for their pictures.

The car cemetery also inspires artists; one of them is Dieter Kunz. In an exhibition in April 2005 in Väsby Konsthall, north of Stockholm, he presented a large collection of oil paintings with motifs from Kyrkö Mosse. Kunz also made an installation of parts from an old Volvo and a painting showing what the car looked like when it was new.

The explicit idea was to remind the onlooker of the fleetingness of time (Kunz 2005). This connects to the yearly *Abandoned Autos* calendars, published in the US, in which photos of scenically situated rusty relics are juxtaposed with ads and sales literature for the cars when they were new (cf. Ehrich 1999). The meeting between the optimism once communicated in the advertisements and today's material remains raises many thoughts: how much has not changed in a few years time? The 'before and after' theme reminds us that the present 'now' will also later become 'past'. How will we then look back on the present? What will appear as important and what will have proved to be insignificant? Reflecting on this may actually change our present priorities. And then not only the present but also the future will be different.

The well-established Swedish artist Ulf Wahlberg has been working with abandoned and stripped car wrecks and car dumps as a much-appreciated theme. His paintings, whose subjects are taken from the Nevada desert in the US as well as the Uppsala plain in Sweden, have been described as modern *vanitas* symbols, reminders of the transience of all things (Edwards 1994: 14). The cars have been transformed from proud examples of industrial society's technical ability and optimistic belief in the future into crumpled reminders that nothing lasts forever. The motors have fallen silent and the finish is flaking off. Despite the fact that it is precisely cars that change so reliably from annual model to annual model, Wahlberg's images mediate a striking, timeless atmosphere. It feels as though the images could just as well be capable of representing the remains of a civilisation that disappeared very long ago.

Figure 7.3 A twentieth-century vanitas *symbol. Photograph: Åsa Nyhlén.*

Marianna Agetorp, the private individual who was the first to draw the local authority's attention to the cultural qualities of Kyrkö Mosse, is one of the contributors to a book that in a number of texts, poems, and aesthetic photos deals with the site (Lindell 2004). The car wrecks trigger personal life histories as well as reflections about human existence more generally. In it, one author, Olle Lindell, testifies that he does not know what happened later in life to a Jaguar Mk X he once owned, but assures the reader that he honestly does not miss the flashy car. He concludes, however: 'But I think now and then of my first wife' (Lindell 2004: 105, my translation). It was she who, as a newlywed, did not get a Christmas present one year because of an expensive cylinder head gasket that had to be replaced in the Jaguar.

The memories and reflections awakened by old car wrecks are obviously of many different kinds. The fact that many of them are very personal says a lot about the power the material past has to affect people. Remains from the past make us remember and reconsider our own past, and with it also our present and future life. The specific content of these reconsiderations is, of course, different for each and every one but it is important to acknowledge its existence. As scholars we are trained to clear away all personal aspects in our interpretations in preference for the general that is supposedly typical and common to most people. In doing so we paradoxically clear away something that all people have, that is the personal dimension. As a result, archaeology is losing some of its most significant potential.

In recent years, there have been several books published in Sweden dealing with car cemeteries and old car wrecks. One of them has the telling title *The Car Dump — the Lost Paradise* (my translation, Carlsson and Lundgren 1996) and is written by a couple of car enthusiasts who give expert comments on the marks and models they find. The book reports nostalgic expeditions to car cemeteries not only to different parts of Sweden but also to Austria, Denmark, New Zealand, Mexico and the US. The authors make judgements whether or not the cars they find would be possible to renovate and their disappointment is apparent when it is too late.

Other authors have no interest whatsoever in renovating the car wrecks they find. On the contrary, they are interested in just the process by which the car wrecks are slowly swallowed by nature and — once more — made a part of it. This is, as Sjöstrand (1989) argues, a fate that awaits cars and humans alike. In another book (Berg and Tuuloskorpi 1993) the car wrecks awake the poet's memories from his childhood and start a remembering journey that includes all dimensions of existence. Car wrecks have indeed proved to be good to think.

The large number of visitors to the car cemetery on Kyrkö Mosse, all internet sites, books, calendars, painters, photographers and poets dealing with car wrecks show an interest or even a fascination that needs explaining. What is it with old car wrecks? Is it merely a romantic fascination for ruin? And, if so, what is it with ruins?

The existential dimension

There are many examples in the past of how people have been affected by the ways in which material culture bears witness to the passage of time. An obvious example is the occupation and fascination with ruins shared by the Romantic artists, poets and gardeners. The British art historian Christopher Woodward (2001: 2–3) has described the interest in ruins:

> When we contemplate ruins, we contemplate our own future. To statesmen ruins predict the fall of Empires and to philosophers the futility of mortal man's aspirations. To a poet, the decay of a monument represents the dissolution of the individual ego in the flow of Time; to a painter or architect, the fragments of a stupendous antiquity call into the question the purpose of their art. Why struggle with a brush or chisel to create the beauty of wholeness when far greater works have been destroyed by Time?

Although Woodward's examples obviously refer to high culture rather than old car wrecks it would seem that the latter hold the same kind of potential for existential reflection concerning the passage of time, the perishability of the material world, and the conditions of our human existence. As a matter of fact, the relatively young age and everyday character of the car wrecks seems to increase their imaginative power. As relics of our own time and our own experience they strike us all the more powerfully; we recognise grandpa's old car, we remember the smell and sound of it, we remember trips we once took, and all of a sudden we are back in our childhood or at the time of our first car — we remember people who are now long gone. It is as if the car wrecks are sufficiently young to strike us with full power of ruination. This may indeed be an important reason behind the growing interest for the contemporary past. The relatively short time span that separates now from then in the recent past makes the marks of time all the more powerful. This has also been clearly shown by photographers working with material remains and ruins of the twentieth century (e.g. Hamm and Steinberg 2000; Kobayashi 2001).

Throughout history the interest in how time makes its mark and eventually breaks down what humans have created — sometimes intended for eternity — has been worked out in many different ways (cf. Burström 2004). Seen in a wider perspective, archaeology belongs to this cultural field. As archaeologists we have extensive knowledge of how time and the passage of time materialise in people's existence. In spite of this, we very seldom approach the existential questions that in other contexts have attracted so much interest. Instead we tend to reduce our perception of ancient remains so that they appear merely as potential sources of information of what once was.

Already half a century ago the Finno-Swedish author Göran Schildt made some clear-sighted observations concerning archaeologists' attitudes toward ruins (1957: 157, my translation):

> As a matter of fact, archaeologists and ruins are, in a way, enemies. The archaeologist sees in the ruin just what it was before it became a ruin, he wants to search into the practical purpose of

the building and he does everything he can to *conserve* what he finds, he lifts the remains that have been severely damaged by time out of time so that they will not be more ruined.

Schildt admits a certain sympathy with this attitude but points out that it none the less leads to the loss of something essential (1957: 159, my translation):

> From the specific point of view of what could be called the poetical or philosophy of life, all conservation is a loss, because it deprives the ruin its most important characteristic, the relation to Time.

Archaeologists generally avoid the poetical perspective and consider the existential dimension of archaeological objects to belong to a personal and subjective sphere that falls outside the field of the discipline. So even if we are affected by things from the past, we keep this to a personal sphere and avoid blurring our archaeology with our private lives. I believe this is a mistake. If we are to understand not only what people in the past did with material objects, but also what these objects do with us, it is necessary to consider the emotive and reflective potential in things (cf. Buchli and Lucas 2001).

When we take an object from the past in our hands we create a direct link with that which no longer exists. Those who once used the objects are usually long since gone, but they have not vanished without a trace; some of their things remain and bear witness to the world that once was theirs. To encounter such remains is a strong experience that can give rise to thoughts and sentiments. It makes us reflect on human existence, the passage of time, and the material world. What remains from those passed and what has disappeared? What will we leave after us? How will the future remember us? How would we like to be remembered? The thoughts carry, often far beyond the objects themselves, but never the less it is the material remains that give rise to such existential reflections. And the questions they raise may indeed be more important than the answers we find.

Walking around the car cemetery at Kyrkö Mosse I find myself looking for marks and models of which I have memories of my own: the Saabs my parents used to have when I was growing up, my grandpa's old Opel. The latter, a blue 1962 Opel Olympia Record 1700, was the car I drove during my first archaeological fieldworks, surveying ancient monuments for the Swedish National Heritage Board in the mid 1980s. Why am I looking for that model now at the car cemetery? I do not know, but it feels like a nice idea to meet again after all these years.

Acknowledgements

The formal handling of the case of Åke Danielsson's old junkyard was studied in a student paper, by Jonas Samuelsson (2001). I have benefited from using this as a source of information, especially for many of the official documents that are unpublished. I would also like to thank Birgitta Johansen at the Swedish National Heritage Board who drew my attention to Göran Schildt and his reflections on archaeologists and ruins.

Bibliography

Agetorp, M (1998) Brev till Tingsryds kommun, unpublished letter, Tingsryds kommun, Dnr 970654-451/12.

Berg, B and Tuuloskorpi, H (1993) *Drömmar i plåt,* Torsby: Heidruns förlag.

Bergman, F (1999) 'Tillbaka till naturen' *Tidevarv. Riksantikvarieämbetets nyhetsmagasin nummer 1/99,* Stockholm, 8–11.

Buchli, V and Lucas, G (2001) 'The archaeology of alienation: A late twentieth-century British council house', in Buchli, V and Lucas, G (eds), *Archaeologies of the Contemporary Past,* London and New York: Routledge, 158–67.

Burström, M (2004) 'Archaeology and existential reflection', in Bolin, H (ed.), *The Interplay of Past and Present,* Stockholm: Södertörn Archaeological Studies 1, 20–28.

Burström, M, Elfström, B and Johansen, B (2004) 'Serving the public: ethics in heritage management', in Karlsson, H (ed.), *Swedish Archaeologists on Ethics,* Lindome: Bricoleur Press, 135–47.

Edwards, F (1994) *Ulf Wahlberg. Målningar, teckningar, skisser, objekt, foto, 1955– 1994,* Älvsjö: Published by the author.

Ehrich, T (ed.) (1999) *Abandoned Autos,* Vermont: Hemmings Motor News.

Hamm, M and Steinberg, R (2000) *Dead Tech: A Guide to the Archaeology of Tomorrow,* Santa Monica: Hennessey + Ingalls.

Kobayashi, S (2001) *Ruins,* Tokyo: Kabushiki Kaisha Magajin Hausu.

Krantz, K J and Jönsson, S (1999) *Underlag rörande Danielssons skrotverkstad och bostadshus på Kyrkö mosse,* Unpublished report. Växjö: Smålands museum .

Kunz, D (2005) *Dieter Kunz i Väsby Konsthall 9–29 April 2005,* exhibition catalogue, Väsby: Väsby Konsthall.

Lindell, O (ed.) (2004) *Skrot,* Markaryd: Kaffebord.

Samuelsson, J (2001) *Från skräp till industriellt kulturminne,* unpublished student paper, Linköping: Linköpings universitet, Institutionen för tema.

Säverman, O (1999) Sista striden om Ryds rosthögar, *Dagens Nyheter,* 27.03.1999, daily paper.

Schildt, G (1957) *Ikaros' hav,* Stockholm: Wahlström and Widstrand.

Shanks, M (1998) 'The life of an artifact in an interpretive archaeology' *Fennoscandia Archaeologica* XV: 15–30.

Sjöstrand, S (1989) *Skrotbilar,* Hässleholm: published by the author.

(07.04.1999) (31.05.1999) (28.06.1999) (08.07.1999) *Smålandsposten,* daily paper.

Wahlberg, U (1981) *Skrotbilar,* Jönköping: Svenska Budskap AB.

Woodward, C (2001) *In Ruins,* London: Chatto and Windus.

(27.06.2003) *Ystads Allehanda,* daily paper.

Into the Space of the Past: A Family Archaeology

Jonna Ulin

In the following text you will be taken on a journey into a process of postmemory work (Hirsch 1997). You will follow me into the walkscape (Campbell and Ulin 2004) of my biographical past and meet with histories, forgotten things, secrets and memories that lie hidden in the ruins of my grandmother's childhood home; a small croft in the north of Sweden, officially registered as Åsen 5:18, Liden Parish, in the County of Västernorrland, in the Province of Medelpad, but more commonly referred to as 'Per Johan's place' (Hansson 2000; 2001).

In the summer of 1997 I began to collect and adopt pieces of information regarding my family past. What I did not know at the time was that my grandmother was dying of cancer and that it would be my last chance to gather her memories of the family landscape. In my attempt to get closer to my family past I persuaded her to let me excavate the remnants of her childhood home — 'Per Johan's place'. In the summer of 1999 the excavation work began and it was decided that focus would be placed on the main house, which began its history in 1851 and was abandoned in 1938 (but with a hope of a return). During excavation things were found everywhere, belongings that had been placed and displaced, broken and used over and over again. By the year of 2000 the excavation of the main house was completed and 497 artefacts were registered.

This project of exploring the walkscape of my biographical past has been and still is a process that subjectively engages me with the material of my investigation, in that it juxtaposes my recollections of my past with the memories of my grandmother, the family archive and with the artefactual information excavated from Per Johan's place. It is a process of transposing memory-images as after-images of the experienced, the remembered, the forgotten, the real and the unreal, after-images that I project back onto the landscape of my family. In doing so I position myself in-between the past and the present and as a consequence thereof I set in motion a process of exploring '...to what extent reality itself is always a kind of ongoing fabrication — not as a kind of fiction but more literally as that which is constantly being improvised, moment by moment' (Young 2000: 45).

***

I walk in the landscape of the dead. I try to follow footprints, paths made by people that I once knew. This work, this process of walking in the landscape of my family history is a process of recognition and representation.

I am a deep map, there to be read, not in a linear fashion but as fragments of layers, as pieces of happenings and events that took place somewhere else at another time. When walking in the landscape of my childhood I see that it is a story with no beginning and no end. I find myself in the near and the far, side-by-side with the past and the present. I am the story of many stories. I locate myself through the retelling, the unearthing of the past.

I rewrite the silent words of the past in order to make sense. When descending into the memories of times long gone, it is as if I sense my memories through somebody else's eyes. It is as if there is someone else standing in front of the looking glass, viewing, seeing me, there, as a transparent image, as an illusion. Everything is blurred and out of focus. It is as if the things I remember never happened. It is as if they are somebody else's memories, not mine.

This work is a 'memory-work', a practice where the body of material consists of remnants excavated from the home-place of my great-grandmother as well as my own recollections, family photographs, family stories, lies and secrets. It is a method and a practice of unearthing and making public untold stories and unseen material remains.

Places are constructed, they are stories. They are verbal as well as spatial. All the landscapes, places and homes of the past contain traces of lived experiences, memories and personal geographies. They are made of a mosaic of stories, they have something to tell. In the process of conducting excavations into the memories of places and people, the personal experiences of the local are being surfaced. In this act depth is created.

There is no 'there' there. 'There' is nowhere but here, in the present. When sitting in my chair, it is as if I can feel how my body explores, senses and meets the place of my imagination. It is as if it exists within my bones. The re-membered story is being transformed through the re-telling of its memory. It is transformed into a presenced place, a 'here', and things start to happen 'there'. Through the process of putting together the pieces of stories, of times long gone, a locus of stability has been created, a reality upon which our multicentred bodies might find some rest.

*

When looking at old photographs, we transcend into a hybrid state, a state of juxtaposition of being far and near, side by side with the past and the present. The process of reminiscence allows the picture to change its context, shifting the notion of distance into an intimate moment of recollection.

I am eleven-years-old, when Hulda, my great-grandmother, is visiting us. We are sitting closely together I can feel her warmth, she is so big it is almost possible to hide in her body. I am touching her hand, it is old, her skin is transparent, her veins are blue and all so full of blood, it is as if they were free floating, as if they are out of context, a map of blue rivers. I look at my hands to see if they are as hers, I want them to be, and once again I ask her to tell me the story of her past.

If I keep perfectly still
then I can feel
the skin of my body
stretching

        over a pattern of fine branches
              then I can feel
       how my skin is the surface
      that holds it all together

      if I alter my vision of sound
          towards the inside

        if I listen a bit more
            carefully
          then I can hear
       the sound of my veins
how they sigh the memory of the past
         it is a faint sound
        like a pulsating wind
           a puff of air

         if I close my eyes
            extra hard
          then I can see
how my eyelids make out the inside of a whole universe
              here
           I can enter
            on a path
towards a vast and endless landscape
             of tales
             stories
             hidden
and forgotten histories about us

I am thirteen-years-old. She is sitting in her sofa, she is silent. She is tired, she is, after all, ninety-three-years-old. I want to ask her some more questions, I want her to tell me again and again who she was and how it was to live in the early 1900s, but I choose not to, I know that I have to be silent now, as silent as she is. Her voice is ending, she is out of words, it is as if they have all been spoken. We both know that time is running out. She says that yesterday she saw a sign, a black bumble bee in the waste bin, I know she is telling me the truth, she has always seen things out of place. She lays her hands on the table and looks out of the window, it is winter and very cold and as always she pats her hand in her specific manner, it is as if they were dancing. One hand stroking the other one time and then clapping it two times, over and over again. That sound is a memory sound. And today, when I do the same movement, I travel through time, there becomes here and here becomes there, I am distant but close. I become placed in the mere act of being displaced. That sound and that touch transcend me back to the stories of her life, back to the personal landscape of her experience.

Letting yourself be displaced in order to be placed is one way of coming closer to the stories of past and present places. A photograph, like a specific site, gives places and memories back to the people who no longer can see them, whose memories are too far away to be brought up without the help of others.

*

The geography of my genealogical past has many locations, some visible and some not. I stand on the south-west coast of Sweden facing north and there on my right, quite a bit further up, that is to the north-east, the local landscape of the family is to be found. *Medelpad* is the landscape and the place between two paths; it is the landscape of middle-path.

In the summer of 1999 I am going back for the first time in almost twenty years. I want to map and excavate the invisible landscape of my family. I hope to find some clues to the answers I never got.

Figure 8.1 Family photograph taken at Jonna's great-grandmother Hulda Ulin's apartment in Nynäshamn, Sweden.

Just before my grandmother died I asked her to draw me a picture of the home where she was born.

The way she holds the pen as she etches her way back into her past, makes me think about my great-grandmother — Hulda, her mother, and that even though they were so different in character they are still similar, to me. I can see how she is forcing the pen to move all over the grey piece of paper, revealing not only a passageway for me to step through but also an image of her childhood home and what it looked like. And she talks and talks: about the rabbit hutch behind the house, about the hollyhock that grew by the right corner of the house and about the arch of birch that he brother Ivar planted shortly before he died; about the waterwheel that the same brother built down the creek, to generate enough electricity for an outdoor lamp. About the two goats and the three cows that grazed the fields. About the cowshed, how it had to be kept as clean as the house, in case they were to have guests. About the wild strawberries, the ones that grew on top of the earth cellar, and about the water·they drank and used for cooking, how it was so full of iron that it almost made everyone lose their teeth, how her mother actually did lose them, all of them except for the two she used when eating.

And it makes me see things, like the fact that each and every corner she remembers is a place of activity, a place of happenings, events and a place of the senses. And I realise too, that for her, a tree is not just a tree, but a part of an image of sight and site, of seeing others sitting there inside the arch of which that specific tree is a part. I realise that for her, an earth cellar is not just a place for storage, but a place of sensibilities, a place where she could stop on her way down the field and put a wild strawberry in her mouth, chewing it slowly and letting the juice colour her lips. And it makes me think about place as a 'somewhere' to be located through the memories of processes of activity. Look at her, as she adds the final touch to her map by writing explanatory words like forest, well, cowshed and barn.

With this drawing, this dream map in my backpack I try to relocate the home-place of the past. To my surprise it is amazingly accurate. Her memory of a place she had not visited since she was a child helps me to descend back into her home of the past. That gap between her and me, there and then, here and there, that gap between my image and her lived experience offers a space for me in which to dream and create ideas of a past present.

Here in the landscape of my family I begin uncovering layer after layer a home-place, a ruin where children, men and women had once lived, people of whom I had only met a few. I get to meet the others now.

Like a place, a map hides as much as it reveals. But what secrets lie hidden here, out of sight, protected from the naked eye? What words have been spoken, what sorts of lives have they lived, here in that land/scape so distant in time but still so close? Here in this place, where they walked the same path on which I am now standing, where they planted those birches just over there. Here where someone for some reason left that metal bucket in the meadow and then forgot about it. These people, my ancestors, once spent hours of conversation dreaming about this place, once bent and moulded and worked it into a home with their bare hands. In this home of a time long gone, I now stand, knelt and bent down over a floor that was once there, but which can now only be seen in earthy colours of red. Here I am, touching the first of a home that began its history in 1851 and was abandoned so abruptly in 1938.

Here the biography of a family past is to be found. Somewhere under all this, I hope to find some clues, detect some signs that could help me come closer to an understanding of the autobiographical record of the family.

I begin the process of unmasking the family face, I begin the process of unearthing the home-place of my great-grandmother, my grandmother, her brothers and sister and last but not least their father, her husband.

During this excavation I meet with silent words, images buried beneath the ground, answers that I am not prepared to hear, answers to questions I have not asked. Here I am, revealing bit by bit a place which has been hidden behind the shadow of time, slumbering the sleep of a thousand sleeps, under the cover of dirt, roots and grass.

*

If I take one more step, if I walk just one step closer, will I then be able to see what you see, hear what you hear, think the thoughts you think, here in this place, here in the abyss of the incomprehensible, here where I am, now?

Can you hear me? Can you hear my voice, can you sense how it is trying to find its way, how it fades out and then, how it comes back again, but stronger this time? It is forcing me to open my eyes, to confront what lies ahead, to see the footprints of the past, to look at the remnants of decay that surround me, to keep an eye on the remains of time as they are being absorbed by my body.

Can you see what I see; can you see the reflections in the ground, the mirror images of now and then, how they keep themselves in motion? Can you see the grass and the leaves how they cover the ground of their past? Can you see them there, underneath the moss and the dirt? Listen to the sound they make as they are chewed into pieces by the worms. Can you sense them? I can.

Can you see what I see? Can you see how the worms make their way through the soil, how they eat the memories of time, how they create tunnels through the past-present. Tunnels that link me to this place, to this soil of which I think I am a part. I am getting short of breath here, and the earth is filling my ears with whispers of past experiences and memories, whispers that slowly penetrate my soul. Can you feel them; can you feel how we are connected to one another, like flesh to bone?

Can you feel how it is beginning to get a bit cold, how the moisture of the soil lowers my body temperature, how it lowers my force of resistance towards this place that surrounds me, lowers my force of resistance towards the memories of my family past? I can. I can feel how it supplies my eyes with images of times that I cannot remember, images of family landscapes that I have never visited. I can feel them leaking through my skin, soaking me with dreams, broken hopes, lies, fantasies and with the secrets of the family. I wonder, am I finally here? At the moment when it all begins? Am I on the right track? Can you see me? Have I finally managed to come closer to the place where you are?

This is the place in which I am to excavate and reveal the layers that make it hard to see; that cover the things that are forgotten, that cover the things that are still close enough to be touched, the things that you touched. This is the place in which I will be able to taste the breath of my family, to utter the sound of their words, whilst letting them roll on the tip of my tongue.

Now can you sense it? Can you sense how something is finding its way inside my mouth? Can you sense how it is preventing me from closing my lips? Whatever it is, it is making me realise that now is the time to free my voice, that now is the time to rid myself of the things that block my speech, that now is the time of incorporation and adoption, that it is now that I should begin to turn them into other pieces of me. Can you sense how it is making me realise that the memories of my family landscape need to be visualised as embodied re-presentations of the past present, as reflections of you that are incorporated by me and not as archives of the past that are packed away for future use?

*

I begin to dig myself closer, down, underneath the skin of the ground, in between the spoken and the unspoken. And I can feel how we are getting closer to each other, how I am making contact. And I realise that I am sinking deeper and deeper down through dark and damp layers of time, memories, events and experiences.

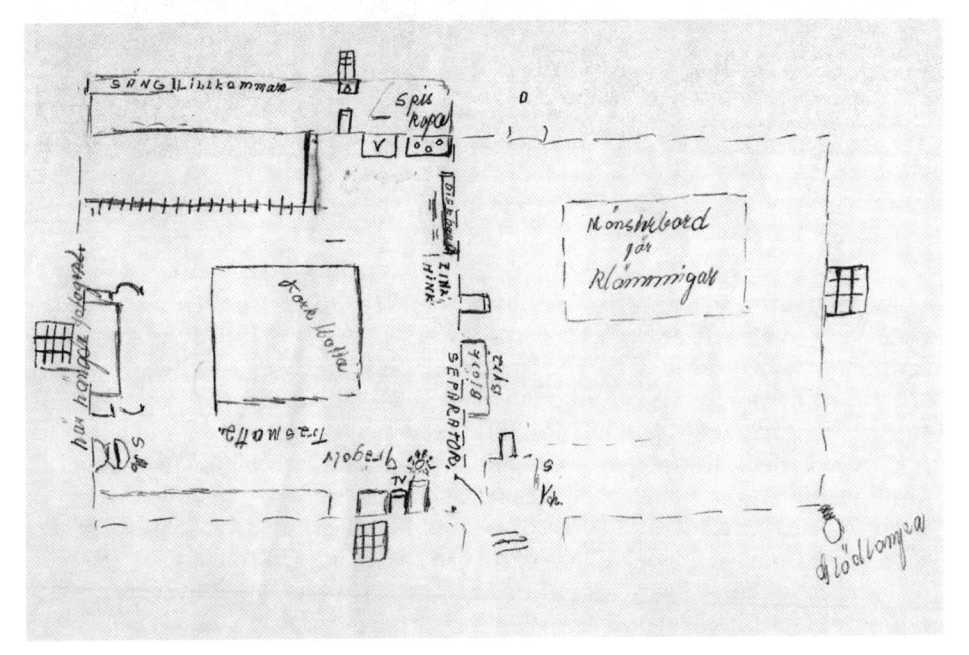

Figure 8.2 Memory map of the interior of 'Per Johan's place — Åsen 5:18, Liden Parish, Västernorrland County, in the province of Medelpad, Sweden, drawn by Jonna's grandmother Ingrid Nilsson.

151

Can you see how it smells in this place? It is the smell of things long gone, the smell of mouldy thoughts and dusty shoes, hats, gloves, bottles, cooking utensils, broken cups and plates. Can you smell the odour of family leftovers, how they are rotting away inside this soil, and how some of them have already disintegrated into a state of oblivion? I can.

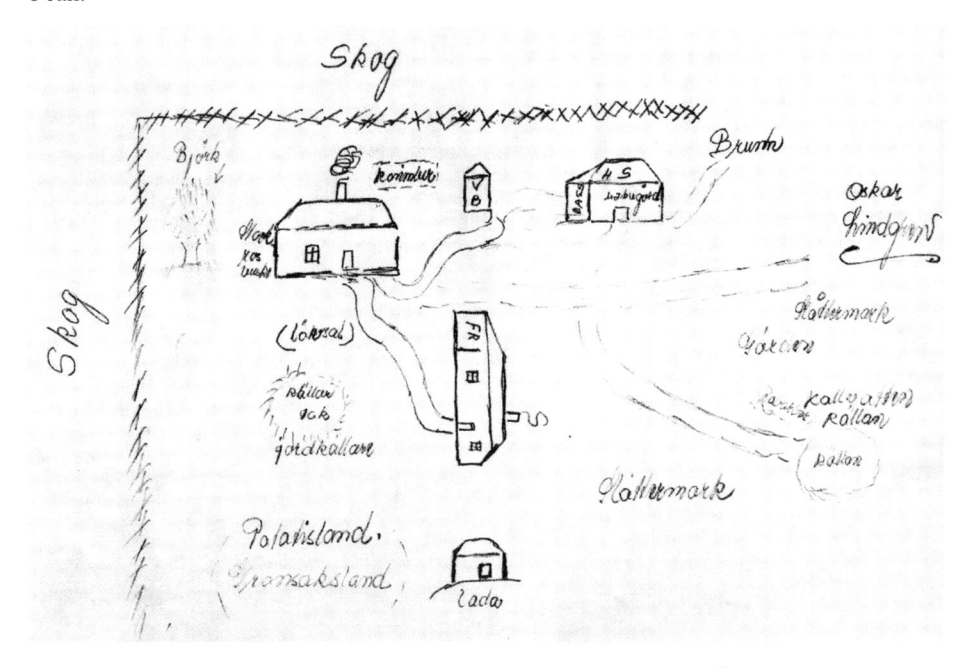

Figure 8.3 Memory map of the surroundings of 'Per Johan's place — Åsen 5:18, Liden Parish, Västernorrland County, in the province of Medelpad, Sweden, drawn by Jonna's grandmother Ingrid Nilsson.

Can you see the stones? The ones that are above me, the ones over there, the ones that have been placed into the ground by the touch of someone's hands, laid down next to the other, in a rectangular form. If they are what I think they are, then they are the remnants of a house, of a home, of comings and goings, of dreams and broken fantasies, of lies and secrets, of longings and happiness, of sorrow and pain.

Can you see the hallway, the small chamber and the two rooms? I can. Can you see what it is that seems to be stuck, not there, not among the roots, but in-between two of the larger stones? Is it what I think, a coin, one 'Riksdaler' from 1857? Can you see if there is a face, one of Swedish King Oscar? I know that it is difficult to see.

There are so many things that cover my sight that it makes it hard to concentrate. As a matter of fact they are no less than 497 to the number. And they surround me. Can you feel them moving, how they touch me, how they cut and carve me into pieces, into pieces of stories, into strings of thoughts, into a family etching? Can you feel how they once again are making themselves a home, how they dig their way through, how they grate themselves underneath the surface of my skin, how they break my bones open, how they germinate inside my body? I can.

Look at them; look at the ones that lay there in the rips and cracks of the soil, in the fissures of stones and roots. Look at the clock that keeps lacerating the skin of my body. It is an alarm clock with big black numbers on a clock face that once was white, but now shifts in various colours of rust. This clock, it runs by its own time, hiding behind the figure of 10:29, a.m. or p.m.? No one will ever be able to tell. Can you feel how it is turning my skin inside out and then back again, how it is moulding it into a million narratives about time, events and experiences? Can you sense how it is turning my body into strands of stories, running from the top of my head and down to the bottom of my feet, and how they are deeply rooted into the geography of my personal past, my family landscape?

And I do not only see the shoe that has grown into my retina but I can see to whom it belongs as well, my grandmother. Look, can you see the bicycle wheel that has grown into my leg, the braces that used to be striped in the colours of white and red, the black hats, the starched collars? Can you see what I see?

But I can see other things too. Like the thermos flasks next to me, the pocket watch to my right, the white porcelain jar for the shaving soap, the leather gloves, the starched cuffs, the medicine bottles, the shoes that have been repaired over and over again, the snuffbox, the eye glasses, the writing kit, the bottles of mouth wash, the tube of toothpaste, the two pocket watches and all the jars of shoe polish ... And all of them make me think things about their ways of living.

Look at those objects as they catch my attention, as the keep telling me that even though they are stuck in a geography of the past-present, in a family landscape that just happened, they know how to talk the sound of now and then, of different and same, of familiar and unfamiliar, of known and unknown, of past and present.

There she is, Hulda Ulin, my great-grandmother, in the kitchen by the window, close to the paraffin lamp. Can you see how she sits there by the sewing machine, hiding the truth in the seams of the dress she is about to make; hemming away the questions she doesn't dare to ask? Can you see how she keeps pressing the treadle of the sewing machine fast and hard as if persuading herself that it doesn't matter, that the words in her golden ring don't speak the sound of truth? I can.

But I can see other things too. Like the fragmented sugar bowl of glass, the broken but nicely decorated coffee cups, teapot and coffee pot, all made of porcelain. And I see the broken pieces of an old record, the purse that is about to fall apart, the tiny shoe of leather, the pieces of cloth, the finer looking buttons, the jar of ginger and the bit that was left inside, the broken flowerpots, the glass bottle that reads 'Mellins food', the empty tins of sprats, the rolling pin for making crispbread, the small metal case that is decorated with a butterfly on the lid... And all of them make me think things about their ways of living.

Look at the comb for the lice, how it still carries the memory of her hair. Can you see the small milk pail, the one she used to carry up and down to the house? Can you see the big stone, the one she and her friends used to hide behind whilst telling secret stories of an intimate kind? Can you see that the things in her mind are things that mattered to her as a child? I can.

But I can see other things too. Like the bread-forks made by vagrants, the can of pesticide, the broken bicycle tyre, the small container of birch-bark, the tiny plastic doll made in Japan, the rusty scythe blade, the strainer, the padlocks, the key, the horseshoes. And all of them make me think things about their ways of living. And as I take an extra close look, I begin to wonder if some of them don't have their home a bit deeper down in the ground than the others. Like the horseshoes for example; from what I can see in the layer of time that belongs to my grandmother's childhood, they never had a horse.

In this place I journey through layers of the same and the different, I confront and approach difficult and unspeakable matters, I travel amongst things that have been addressed and spoken but I also move within the silence of the past-present. And I have to be careful on my journey not to push something that might break. I have to be careful on my journey not to grab on to something too forcefully, and I have to make sure that I keep my mouth open; wide enough to let the different sounds of my family past pass in and out. But it is hard. Because whenever I move I feel how they are crushed under the weight of my search, how they break apart and stick to my body, forcing me to change my perspective into one that sees things from another perspective — from the perspective that looks at the remnants of you and all the others from the edge of time, from the edge of the remembered, from the edge of the real and the imaginative.

*

This is the place of the unknown-known, this is the place of decomposition; this is the place of the unexpected. In this place anything might happen if I only let myself walk along the edge of the things that I don't understand, along the edge of everything that I have never experienced, everything that I cannot explain to the full.

Here I meet, for the first time, with a woman of my own age, perhaps even younger than me but still older in time and place. I do not know her. Here she is someone else. In this place she is not my great-grandmother born in the year of 1888, a woman who was eighty years old when I was born. In this place she is the mother of five children, three boys and two girls, she is the wife of a man ten years older than her, who has already deserted another woman and their two boys, a story she claimed she did not know about until after his suicide in 1938.

Here she is the woman — who grabs the children and runs to her own mother and father in order to hide from him and his violence. Here she is the woman — who goes into his small chamber when he calls. Here she is the woman — who comes home late at night in the dark, in a landscape so black, walking on that hillside sloping so much that it feels as if you are going to fall off. In this home she wakes her children at night asking them to help her to thread the needles so she could finish the ordered dress. Here she is beginning a story of loss, a story of pain, of losing her children one by one, all of them except my grandmother, the only one to outlive her.

>   We share each other
>   you
>   and
>   I
>   we are
>   collected memories
>   stirred by the winds of time
>   we are
>   invisible patterns
>   on a map
>   of voices
>   and
>   I was born
>   too far
>   from your beginning
>   you were
>   already
>   the time
>   the place
>   the room
>   in which
>   I
>   came
>   to be
>   I was born
>   along footprints
>   along the rootprints
>   of you

But who is he then, the man I meet as a reflection in the things left behind, in the bottles, the shoes and the hats? Her husband, Per-Johan Lindström, the man in the family album, looking straight ahead into the camera, the man who left the home of his father, who travelled around selling clothes to the men and women of the north. Why did he abandon that other woman and their two boys, the younger one only one year of age? These boys who would return, reclaiming their rights after his death. What is his story? That man, the father of many children. The boy with a younger sister Kristina. The half brother of his two older sisters. The first of the family, born by the second wife of his father. What did he witness, which words did he hear, this boy, the bearer of his father's name, but with a hand so different? To what can he confess, what statements may he sign? Who is he, my great-grandfather, that invisible man? That man who is ever-present but of whom no one has really spoken, that man of silence.

Look: there he is, in the guise of a travelling salesman, a man dealing not only with women's clothing but with their bodies too. There he is, dressed in a well-cut suit, holding a cigar between his fingers. Can you see how he is walking up the road that leads to his father's house, to 'Per Johan's place'? There he is, sitting on his bed in his chamber by the kitchen. Can you see how he looks through the bottle and down on himself? Per-Johan Lindström, the father of my grandmother Hulda's husband; a man struck by the sound of silence, a man whose words bite. Can you see how the face of his father covers him and how he is searching for another mask to wear? I can.

*

The landscape of my genealogical past has outlasted itself. The voices of the past have once again been heard, but are their words a copy of what was really said or have they become a myth, a legend of something that never happened? Does it matter? I am the one uttering the words, taking them into my mouth, formulating them, letting them stroke my lips, roll on my tongue, take shape and form into a meaning, a sense of place, of a memory, of a story.

Is it not so that one reason for us to know our own histories is so that we are not defined by 'others'? Is it not so, that in the end we are the ones who choose what to tell, which memories to display? At the same time, however, the re-membered story might lead us in a direction different from the one we thought we were following, translocating us into a state of juxtaposition, a state of being side-by-side with the near and the far. It is in this movement of placement through displacement that stories of a past present are forever being created.

Figure 8.4 Excavation of 'Per Johan's place' — Åsen 5:18, Liden Parish, Västernorrland County, in the province of Medelpad, Sweden.

Figure 8.5 Shoe excavated at 'Per Johan's place' — Åsen 5:18, Liden Parish, Västernorrland County, in the province of Medelpad, Sweden.

Figures 8.6, 8.7, 8.8 Artefacts excavated at 'Per Johan's place' — Åsen 5:18, Liden Parish, Västernorrland County, in the province of Medelpad, Sweden.

Bibliography

Campbell, F and Ulin, J (2004) *BorderLine Archaeology: a Practice of Contemporary Archaeology — Exploring Aspects of Creative Narratives and Performative Cultural Production*, Göteborg: Göteborg University, Department of Archaeology.

Hansson, J (2000) 'Unearthing the local', in Campbell, F and Hansson, J (eds), *Archaeological Sensibilities*, Göteborg: Göteborg University, Department of Archaeology, 58–70.

Hansson, J (2001) 'Längs stigar in i det förflutnas rum', in Lind, H, Svensson, E, Hansson, J, *Projekt Uppdragsarkeologi: Sentida Bebyggelse i Antikvarisk och Arkeologisk Verksamhet*, Stockholm: National Heritage Board, 89–102.

Hirsch, M (1997) *Family Frames: Photography, Narrative and Postmemory*, Cambridge, Mass.: Harvard University Press.

Young, J E (2000) *At Memory's Edge: After-images of the Holocaust in Contemporary Art and Architecture*, London: Yale University Press.

Beyond the Space Race: The Material Culture of Space in a New Global Context

Alice Gorman

Introduction

With the launch of Sputnik 1 in 1957, human material culture entered the realm of interplanetary space. Since then, the twentieth-century world has been transformed by satellite-delivered services such as telecommunications, navigation, mapping, meteorology and surveillance. Places and objects associated with this technology have proliferated on Earth and in space. Over 10,000 objects orbit the Earth alone, including satellites, upper rocket stages, mission-related debris, human waste and 'space junk' (ESOC 2005). On Earth, space-related sites include rocket ranges, tracking stations, research and development facilities and domestic satellite dishes.

The development of space technology occurred in tandem with two other major processes of the post-war world: decolonisation and globalisation. More than 140 new states came into being between the Second World War and the turn of the millennium (UN 2005). As the great European empires disintegrated, colonial aspirations were transferred to the 'High Frontier' of space. However, terrestrial colonies still played a significant role in the exploration of space, as emerging space players took advantage of 'empty' regions to locate launch facilities, such as Woomera in South Australia. At the same time, the potential of satellites for telecommunications was realised, connecting almost the entire terrestrial surface through orbital hardware. At the very stage that new nation-states were proliferating, the ability to transmit information almost instantaneously across the world began to undermine their coherence (eg. Robinson 1998: 564).

Space exploration starts on the surface of the Earth but leaves its traces in the vastness of interplanetary space. Syncom 3, launched in 1964, was the first satellite in geostationary orbit (table 9.1) and provided live coverage of the 1964 Olympic Games in Tokyo. Rapidly superseded by new generations of satellites, it is now technically classed as orbital debris. Syncom 3 and Woomera played a part in the narrative popularly known as the Space Race, celebrated in films, books and museum exhibits. The Space Race story assumes that the interests of the USA in conquering space represent those of all humanity. But places like Woomera, and objects like Syncom 3, can reveal a more complex significance that takes account of the interests of non-spacefaring nations and Indigenous people.

The material culture of space exploration

In 1936, the first of a new kind of industrial installation was established in Germany, at the former resort town of Peenemünde on the Baltic coast. Here, a dedicated team under the direction of Wernher von Braun took the science of rocketry to, quite literally, new heights. Research, development, manufacture and launching of the V2 missile took place at Peenemünde, until Allied forces bombed it in 1943. Both at Peenemünde and the later factory site of Mittelbau, slave labour drawn from concentration camps enabled the war-time pace of rocket production (Neufeld 1996: 188–89, Sellier 2003).

In 1946–47, four new rocket launch sites were set up as V2 technology was distributed as the spoils of war. The USA launched its first V2s from the White Sands Proving Ground in New Mexico. In the USSR, an area extending from the Volga River into Kazakhstan became the Kapustin Yar range. France used the former Foreign Legion outpost of Colomb-Béchar in Algeria, and the UK entered into an agreement with Australia to establish the Woomera rocket range. The purpose of these ranges was to develop missiles as armaments; but other possibilities were acknowledged. As early as 1945 Arthur C. Clarke highlighted the possibility of telecommunications from geostationary orbit, positing that three equidistant spacecraft could provide television and radio coverage for the entire planet.

By the early 1950s, rockets had become sufficiently powerful to launch an 'earth-circling spaceship'. In 1954, the International Geophysical Year committee adopted a satellite launch as part of its official programme (Chapman 1959: 105). Although at this stage it was possible that the USA, USSR, UK, Australia, Japan or France might be able to launch a satellite (Wyckoff 1958: 107), the field quickly narrowed to the USA and the USSR. In 1957 Sputnik 1 was successfully injected into Low Earth Orbit (see table 1). Now the nature of space had changed irrevocably: no longer enclosed in the envelope of the atmosphere, the artefacts of human activity were joining the celestial population. In January 1959, the USSR launched Lunik 1, the first object to approach the moon, and in September that year Lunik 2 crash-landed on the lunar surface, becoming the first human artefact on another celestial body.

A human presence in space was not far behind. In 1961, Yuri Gagarin successfully orbited the Earth in the Vostok 1. And Arthur C. Clarke's prediction was finally realised: in 1963, the first geosynchronous satellite, Syncom 2, was launched by the USA. This decade also saw the first human planetary landing sites. A mere eight years after Gagarin proved that humans could venture into space and survive, the Apollo 11 mission placed humans on the surface of a celestial body, leaving a scattering of artefacts such as the descent module, cameras, gloves, cables, lanyards, Mylar fragments, and canisters (Burton 2000). It was followed by five more lunar missions, until the Apollo programme was cancelled in 1972.

The 1970s was the decade of space stations and the exploration of the solar system, with probes travelling to all the major planets. The first space station, the USSR Salyut 1, was launched in 1971, followed by the USA Skylab in 1973. Six Salyuts were placed into orbit between 1977 and 1982. All were de-orbited successfully, but Skylab had a more spectacular end, with an unplanned re-entry in 1979. Debris from the space station were scattered in a broad footprint from Esperance to Rawlinna in Western Australia. Also in this year, the European Space Agency launched the first Ariane rockets from the tropical base of Kourou in French Guiana. Unlike the space programmes of the Cold War powers, the Ariane was aimed at commercial and civil markets.

In the 1980s, the USA successfully flew a new type of spacecraft, the returnable space shuttle designed for use in Low Earth Orbit. (The USSR's Buran shuttle programme was cancelled before a crewed flight took place.) The USSR continued to maintain a human presence in LEO, launching the core module of the Mir space station in 1986. The Ariane 4 rocket, operating from 1988, made ESA a leader in commercial satellite launching.

The 1990s brought new challenges. Interplanetary space was accumulating a population of debris that created hazards for crewed missions and satellites. In 1995, NASA formulated guidelines for minimising the creation of orbital debris, followed by the UN's guidelines in 1999. As the Soviet Union disintegrated, international co-operation came to be more prominent in space enterprises. The first two modules of the International Space Station were launched in 1998. This was a major impetus for continuing the USA space shuttle programme, increasingly under attack after several high-profile disasters.

In the first decade of the twenty-first century, the geography of spacefaring is changing rapidly. Both China and India are aiming their space programmes at the Moon, while the USA has shifted its focus to Mars exploration. Space tourism appears nearer than ever as private and commercial ventures strive to lower the cost of taking people into orbit.

Orbit	Description	Function
Low Earth Orbit (LEO)	250 km–1200 km, low inclination	Crewed missions, remote sensing
Medium Earth Orbit (MEO)	1200 km–35 000 km	Global Positioning Systems
Geosynchronous	At least 35 000 km, period of 24 hours	Telecommunications, meteorology
Geostationary (GEO)	35 786 km	Telecommunications, meteorology
High Earth Orbit (HEO)	Above 35 786 km	Disposal orbit for GEO
Polar	LEO, inclination near 90°	Earth observation and mapping, reconnaissance
Molniya	Highly elliptical, inclination 63°	Used mainly by former USSR for coverage of high latitudes
Sun-synchronous	LEO or MEO	Meteorology, remote sensing, surveillance

Table 9.1 Commonly used orbital configurations

From 1936 to 2006, a body of material culture related to the exploration of space has grown both on Earth and in space. These sites and objects include rocket ranges and launch facilities, research, development and manufacture sites, and ground stations on

Earth; space stations; satellites, upper rocket stages and debris in Earth orbit; lunar landing sites and lunar orbital material; and satellites, probes and landers on and around nearly every other body in the solar system. New materials and technologies have been utilised, and new industries based on assets in orbit have developed. In this paper I want to look at how we currently understand the significance of this material culture, and the implications of regarding it as heritage.

The Space Race model

In this period, the dominant interpretation of space material has been what I have called the Space Race model (Gorman 2005a). This is a shorthand way of referring to the early history of space exploration that everyone understands, and alludes primarily to three phases where the USA and the USSR, the Cold War superpowers, went head to head in space: 1945, with the mad scramble to obtain rocket technology from the ashes of Germany; the 1950s, when they competed to place the first satellite in orbit; and the 1960s where landing humans on the moon became the focus of competition. The USA 'won' the Space Race with the Apollo 11 moon landing, and since the diffusion of the Cold War ideological and nationalist motivations for space exploration have weakened. But the Space Race continues to capture the public imagination, as evidenced in books like Deborah Cadbury's 2005 *Space Race*, and films such as *The Right Stuff* (Philip Kaufman 1983) and *Apollo 13* (Ron Howard 1995). It is celebrated in museum exhibits such as the National Air and Space Museum's hugely popular Space Race gallery (Washington DC).

Although the Space Race model concerns two opposing empires and ideologies, it is presented as the story of the human species, having the same meaning whether you live in Washington DC or Dakar. The interests of largely white, male Americans are assumed to be universal human goals. In this 'master narrative', heroic acts of discovery in space are the outcomes of a natural human urge to explore (Bryld and Lykke 2000; Logsdon 1983: 3; Jones and Benson 2002: 62). Thus, space objects are perceived to have a universally understood meaning that appeals to our common human nature (Gorman 2005b).

The Space Race model suggests that technological change is driven by competition, that entry into space represents progress for the human race, and that the USA and the USSR alone bore the risks and the glory of space achievements, the rest of the world being elevated into the Space Age by the coattails. In this model, the significance of space objects and places relates to their role in affording an edge to the Space Race players, or in contributing to the eventual victory of one. 'Firsts' become paramount: the first satellite, the first human in space, the first planetary landing (indeed it is difficult to describe space history without this emphasis, see section above). Milestones like being the first, second, third or fourth country to place material in orbit are still hotly debated and defended.[1]

One effect of viewing space exploration as the outcome of the 'natural' human urge to explore is to decouple it from its historical context. There is no need to explain 'why here? why now?' as these are supposed to be self-evident: as soon as the technology emerges, humankind will spread its wings and leave the confines of the Earth. Russian rocket pioneer Konstantin Tsiolkowsky's line about the Earth being 'the cradle of mankind', drawing an analogy with Africa and the Fertile Crescent, is often quoted.

In essence, then, space industry interprets its own history as a form of vulgar Darwinian evolution in which progress is the result of immanent properties within the human species itself. Implicit in this view is the assumption that spacefaring states have demonstrated their evolutionary fitness through the successful pursuit of space exploration. It is almost an expression of nineteenth-century unilinear cultural evolution, as propounded by early anthropologists seeking to explain the differences between European imperialists and their Indigenous subjects. In the 1960s, Bruce Trigger has suggested, a neo-evolutionist view of cultural change developed in the United States as an attempt

by a politically dominant country to 'naturalize' their situation by demonstrating it to be the inevitable outcome of an evolutionary process that allowed human beings to acquire greater control over their environment and greater freedom from nature (Trigger 1989: 289).

This neo-evolutionist story of space masks the really interesting questions about the development of space technology, and these can be addressed by contemporary archaeological approaches to the modern world: for example, how space technology has contributed to the growth of global capitalist economies; and the participation in this economy of people usually considered marginal to its operation. Viewing space exploration through the lens of archaeology raises another question: the encounter of the Space Age and the Stone Age as a cultural interaction (Gorman 2005c).

So, while the evolutionary tendencies of the Space Race model might appeal to people living in the USA or in the former Soviet Union, people from the 'non-spacefaring' states might have different views. These emerge from contextualising the material culture of space exploration within other social and political trends of the post-war period.

Colonisation/decolonisation

The period following World War II saw the acceleration of two processes that transformed the complexion of the world: decolonisation and globalisation. As the great European empires disintegrated, myriad newly independent nation-states came into being. At the same time as this proliferation of national identities, the globalisation of

---

[1] I observed this most recently at a history workshop run by the European Space Agency, and in a debate on the Australian Space Research Institute's discussion list.

165

capital and markets was eroding national boundaries and facilitating the creation of transnational corporations and communities. Two space sites relate specifically to these processes: the Woomera rocket range in Australia and the Syncom 3 satellite in geostationary orbit (GEO).

An escalation of decolonisation following World War II saw former dependencies of Western capitalist powers metamorphose into independent states. For the most part, these new nations were non-white ex-colonies (Kay 1967). While decolonisation was a global phenomenon, it was by no means a uniform process, manifesting itself in numerous complex ways (Smith 1978). The process did more than create new states, however: it turned much of the world into a development area (Calvocoressi 1990: 666). The 'Third World', a 'developing' sector as defined by the standards of successful capitalist nations, was also politically non-aligned and thus open to influence from the Eastern and Western blocs. Demonstrating technological superiority through achievements in space was one of the ways that the USA and USSR hoped to influence these new nations (Osgood 2000: 213–14; Green and Lomask 1970: 32). Thus, the very presence of a nationally affiliated craft in space was thought capable of swaying hearts and minds among the non-aligned.

The proliferation of new nations is usually measured by calculating the rate at which new members joined the United Nations. Between 1945 and 1955, ten nations joined. In 1960 alone, 17 new members were admitted. By this time, imperialism on the basis of racial or social superiority was no longer a legitimate rationale for international action and was interpreted as contrary to human rights (Strang 1990: 848; Strang 1991: 440).

The trend towards decolonisation was balanced by another: the idea of interplanetary space as open for conquest. While imperial ambitions on Earth were no longer seen as acceptable, they could readily be admitted for the unpopulated regions beyond the atmosphere. 'The Conquest of Space' was a term almost universally used. In one sense, this conquest was technological, using scientists rather than soldiers to tame a hostile environment. In another sense, the term was redolent of a new New World, with resources like minerals, territory and strategic positions, waiting for the bold and enterprising (Gorman 2005a). Space was a frontier to be pushed back, just as it was in the American West (McCurdy 1997: 159).

Despite the growth of decolonisation, retaining an interest in colonies and former colonies was vital to the capacity of developed industrial nations to further their missile and space programs. For the USA, USSR, Britain and France, the beneficiaries of German rocket science, the problem was to find locations at which to develop nuclear-warhead bearing missiles that could guarantee security and safety. For this purpose, remote desert locations were ideal, especially as they could also assure clear skies and predictable weather conditions. The USA used land in New Mexico that had been cleared of its previous inhabitants: Mexicans, the Pueblo Indians and the Mescalero Apache (Gorman 2005d). The 'empty' steppe land in Kazakhstan that became part of the Kapustin Yar range was only so because of the Russian policy of removing former nomadic pastoralists to create land for cotton cultivation (Gorman 2005e). France's situation was slightly different. Since 1830, when France annexed Algeria, there had been a continual state of war that necessitated a high military presence (including the famous Foreign Legion). Algeria was not politically stable, but it did provide the desert and the infrastructure needed to test rockets. Within the Commonwealth, the UK rapidly found there was really only one choice: the Australian outback.

Woomera

Australia, colonised by Britain in 1788, had become a self-governing Commonwealth Realm by 1942. The head of state was the King of England, and the Governor-General had the power to dismiss Australian governments (as famously occurred in 1975). In 1945, the British Government approached the Australian Government with a proposal to establish a rocket range.

Australia's motivation in accepting the proposal was far more complex than a traditional loyalty to Blighty. In 1943, the Government had been shocked to realise that despite major Australian contributions in both wars, Britain was not prepared to assist Australia in defending itself against imminent Japanese invasion. Prime Minister Ben Chifley was determined that Australia would never again rely on foreign armaments for its defence. Accordingly, the agreement was to be a joint agreement: Australia would be privy to technological developments that would allow it to build its own armaments capacity (Morton 1989: 11–12).

Figure 9.1 The Redstone rocket that launched WRESAT-1, recovered from the desert, at the Woomera Missile Park. Photograph: Alice Gorman.

Over the next four decades, the Woomera rocket range grew in the red desert. A village was surveyed in 1946, and was followed by roads to the launch pads and the firing line: in the testing of new rocket and missile technology, recovery of the vehicle was vital to analyse the reasons for success or failure (figure 9.1). These roads opened up a vast area of desert to European access. As launch programmes extended — Woomera tested rockets for both the USA and UK — more launch pads with associated infrastructure were constructed. Among the most impressive of these are the ELDO launch areas on the edge of Lake Hart, a lake not of water but pure snow-white salt (figure 9.2). Here, the precursor of the European Space Agency's Ariane rocket, the Europa, was launched in the 1960s. Woomera had one of the first satellite tracking stations in the world, and later tracked the Gemini and Mercury missions from stations at Red Lake and Mirikata. At the range head, there were instrumentation buildings, workshops, storage areas and offices. Between the village and the range head, a golf course was sculpted out of red sand: no spare water here to create a perfect village green. In the 1950s and 1960s, it seemed that Australia had become a spacefaring nation, especially after it launched WRESAT-1 in 1967, becoming the fourth nation to launch its own satellite by some reckonings. It did not seem too far-fetched to suppose that, one day, crewed missions would be launched from Woomera (Eliott 1955).

Figure 9.2 Remains of the ELDO Launcher 6a at Lake Hart, Woomera Prohibited Area. Photograph: Alice Gorman.

But there was another layer of colonial infrastructure to unravel at Woomera. The desert regions of Central Australia were seen as empty, barren and remote, the most inhospitable country on Earth. This was the true outback: a red gibber plain with vast salt lakes and sparse mallee scrub. Only it was far from empty and barren. The place where the Woomera Village was surveyed was the traditional country of the Kokatha people. A large part of the Woomera Prohibited Area overlapped with the Central Aborigines Reserves, an area that crossed three state boundaries, and was home to Pitjantjatjara and related groups. A factor in the perceived emptiness of the landscape was the fact that drought, pastoral occupation and removal to missions had already begun the process of dispossession from country. The establishment of the Woomera Prohibited Area would accelerate this process.

The Kokatha and Pitjantjatjara had no land tenure recognised by the Australian Government and could not negotiate the conditions of use of their land. Some white Australians thought that the rocket range would provide employment opportunities for Aboriginal people, especially Aboriginal servicemen, but this does not seem to have happened (Morton 1989: 73). In 1947, Aboriginal people were not citizens and their movements were controlled by an oppressive pass system.

Space, race

For the emerging spacefaring nations, the possession of 'empty' colonial territories was a crucial element in developing the technology to conquer space. The perceived 'emptiness' of these places was, however, a perception based on colonial ideas of race and progress.

The construction of rangeheads, roads, launch pads and accommodation for the early rocket ranges did not take place in a pristine landscape. At Woomera, these facilities were interpolated between campsites, rock art sites, quarries, tracks, and places of mythological significance to Kokatha and Pitjantjatjara people. Aboriginal people continued to live in the Prohibited Area, where the new roads allowed ever greater numbers of Europeans to enter their country, bringing alcohol, disease, guns and flour. Spacefaring ambition was not acknowledged by Aboriginal people as a universal human urge; rather they saw the imposition of the rocket range as another strand of colonial practice that alienated them from country (Gorman 2005a).

The material remains on the Woomera range can tell us something about this interaction. Was the operation of the rocket range similar in its impact to other white activities, whether pastoral or industrial? Did it merely hasten a process of 'detribalisation' already initiated, as proponents of the rocket range argued, or did it significantly alter the ability of Aboriginal people to maintain their cultural practices, as the vocal protestors against the range claimed (Gorman 2005a)? Conversely, Aboriginal culture could be argued to have made an impact on the lives of Europeans in the Woomera village: they adopted words and symbols of Aboriginal culture to define their identity in the desert; they traded in souvenirs like woomeras and spears; and they employed 'half-caste' women as domestic servants.

Places like the remote Giles meteorological station, established in 1955 within the Central Aborigines Reserves to monitor weather conditions for rocket launches (and later, for nuclear tests), perhaps illustrate this process most clearly. Giles was located on a permanent water source known to Aboriginal people for millennia (Morton 1989: 85). Here, the scientific outstation and an Aboriginal fringe camp existed side-by-side. The Native Patrol Officer, R.A. Macauley, saw the situation as something like a controlled experiment (Morton 1989: 87). There was competition for precious water and game, which impacted on the ability of the Aboriginal group to survive. Despite this, station staff were forbidden to provision the Aboriginal camp. They chose to ignore official regulations, and distributed flour and shot kangaroos for the Aboriginal families in times of obvious shortage. The station rubbish dump became a source of raw materials eagerly used by the fringe camp. One could surmise that excavation at Giles would demonstrate a radical discontinuity in patterns of mobility, technology and population size for Aboriginal occupation. Inside the Giles compound itself, Aboriginal influence would be more subtle: supplementation of imported supplies with local resources, artefacts testifying to the presence of fringe camp people.

Neither the white colony of Australia, nor the Traditional Owners of Australia, became spacefaring by virtue of having hosted a launch facility; nor did they gain an equal share in the technology and resources of space exploration. This is vividly illustrated in a painting of the Europa rocket by Munggurrawuy Yunupingu, now in the South Australian Museum. Yunupingu was a Yolngu elder from the Gove peninsula in Arnhem Land, where there was a tracking station for Europa. In the painting, the white people inside the rocket ascend into space while Yolngu people remain behind, forever, with their Dreaming ancestors (Gorman 2005f). In effect, despite the rhetoric that space was available for all humanity, the former imperial centres embarked on the conquest of space by exploiting existing inequalities between them and their colonies.

A Space Race interpretation of the significance of Woomera would stress Australia's launch of the WRESAT satellite, third or fourth in the world, and the role Australia played in the research and development of four major space programmes: Mercury, Gemini and Apollo, and Ariane. Placing Woomera in the context of colonial relations after the war brings different aspects to the fore, in particular the relationship between the British Government, its Australian citizens, and Indigenous Australians. It highlights the relationship between the haves and have-nots of space. Aboriginal people may not have financed the Australian, American or British space programmes, but they paid a cost all the same.

Globalisation

While decolonisation has led to the birth of dozens of new nation-states, globalisation runs counter to this trend through the creation of transnational entities. Some regard globalisation as the mechanism of increased wealth, freedom, democracy and diversity (eg Friedman 1999). The disadvantage, as others argue, is

...increased domination and control by the wealthier overdeveloped nations over poor underdeveloped countries, thus increasing the hegemony of the 'haves' over the 'have-nots' (Kellner 2002: 286).

Globalisation and decolonisation are thus deeply entangled. There is an added dimension of this entanglement: the role of telecommunications technology in sustaining late nationalist movements (for example, in Hawai'i, Andaluz and Alaska: Saxton n.d.).

Some argue that globalisation was initiated literally when the Earth was first circumnavigated, developing concurrently with the spread of colonial and capitalist economic systems from the fifteenth century (eg Osterhammel and Petersson 2005). But it is also a distinct feature of the post-war world, accelerated by the accessibility of international aeroplane travel, and by the growth of computer and telecommunications technology. Castells (1996; 1997; 1998) defines the global economy as grounded in the new communication and information technology. Although rarely discussed explicitly by theorists of globalisation (but see Kellner 2002: 287), effectively this means satellite-based telecommunications. Global satellite and computer networks have provided the technological infrastructure for an economy characterised by a severing of production from territorial entities. Transnational corporations, rather than nation-states, have assumed control of production.

As a new global (Americanised) culture is distributed through television, telephone and the Internet, Indigenous and local cultures, traditions and languages are under threat (eg Barber 1996). Corporations and governments promote globalisation, but there is also a strong resistance to it, especially from Indigenous people, environmental groups and human rights activists. They condemn its homogenising affects, the impact on traditional cultures and the reinforcement of the divisions between the wealthy industrialised nations and the developing world — which, as we have already noted, is partially a result of decolonisation. On the other hand, access to the technology of globalisation also creates opportunities, heterogeneity and hybridity, breeding difference and creativity in a new way (Kellner 2002: 292; Luke and Luke 2000). Globalisation can give power to previously marginalised individuals and groups by increasing access to education and media networks. Increasingly, the antiglobalisation movement makes use of the same technology as proponents of globalisation to promote its call for social justice.

The beginning of the modern impact of globalisation can be dated to a specific year and a specific object: the Syncom 3 satellite.

Syncom 3

In 1959, two years after the launch of Sputnik 1, the Hughes Aircraft Company began work on a geosynchronous satellite project. At this time, communications satellites orbited in the Low Earth region. These satellites required a massive ground-based infrastructure, as they only remained within reach of a receiving station for a short period of time. By contrast, at the much higher geosynchronous regime, the height and speed of the satellite meant that its swath width was much broader, and far fewer receiving stations were needed, reducing the ground segment cost.

The Syncom satellites were designed by Dr Harold Rosen, Donald D. Williams and Thomas Hudspeth at Hughes. They devised innovative technology for the satellites, using a spin-stabilisation system and frequency multipliers (Boeing 1995–2005). At the Paris Air Show in 1961, they demonstrated how a Syncom could be used to relay television pictures. They displayed the prototype on top of the Eiffel Tower, and a passing wit commented that this was as high as the satellite would ever get (Boeing 1995–2000). Despite such scepticism, Hughes Aircraft won a contract to build geosynchronous satellites from NASA and the USA Department of Defense that year.

In 1963, the Syncom was ready for launch. Syncom 1 reached its transfer orbit, but systems failed before it could be injected into the final geosynchronous orbit. Rosen and his team redesigned some components for Syncom 2, which successfully reached geosynchronous orbit in July 1963. For the first time, instant global communication was possible. Later in 1963, Nigerian Prime Minister Abubaker Balewa spoke to USA President John F. Kennedy via Syncom 2.

Figure 9.3 The Syncom 3 satellite. Photograph courtesy of NASA.

Syncom 2's orbit was inclined at 33^0 to the equator. From the surface of the Earth it did not appear stationary; rather, it moved in the classic figure-of-eight relative to the observer (see table 1 for orbit definitions). Syncom 3 would achieve the first true geostationary orbit (figure 9.3). It was launched in August 1964, one month before the Tokyo Olympic Games, which it was to broadcast to Europe and North America. The broadcast was a turning point in the popularity of the Olympic Games, and a watershed for the Japanese television industry. Between them, Syncom 2 and 3 provided direct, 24-hour communication access to two-thirds of the Earth.

Arthur C. Clarke, ever prophetic, suggested that whoever was first able to harness the power of geostationary telecommunications could determine whether the *lingua franca* of the future was Russian or English. Intercontinental television broadcasts relayed through satellites would be mightier weapons than intercontinental ballistic missiles (Clarke 1962: 190). The Syncoms ensured that it was English language and capitalist ideologies that were broadcast from orbit. Despite its outwardly benign function, Syncom 3 was also a Cold War weapon; and with its sister was a primary communications link for the USA in the Vietnam War (Gorman 2005b).

Syncom 2 and 3 were small by comparison with USSR satellites of the same period. They were 0.71 m in diameter, and 0.39 m high, weighing 35 kg. They carried solar cells, transmitting and receiving antennae, and telemetry and command antennae. While the Syncoms were decommissioned in 1969, the design was tremendously successful and remained in use well into the 1990s. The AUSSAT and Optus B series utilised exactly the same design.

Satellite television and Indigenous identity

What changes to life on Earth did Syncom 2 and 3 effect from their distant eyrie in space? To many new and old nations, the ability to receive television from wealthy countries like the USA seemed a form of 'cybernetic colonialism' (Miskin 1995). In some remote Aboriginal communities, television was called 'the Third Invader', after Europeans, and alcohol (McGregor 1988: 35). Ginsberg (1991: 96) calls the advent of satellite-based television a Faustian dilemma for Indigenous and minority people:

> On the one hand, they are finding new modes for expressing indigenous identity through media and gaining access to film and video to serve their own needs and ends. On the other hand, the spread of communications technology and satellite downlinks threatens to be a final assault on culture, language, imagery, relationships between generations, and respect for traditional knowledge.

In 1982, the Australian government commissioned the Hughes Aircraft Company to build the AUSSAT satellites, a new generation of the Syncom design. The idea was to provide remote parts of Australia with same television and telecommunications services as the rest of the country. This was not viewed as a universally positive move. The Australian Institute of Aboriginal Studies (AIAS) was concerned about the impact on settlements and communities who would receive television for the first time (Ginsberg 1991: 99). One of the projects initiated by AIAS in 1982 led to the formation of the Warlpiri Media Association. The WMA made its own videos, and by setting up their own satellite downlink they were able to insert these programmes into the signal.

The launch of AUSSAT in 1985 (figure 9.4) brought another level of Indigenous involvement in satellite broadcasting. The Central Australian Aboriginal Media Association (CAAMA) had developed from a small radio station founded in 1980, promoting Aboriginal languages and music. Like the WMA, they began making their own videos. CAAMA was concerned about the impact of AUSSAT on traditional languages and culture, and made a bid for AUSSAT's downlink license to Central Australia. Despite competition from much larger commercial interests, CAAMA was successful in winning the license. In 1988, the Imparja television station began broadcasting, including Aboriginal news and magazine programmes as well as mainstream content (Ginsberg 1991: 99). Nineteen years later, the station is still going strong, and the Warlpiri Media Association is one of its shareholders (Imparja 2001). Fry and Willis (1989: 163) commented that this active role by an Indigenous group in the new media 'doesn't override the effects of a damaged culture in which it functions, but creates a fissure in which a new set of perceptions can creep in'.

For the WMA and CAAMA, Syncom 3 and its AUSSAT descendents represent a technology of subtle colonialism: a threat to the viability of communities not through overt violence, but through the desire to provide them with the services expected by urban Australians. This threat and their response illuminate the Faustian dilemma of globalisation as expressed by Ginsburg, and these uneasy meanings are embodied in Syncom 3 satellite, now just one more piece of space junk in the densely populated geostationary ring.

Figure 9.4 The deployment of Aussat. Photograph courtesy of NASA

One (GEO) ring to rule them all

The satellite revolution inaugurated by Syncom 3 has also had a significant effect on the built environment. Buildings both ancient and modern now sprout satellite dishes. In Australia and the UK, regulations control the size and location of satellite dishes to protect the visual impact on heritage buildings and landscapes. In the developing world, travellers delight in (or deplore) tales and images which juxtapose crumbling mud brick houses with satellite dishes (eg Yeomans 2002; Elisabeth and Teije 2003). For some, the presence of satellite dishes is an impediment to their enjoyment of an authentic traditional culture. Of Casablanca, one traveller says 'A visit to this country can take you back in time hundreds of years ... numerous satellite dishes that look out of place in this African city' (Salant 2003; Figure 9.5).

Figure 9.5 Satellite dishes in Casablanca. Photograph courtesy of Sat 7

And yet, these offending dishes are a link to orbital space. In a sense, they could be considered a part or extension of the satellites whose signals they receive. Not only the dishes, but also the millions of televisions, computers, telephones, GPS receivers etc are networked with a handful of satellites in orbit, visible components of an invisible web of information.

The effect of satellite television may extend beyond the scattering of dishes in the desert. In the Woomera Prohibited Area, the sudden appearance of European settlements like Woomera village and the Giles weather station had an immediate impact on the everyday life of the local Aboriginal families. The effect of exposure to television through satellite downlinks, one might expect, would be more gradual. Advertising, and the representation of American culture (Australian television has far more USA content than the European networks) may alter patterns of consumption. By assessing the changes in the material record in communities in the far north, an aspect of globalisation can be explored that is accessible in no other way.

Syncom 3 is the ancestor of the satellites that provide telecommunication services today. Technologically, Syncom 3's design and mission helped shape the world of the second millennium where nearly everyone is within reach of almost every point on the globe, and transnational entities assume a greater and greater role in the structuring of everyday life. Syncom 3 was a major step in the process of globalisation that has been developing since the 1400s when navigation connected previously separate old and new worlds. For some, globalisation has meant new possibilities and opportunities; for others, it has meant the erosion of identity in contexts where colonial exploitation has already exacted a high price.

Conclusions

In 1965, Lincoln Bloomfield recognised a tension between the forces of neonationalism and internationalism — by which he meant transnationalism — being played out in space (1965: 603). He noted that outer space was an arena for virulent forms of nationalism. But he also noted that

> if anything makes a nonsense of national boundaries, however useful and meaningful they may be in other ways, it is the earth satellite, orbiting the earth every 90 minutes or so over different countries, transiting their boundaries, without passports, travel documents, customs inspection or even permission (Bloomfield 1965: 605).

Space objects and places embody this tension. On the one hand they can represent nationalist ideologies and agendas; on the other, they are the very instruments of a process that reduces the economic relevance of nation-states.

The material culture of space exploration illuminates both these processes. The distribution of ground sites like rocket ranges and tracking stations reflects colonial power relations: thus we have a rocket range in Australia, but only one existing Australian-made satellite in orbit since WRESAT-1. The installation of satellite dishes in impoverished communities from Australia to North Africa demonstrates the material impact of globalisation. In particular, looking at globalisation and decolonisation opens space exploration to the area where contemporary archaeology is strongest: connecting global processes with the local scale through material culture.

The Space Age did not take place only in space, or only in the spacefaring nations. It left its traces in every country with a satellite dish or a tracking station. Hidden from view beneath the triumphal sagas of launching satellites and crewed spacecraft, there are smaller events and interactions: the crash of a rocket into a landscape shaped by the flight of the Seven Sisters (the Pleiades); the sudden construction of a meteorological outstation on land once deemed worthless for European exploitation; the response of CAAMA to the problem posed by AUSSAT for the survival of Aboriginal culture in Central Australia. These also tell a story of the Space Age, where Indigenous people move from dispossession by to active engagement with space technology.

The basis of success for spacefaring states is rooted in inequalities arising from the period of empire-building, and subsequently, post-war decolonisation. So the material culture of space exploration cannot be interpreted as global in its significance because, as the cases of Woomera and Syncom 3 so clearly demonstrate, participation in and impact from space ventures depends on where you are and who you are. And yet, by placing space exploration in the context of decolonisation and globalisation, it can be seen that developing nations and Indigenous people have participated in space exploration in ways that have previously gone unrecognised.

Through an investigation of the material culture of space exploration — for example in the landscape of Woomera, in the nexus of satellites and satellite dishes in Central Australia — archaeology can effect a shift of perspective that moves beyond the evolutionary, progressive, colonial framework captured by the 'Space Race' model to a more inclusive view that takes account of all participants in the development of space technology. Contemporary archaeological perspectives that explore culture contact, as, in this case, between 'the Stone Age' and 'the Space Age' (Gorman 2005c), are critical in understanding how space industry has created, and impacted on, a world transformed by decolonisation and globalisation.

The United Nations Committee on the Peaceful Uses of Outer Space has defined a goal of breaking down barriers to participation in space exploration of the 'have-nots': non-spacefaring states, the developing world, Indigenous people, women. Within the paradigm of the Space Race, the participation and contribution that has already been made by these groups is unacknowledged. It is only by looking at space material culture outside this framework that it is possible to make an argument for global significance of space sites, and make space material relevant to non-spacefaring, Indigenous and developing countries. Moving beyond the Space Race is a first step in decolonising space itself.

Acknowledgements

An earlier version of this paper was presented at the Society for American Archaeology conference in Montreal, 2004. I would like to thank Andrew Starkey, Kokatha representative, for discussions on Kokatha culture, and Angela Piccini and Cornelius Holtorf for their encouragement and insightful comments.

Bibliography

Barber, B (1995) *Jihad vs McWorld,* New York: Times Books.
Boeing (1995–2005) Syncom factsheet, *www.boeing.com/defense-space/space/bss/fact sheets/376/syncom/syncom.html* (01.12.2005).
Bloomfield, L (1965) 'Outer space and international cooperation' *International Organization* 19 (3): 603–21.
Bryld, M and Lykke, N (2000) *Cosmodolphins: Feminist Cultural Studies of Technology, Animals, and the Sacred*, New York and London: Zed Books.
Burton, J M (2000) 'Tranquillity Base Today', *http://members.aol.com/TranBaseDiorama/TBDetails.htm*, (01.11.2003).
Cadbury, D (2005) *Space Race*, New York: HarperCollins.
Calvocoressi, P (1990) 'World Power 1920–1990' *International Affairs* 66 (4): 663–74
Castells, M (1996) *The Information Age: Economy, Society and Culture. Volume 1: The Rise of the Network Society,* Oxford: Blackwell.
Castells, M (1997) *The Information Age: Economy, Society and Culture. Volume 2: The Power of Identity,* Oxford: Blackwell.
Castells, M (1998) *The Information Age: Economy, Society and Culture. Volume 3: End of Millennium,* Oxford: Blackwell.
Chapman, S (1959) *IGY: Year of Discovery. The Story of the International Geophysical Year*, Ann Arbor: University of Michigan Press.
Clarke, A C (1945) 'Extraterrestrial relays: can rocket stations give worldwide radio coverage?' *Wireless World*, October.
Clarke, A C (1962) *Profiles of the Future,* New York: Harper and Row.
Eliott, E C (1955) *Tas and Postal Rocket,* London: Thomas Nelson and Sons.
Elisabeth and Teije (2003) *Elisabeth and Teije's Travel Website, www.teije.nl/2003/mar/0809_en.htm* (01.01.2006).
European Space Operations Centre (2005) *Space Debris Spotlight*, www.esa.int/SPECIALS/ESOC/SEMHDJXJD1E_0.html, (01.01.2006).
Friedman, T (1999) *The Lexus and the Olive Tree*, New York: Farrar Straus Giroux.
Fry, T and Willis, A-M (1989) 'Aboriginal art: symptom or success?' *Art in America* 77 (7): 108–17; 160; 163
Ginsburg, F (1991) 'Indigenous media: Faustian contract or global village? *Cultural Anthropology* ' 6 (1): 92–112
Gorman, A C (2005a) 'The cultural landscape of interplanetary space' *Journal of Social Archaeology* 5 (1): 85–107
Gorman, A C (2005b) 'The archaeology of orbital space', *Proceedings of the Fifth Australian Space Science Conference*, Melbourne: Royal Melbourne Institute of Technology.
Gorman, A C (2005c) 'From the Stone Age to the Space Age: interpreting the significance of space exploration at Woomera', unpublished paper presented at *Home on the Range: the Cold War, Space Exploration and Heritage at Woomera, South Australia*, Flinders University, Adelaide.

Gorman, A C (2005d) 'Space cowboys: the Wild West and the myth of the American hero' *The New England Review*, February, 10–12.

Gorman, A C (2005e) 'Everybody wants to rule the world: the archaeology of the early Cold War rocket ranges', unpublished seminar presentation, Department of Archaeology, Flinders University.

Gorman, A C (2005f) 'From the desert to the tropics: European space exploration at Woomera', unpublished seminar presentation, Centre Spatial Guyanais, Kourou, French Guiana.

Green, C M and Lomask, M (1970) *Vanguard: A History*, Washington D C: NASA SP-4204, The NASA Historical Series.

Imparja (2001) *www.imparja.com.au/* (01.01.2006).

Jones, T D and Benson, M (2002) *The Complete Idiot's Guide to NASA*, Indianapolis: Alpha Books.

Kay, D A (1967) 'The politics of decolonisation: the new nations and the United Nations political process' *International Organization* 21 (4): 786–811.

Kellner, D (2002) 'Theorizing globalization' *Sociological Theory* 20 (3): 285–305.

Logsdon, John (1983) 'Introduction', in Needell, A (ed.), *The First 25 Years in Space*, Washington DC: Smithsonian Institution Press, 3–5.

Luke, A and Luke, C (2000) 'A situated perspective on cultural globalization', in Burbules, N and Torres, C (eds), *Globalization and Education,* London: Routledge, 275–98.

McCurdy, H E (1997) *Space and the American Imagination*, Washington and London: Smithsonian Institution Press.

McGregor, A (1988) 'Black and White television', *Rolling Stone* 415: 35ff.

Miskin, A (1995) 'Mediations: globalization and its discontents' *Middle East Report* 193: 28.

Morton, P (1989) *Fire Across the Desert. Woomera and the Anglo-Australian Joint Programme, 1946–80*, Canberra: Australian Government Publishing Service.

Neufeld, M J (1996) *The Rocket and the Reich: Peenemünde and the Coming of the Ballistic Missile Era,* Cambridge, MA: Harvard University Press.

Osgood, K A (2000) 'Before Sputnik: National security and the formation of US outer space policy', in Launius, R D, Logsdon, J M and Smith, R W (eds), *Reconsidering Sputnik: Forty Years Since the Soviet Satellite*, London: Harwood Academic Publishers, 197–229.

Osterhammel, J and Petersson, N P (2005) *Globalization: a Short History*, translated by Geyer, D, Princeton: Princeton University Press.

Robinson, W I (1998) 'Beyond nation-state paradigms: globalization, sociology and the challenge of transnational studies' *Sociological Forum* 13 (4): 561–94.

Salant, D (2003) *Charmed, I'm sure! In Morocco, www.escapeartist.com/efam/52/ Travel_Morocco.html* (01.01.2006).

Saxton, G D (n.d.) 'Nation, nation building and nationalism in the Catalan-speaking cyberspace', paper prepared for delivery at the annual Meeting of the American Political Science Association, September 3–6, Boston, MA *www.nd.edu/~dmyers/cbsm/vol2/saxton/apsa98.htm#fn3* (01.01.2006).

Sellier, A (2003) *A History of the Dora Camp,* translated by Wright, S and Taponier, S, Chicago: Ivan R. Dee, in association with the United States Holocaust Memorial Museum.

Smith, T (1978) 'A comparative study of French and British decolonisation' *Comparative Studies in Society and History* 20 (1): 70–102.

Strang, D (1990) 'From dependency to sovereignty: an event history analysis of decolonisation 1870–1987' *American Sociological Review* 55 (6): 846–60.

Strang, D (1991) 'Global patterns of decolonisation, 1500–1987' *International Studies Quarterly* 35 (4): 429–54.

Trigger, B (1989) *A History of Archaeological Thought*, Cambridge: Cambridge University Press.

United Nations (2005) *List of Member States, www.un.org/Overview/unmember.html* (01.12.2005).

Wyckoff, P H (1958) 'The rocket as research vehicle' in Odishaw, H and Ruttenberg, S (eds), *Geophysics and the IGY. Proceedings of the Symposium at the Opening of the International Geophysical Year 28–29 June 1957*, Washington DC: American Geophysical Union of the National Academy of Sciences – National Research Council, Publication No 590, 102–07.

Yeomans, M (2002) 'Ethiopia: architecture, ancient ritual and the satellite dish', *http://travel.roughguides.com/spotlight_display.html?spotlightid=288* (01.01.2006).

Part 4: Into the future

Guttersnipe: A Micro Road Movie

Angela Piccini

> Respect the kerb line — the kerb can be the key to making a street look like a street. It acts like the pediment to a Greek column, it provides continuity between adjoining buildings. Buildings have a typical life of 100–200 years; the alignment of a road can have an indefinite lifetime. Changing the kerb line, or removing the kerb altogether can have a detrimental effect on the appearance of a street.
>
> Institution of Civil Engineers. n.d. Paving Aesthetics Briefing Sheet

58"–1'13"

A long, rusty nail

Lipsticked cigarette

Silver birch leaves

Chewed gum from countless mouths

Worked and painted kerbstone, the presence of nineteenth-century stonecutters and contemporary cable, water, sewer, telephone, road workers.

A drain.

Tarmac and sandstone rub up against each other and hoard the grimy castings of the passersby. Plastic, soot, particulates, the remains of fossil fuels from across the centuries, produced and consumed on a global level. It's what connects my house to yours, my mouth to yours.

This is not a film. I wanted to explore how to practice an archaeology through a video practice but I am not a video practitioner. I work in a university drama department but they think I'm just an archaeologist. I work in a university archaeology department but they think I'm just a drama type. What I do once a week is research and teach archaeology for screen media, thinking beyond the standard broadcast expository documentary. I don't know about available light and white balance, but I am there in the shadows, on those screens, here now.

This doesn't work as I skip ahead and slip behind time. But then that's the point, too.

Figure 10.1 Photograph: Angela Piccini (video still)

2'05"

A ring and an M connecting kerbstones, Neolithic and now. Bob Jones, city council archaeologist tells me that no one's paid much attention to the kerbs. These masons' marks might be saying something about where the stone was quarried or where it was worked or it might indicate a production batch or be a location key. My interest sparks Bob's and he tells me that this is a good field for documentary research.

The above words are the first few minutes of script from *Guttersnipe*, a fourteen-minute video/live-spoken-word performance, which I shot and initially scripted in November 2003. Between 2003 and 2005 I revisited the script for a range of different events, from archaeology conferences to locative media workshops to local arts and music festivals. My aim in the video project was to explore the potentialities and limitations of a photographic practice as archaeological practice, archaeology *in* the modern world. Given the central role of camera-based technologies in archaeology and the generative tensions between the live archaeological 'event' and its various recorded artefacts (Pearson and Shanks 2001; Phelan 1993; Piccini and Rye forthcoming; Reason 2006; Rye 2000; 2003), I wished to attempt a different way of thinking about the relationships between record and event. Rather than seeking to reproduce a 'commonsense' use of camera-based technologies to contain and transmit 'knowledge', I wished to work with John Grierson's famous description of documentary as the 'creative treatment of actuality' (1926) as a starting point. What might the juxtaposition of video and live spoken word specifically contribute to archaeological practice that is qualitatively different from a textual account of place? How is this practice performative of place? How might this practice organise space — screen space, stage space, suburban space, family space, depth and surface, now and then — and place — the specificity of locale, city, neighbourhood, street, gutter, housing, pavement, roadway — as they intertwine variously?

The video comprises a largely unedited tracking shot (there is a fade in from black at the beginning and fade to black at the end) along one unbroken stretch of gutter in Brislington, Bristol.

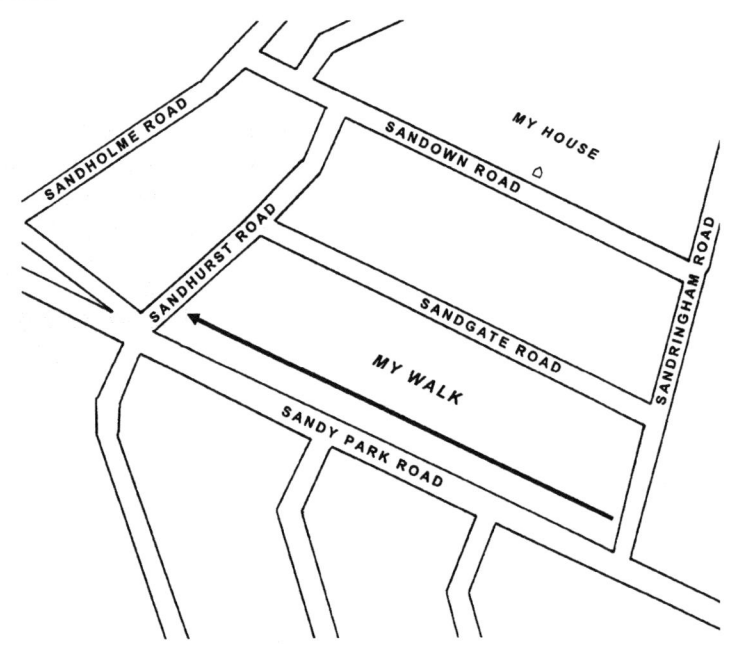

Figure 10.2 A walk along the north side of Sandy Park Road, from Sandringham Road to Sandhurst Road.

The camera focuses in on the 90° angle where the street meets the kerb. I shot the screenwork in one take with a consumer miniDV video recorder, lashed onto a pushchair. In performance I have not used the synchronous recorded sound, but rather a soundtrack composed by Jem Noble, which layers the original synchronous sound with multiple sound recordings of the script. I then read the script in performance.

While the time-base of the screenwork is necessarily absent from these pages, the script reproduced here in the indented passages emerged from the moving image material just as this chapter emerges from the performance. The screenwork was the initial artefact that I used to construct an archaeological narrative that sometimes referenced what I saw on the screen and sometimes became a departure point from which to discuss a broader archaeology. This practice is in the spirit of Benjamin's 'philosophising "directly" out of the objects of cultural experience' (Benjamin and Osborne 1994, xi; Benjamin 1999). The screenwork also refers to the embodied practices that characterise archaeological endeavour: surveying, planning and drawing, fieldwalking, electronic sub-surface survey, excavation, photography, recording, looking (see also Holtorf 2001; Wylie 2002). Thus, a videoed gutter brought me to consider the briefing paper from the Institute for Civil Engineers quoted at the beginning of this chapter, which then allowed me to make a connection between pediments and continuity and the notion of the gutter as performance space with its kerbstone proscenium arch. The practice of making the video together with my watching practice shaped the emergent archaeological narrative. In this way, the forensic camera view framed the markings on top of the kerbs, such that I began to consider the relationships between the contemporary past and the cup-and-ring marks of the late Neolithic and early Bronze Age.

Figure 10.3 Photograph: Angela Piccini (video still)

My writing here in this chapter is clearly not the performance, nor is it intended to be an explanation or representation of the work. My aim here is to organise this writing practice in such a way as to resist the expository drive and yet expand a contemporary archaeology. It is an attempt to write in proximity to the performance piece. In so doing I deliberately and occasionally awkwardly juxtapose discursive registers. Anecdote, informality, opacity sit in relation as do the various artefacts in the gutter. In this way I suggest that the project is cognate with archaeology's recent experiments with the languages of symmetry, situation, relationality, percolation, multivocality (see esp. Buchli 2002; Campbell and Ulin 2004; Hicks 2005; Holtorf 2005; Pearson and Shanks 2001; Shanks 2004).

2'21"

Sweet wrappers. A Bounty bar. Just bought from the Newsagents at the bottom of the road, or maybe leftovers from last night's Halloween treats. The coconut, sugar and chocolate a perfect Bristol snack. The story of slavery and Bristol's wealth all in one convenient bar. But I don't suppose anyone else was seeing it that way, that day. It's always the archaeologist who brings up that kind of thing.

And so for me the contemporary ephemera of consumer litter are performative of a range of themes. Here they articulate a slavery narrative, with which the city of Bristol has grappled. Yet it is not *about* slavery. This is a chance to make a political archaeology, to suggest that the story of slavery is not out there in the received spaces of slavery such as the Clifton area of Bristol, or safely imprisoned in museums; its legacy exists today beyond the 'exotic' of British Afro-Caribbean communities, mediatised as urban, violent. It is here in Brislington, where the BNP campaign and where a large number of slave-dependent Bristol plantation owners and merchants made their country retreats. It is here, under our feet.

Here is James Ireland (1724–1814), sugar refiner and high sheriff of Somerset. His family, the Clayfield-Irelands, built Brislington Hall in the 1770s, with the profits of this 'respectable trade' (Rowe 1986: 6). At the time of beginning this chapter the remains of Brislington Hall were hidden beneath a B & Q hardware superstore. Since then, the hardware store has become a Toys R Us®. In 1733, Josiah Wharton's cousin Michael went to Virginia to start up his plantation (Lindegaard 1994: 18). Another Wharton cousin, Thomas Murray, sailed with Captain Waring in the slave ship Antilope. He later died in 1742, somewhere between Guinea and Jamaica (Lindegaard 1994: 46). On 13 December 1816 John Duncombe Taylor, of Antigua, became a Brislington resident (BRO 8032[3] and [13]). However, some traffic went the other way. On 29 November 1658, before the monopoly of the Royal African Company ended in 1698 and the official slave trade began, James Cogin was one of many indentured servants sent to the New World; he is likely to have died in Barbados in the service of Francis Parsons (Lindegaard 1993: 37). On 27 May 1680 Tobey Grey was sent to Jamaica. And on 12 June 1686 John Purnell travelled on the Maryland Merchant to Virginia (Lindegaard 1994: 60).

Perhaps the most famous of the Brislington slavery links is George Weare Braikenridge (1775–1856), merchant, collector and antiquarian. He was born in Virginia, son of planter and slaver George Braikenridge, who was in turn son-in-law to Virginia merchant Francis Jerdone (1720–71), said to be the originator of the chain store, the precursor to that B & Q hardware store up the road (Stampp 1994: 9). In 1818, young Weare

Braikenridge held title deeds to and was mortgagee on land on the island of Nevis, land that he eventually inherited in 1836 (BCC Libraries, Jefferies collection–Bristol MSS Miscellaneous). Often painted as a quirky Brislington collector (Stoddard 1981) he moved to the area in 1816/17 and in 1823 bought Broomwell House on Wick Road. Demolished in 1928 to make way for early council housing that stood at 240–286 Wick Road — which has, in turn, been demolished in the past four years to make way for semi-private Housing Association houses — the house became known as a museum of local and general antiquities. Unlike Thomas Goldney III (1696–1768) up in Clifton, Weare Braikenridge did not collect and display material directly associated with the West Indies trade but rather sought to create an idealised English heritage. However, both men shared a similar approach to material culture: in keeping with Goldney's Atlantic World bricolage (Hicks 2005), Weare Braikenridge would break up medieval church pews, stained glass and other items and combine the pieces to construct new, hybrid antiquities. Many of these pieces were removed from Broomwell House after Weare Braikenridge's death and installed at the family's summer home on Highdale Road, Clevedon, where it faced west, across the Atlantic.

Figure 10.4 Photograph: Angela Piccini (video still)

Institution of Civil Engineers: Paving Aesthetics

Design from the pedestrian's perspective – pedestrians view paving from a height of 2 metres. A drawing board however provides an aerial view equivalent to about 25 metres when the designer is working to a scale of 1 in 50. Some paving schemes include patterns that can only be appreciated from nearby office blocks, or passing aircraft. The design of many buildings falls into the same trap.

A runoff drain cuts through one of the kerbs.

And in a minute there's a gap coming up, mirroring the change from tarmac pavement to brick paving.

13,598 cm, 168 kerbstones

> This is the north side of Sandy Park Road, Brislington. A short stretch of high street in a once vibrant village, now a rundown neighbourhood on the up again due to the housing boom that confines me forever to tenancy. Further down the road, out of shot, was the Brislington Picture Palace, 1913–1955. There is a late 3rd, early 4th century Roman villa up at Winchester road. During excavations mosaics, a coin and the remains of twelve cattle and four humans were found. And there's the incongruous WW2 pillbox tucked away below street level in the Sandy Park Road car park. Writer and asbestos campaigner Julie Burchill walked down this street when she lived here. And the 60 men and 89 boys from the so-called honeytrap at 49 Churchill Road, just around the corner, walked this street, their secrets safe, for over 20 years. No one had any idea. And perhaps some of those on their way to the Chapel of St Anne in the Woods, the third most important place of medieval pilgrimage, travelled this route. Henry VII visited twice – in 1486 and 1502. The Quakers were here in the 17th century. At St Anne's Woods the State used dogs, whips and guns against the large dissident congregations. It's a multivalent byway, the world in a gutter. The absent have all been down this way.

And I was walking this stretch of my neighbourhood on All Saints Day, 2003.

These archaeological silences, the absent presence of structures, seem to deafen Brislington. St Anne's Chapel was built by Roger la Warre in 1276 to commemorate his marriage to Clarice and celebrate his elevation to First Baron la Warre (Lindegaard 1992: 12). It was reputed to be 58' x 15', with nineteen buttresses and candles renewed yearly at £5 each (ibid.). In 1538, the chapel was surpressed, the roof stripped, the lead given to the exchequer and the windows removed (Lindegaard 1992: 24). Some of the glass eventually made it into George Weare Braikenridge's house (Stoddard 1981). There is also a silence collecting in the gutter. I planned to do document-based research into The Bristol Urban Sanitary Authority, the body responsible for the city's planning and its roadways, but their archives were destroyed in a fire 1969 (Bristol Record Office communication).

Then there is the Brislington Picture Palace. On 18 July 1913, Howard James Usher of 46 College Road, Clifton applied for a licence for '*Singing, Music and Dancing*, at the House and Premises thereunto belonging, now in my occupation, situate at the corner of Belmont Road and Sandy Park Road…to be used as a picture hall and cinematograph house' (Bristol Records Office Pol/L/13/15). By 13 October City Engineer Lessel S McKenzie wrote to Police Chief Constable Jas. Cann that the 'New Cinematograph hall' has been 'certified under Section 36 of the Public Health Acts Amendment Act 1890 as to substantiality and means of egress. The Cinematograph Act and Regulations are also complied with so far as my Department is concerned…' (ibid.). The Brislington Picture Palace fell victim to post-war cinematic decline and became a local bingo hall in

1956. By the 1990s it had been comprehensively gutted and converted into flats. Only the crenellated pediment above the katy-corner door hints at the art deco glory days of early cinema, which, like that Bounty bar, brought the world to Brislington. The enfolding journeys of chocolate bar, cinema and chapel disrupt easy distinctions between global and local, space and place (Massey 2005: 177–95).

Figure 10.5 Photograph: Angela Piccini (video still)

5'34"

There's a small castor encrusted with road grime. The sad social life of a thing. How did someone lose that? I know that out of shot is the end of the terrace, where the houses change to shops. One sold a few months back. Looks like whoever lived there now has a lopsided Ikea coffee table somewhere. No one thought to look in the gutter.

And then there was the circumflex and A carved into one kerb, or was it a theta? There is no pattern to the distribution of these marks, no sense I can make that they were intended for one stretch and not the other. Did the parish council buy up a job lot of different batches in order to complete modernisation? An archaeologist told me that once the kerbs wore down, they were turned over. The mason's marks weren't meant to be seen. But I've looked all round the city and haven't found anything to compare. Are Brislingtonians particularly hard on their kerbs or is something else altogether going on?

A lot of the Pennant sandstone in Bristol kerbs came from Snuff Mills, Stapleton, quarried by Maberly Parker after he bought the place in 1889. Thomas Henry Kinchin ran the mill on Parker's behalf. Is that why in land-locked Brislington it's either Sandy Park, Sandown, Sandholme, Sandwich, Sandhurst? Even the 90-year old keeper of the church crypt key, who's lived here since she was a baby doesn't know why and tells me that her family spent a lot of time once doing some unfruitful research.

The daily shopping at green grocer and butcher, the school trips, visits to the post office, friends, the local funeral director – our retracing the steps of this 19th-century avenue of industrial expansion, itself overlaying those earlier pathways, makes this gutterscape.

In both the screenwork and in this paper objects (and words) are 'circulating temporalities of recurrence and iteration' (Lefebvre 2003: 49). A recurrence of mason's marks on the kerb is given new meaning through iteration: the earlier cup-and-ring referencing is now associated with industrial mass production. I may also re-consider slavery through the appearance of the sand-prefixed roads as they occupy what were the grounds of Weare Braikenridge's Broomwell House. Recurrence and iteration create the conditions by which I evidence how slavery physically underpins the contemporary life of the Sandy Park Road area. But these roads have always been implicated in the performative production of 'normalised and governable individuals' (Marshall 1999: 309). The school walks and daily shopping along Sandy Park Road are performative of this space as suburban high street, with a full array of industrialised public and private conveniences.

This is further evidenced in the records. On 23 June 1902, E Smith of the Bristol Urban Sanitary Authority posted notices of works on Sandgate and Sandhurst roads:

By virtue of the Powers and Provisions of "The Public Health Acts," WE, THE URBAN SANITARY AUTHORITY of the City and County of Bristol, *Hereby give Notice* that so much of a certain Street, situate and being in the Parish of Bristol, in the said City and County of Bristol, within our District and commonly called or known by the name of …as lies between the points marked A and B on a plan of such Street deposited at our Offices, and not being a Highway repairable by the inhabitants at large, having been Sewered, Levelled, Paved, Flagged, Channelled, Metalled, and made good, and provided with proper means of lighting, to our satisfaction *We Hereby Declare* the said portion of the said Street to be a Highway repairable by the inhabitants at large. (BRO 40287/6/29).

And back on 22 June 1215, Brislington men were ordered to make a 'perambulation' of the highways and byways in order to prove which Chases belonged to the King (Lindegaard 1992: 8). Later, after Brislington's roads were described in 1634 as 'founderous and in decaye', a committee was appointed to resolve the matter (1633–34 Quarter Sessions at Bridgewater, Somerset Records Society). It did not work: in 1637 Samuel Magges, Constable of the Hundred of Keynsham, refused his part in the upkeep of the highways (Lindegaard 1993: 27). The recurrence and iteration of roads describes various understandings of their human traffic.

Watch for the boiled sweet wrapper. There's something quite beautiful about the way it blows along the gutter. The plastic is the only stuff that moves here. While kids stick with cola bottles, flumps and the gelatine menagerie these occasional sweet wrappers seem to point to elderly women out for their morning walks, just popping in a humbug to soothe a cough. My gran was one of those and my mum's becoming one. But then again, it was Halloween last night. Maybe the kids get rid of these sweets first so they can get to the chocolate.

8'02"

Out of the corner of your eye is a passing child on a bike.
 Excuse me love, what are you doing walking in the middle of the road? I'm not using the pushchair or the streetscene in the proper way. Who ever heard of putting a pillow in a pushchair and tying a camcorder on to it with pipecleaners? I don't think I've left anything behind, but my wheels grind through the grit, making it hard to keep a steady pace. So I leave subtle tracks in this gutter and embedded in my wheels are the remains of the other people who've gone this way, their traces worked into the fibres of my own front hall carpet.

8'21"

I have to walk around a jeep about now. The jeep and the well meaning woman from Sandy's Diner, the place you can't see with the sausage-eating pigs on the plate glass, force me to acknowledge that I have disturbed the natural order of things with this timecoded walk in the road. My street just another mediatised place. The jeep is the proper American kind. It's parked on the double yellows so it shouldn't be there but it got there via the docks at Avonmouth, row after row of cars fresh off the boat, economic migrants – just like me.
 The creep of the tarmac up the sides of the kerbs makes me want to peel it back, like a scab.

My fascination with ground level, with the boundary separating over and under, with the city's skin calls up the work of Gordon Matta-Clark (1943–78), although I found out about him later. In *Substrait (Underground Dailies)* and *City Slivers, NY* (both 1976) and then *Sous-sols de Paris* (1977) Matta explores the secret archaeologies of the urban, making unprojectable films that mix film stock and still images:

> the next area that interests me is an expedition into the underground: a search for the forgotten spaces left buried under the city either as a historical reserve or as surviving reminders of lost projects and fantasies, such as the famed Phantom Railroad. This activity would include mapping and breaking or digging into these lost foundations. (Matta-Clark in Walker 2003: 163).

Matta-Clark undertook expeditions into New York's networked service spaces — aqueducts, sewers, subway — and into the storage spaces beneath Paris — catacombs, wine cellars, undercrofts — the 'mappings' of which were shown as film in galleries. While the stratigraphy of the cities is clear, images like that of the river beneath the Paris Opera and the catacombs with their bones piled up to the under surface of the Parisian streets serve to make the familiar strange. Matta-Clark's work references Baudelaire's *Le Voyage* — we travel 'deep in the Unknown to find the new' (quoted in Lefebvre 2003: 56) — thus bringing me back to archaeology via Julian Thomas's explorations of the tensions of depth and surface via a modernity seen through a lens of Freudian psychoanalysis (Thomas 2004: 27–29). The objects that we see and feel displace time into things to become 'bearers of the potential of modernity' (Lefebvre, 2003: 58). We 'call to the object in hope and expectation' yet modernity fails when we fail 'to recognise and realise the objective qualities of temporality' (56–8). Matta-Clark calls to the under surfaces, the forgotten objects and spaces, which then call to us. The power of screen-based media within archaeological practice is in such an ambiguous displacement of time, into film and filmic artefact. Archaeology can remind us of the objective qualities of temporality while a mediatised archaeology reminds us of the temporal qualities of objects.

Unlike Matta-Clark I do not go underground. But in the great, decaying, leather-bound building plan volumes at the Bristol Record Office I find elevations and sub-surface drainage schemas. I discover that on 13 September 1899, Thomas Pearce of 117 Wells Road put in plans to build six houses on Sandy Park Road: 'brick, stone, tile, timber, etc, damp proof course, 6" socketed drain pipes flowing into existing 12" sewer' (Building Plan Volume 37 19f:). William Bindon logged similar plans on 24 February 1899 to build numbers 7–13 (Building Place Volume 36: 20d). In December 1900 Henry Crewe of 10 Grosvenor Road put in plans to build numbers 74 and 75 (Building Plan Volume 39: 21b) and in June 1901 numbers 76–79 (Building Plan Volume 39: 33b). But on 4 May 1901 he put in for permission to build an additional drain at number 69 (Building Plan Volume 39a: 73c). And it was during the nineteenth-century excavation of the new drainage system for the housing project on Winchester Road that builders discovered the Roman remains referred to in the video piece. Hints at the importance of these commingled dwelling/sewage, clean/dirty spaces emerge at the 13 June 2005 Institute of Civil Engineers conference 'The Geospatial Future of Buried Services':

> The increasing demand for utilities by society has resulted in examples of a saturation of buried services. In the United Kingdom the infrastructure we enjoy has been created over a very long period. The efforts of great engineers, such as Joseph Bazalgette, has changed the way society deals with the effects of concentrated populations that we now accept as the norm. The use of buried services has supported the development of communities by providing water supply, sewerage systems and energy. With the recent advances in technology we have added telecommunications and cable television to the list of buried services. Paper-based records of where buried services are located have been kept in various formats but generally as a relative position, e.g. gas main in London Road 6ft from kerb. On the map used as a record, is the information accurately positioned? Which kerb is used as the reference? (*http://www.ice.org.uk//news_events conferencedetail_ice.asp?EventID=1478&EventType=ICE&FacultyID=*, 15.09.2005)

Figure 10.6 Photograph: Angela Piccini (video still)

13'01"

A beautifully tied ribbon: surprisingly clean and fresh like it's just slipped out of a little girl's hair or off a Saturday birthday present.

And have you noticed all the tire marks on the kerb? But like I said, it's double yellows all the way so there's some serious contravention of the highway code going on here. The plastic, the soot, the tire marks – it's all about the petrochemicals in this place. This is the quotidian, the everyday of global capital exchange. The kerb and the gutter are where Brislington meets the rest of the world.

A firework casing points to ritualised Halloween behaviours and makes me notice the spectral white face painted on the tarmac.

The 168 kerbstones average 81cm. But the shortest is just 33cm while the longest is 153cm. The ebb and flow of individual measurement reads like poetry: 78, 145, 125, 87, 92, 81, 54 or 59, 46, 92, 91, 91, 91, 91, 92, 45. Those mass-produced 91s tell of the construction of the zebra crossing with its intrusion of concrete kerbs.

As in Matta-Clark's work there is something in both my screenwork and my concerns in this chapter of Bergson's 'matter' as 'existence placed half-way between the "thing" and the "representation"' (Bergson, 1911: xii). Matta-Clark's focus on the 'under surface' and my own fascination with what I suppose I could term the 'over surface' also calls up Bergson's analysis of sensation and perception:

Pain is therefore in the place where it is felt, as the object is at the place where it is perceived. Between the affection felt and the image perceived there is this difference, that the affection is within our body, the image outside our body. And that is why the surface of our body, the common limit of this and of other bodies, is given to us in the form both of sensations and of an image (Bergson, 311).

Figure 10.7 Photograph: Angela Piccini (video still)

What is beneath our feet is concurrently experienced as the sensation of footfall and as image. Matta-Clark's explorations attempted to bring matter 'back into play as an active dimension in our relationship with the world' (Walker 2003: 173). My own attempt works towards unsettling Matta-Clark's understanding of archaeological practice as the uncovering and reconstituting of whole objects; it is all about the lateral movement of the camera coupled with a fascination with things 'down there'. While Matta-Clark actually takes his camera under the surface, I wanted to presence the idea of archaeology existing in the present through the use of the tracking shot along the surface of the tarmac. In my concern with the present presence of material culture I do not uncover or move deeper. While I combine those surface traces with other research activities, my aim is not to show things as they 'really are' (Pleasants 1999: 22, quoted in Dewsbury 2002). I measured these kerbstones, this gutter, as I walked along it, and re-measure them each time I screen the video. However, these numerical folds of space-time are sensate, first through my feet and then via an embodied practice of looking (Merleau-Ponty 1969; Wylie 2003).

Bibliography

Benjamin, A and Osborne, P (eds) (1994) *Walter Benjamin's Philosophy*, London: Routledge.
Benjamin, W (1999) *The Arcades Project*, translated by Eiland, H and McLaughlin, K, Cambridge, MA: Belknap-Harvard University Press.
Bergson, H (1911) *Matter and Memory*, translated by Paul, N M and Palmer, W S, London: George Allen and Unwin.
Bristol City Council Libraries Service, Jefferies collection, Bristol MSS Miscellaneous.
Bristol Records Office 40287/6/29.
Bristol Records Office 4550/10.
Bristol Records Office 8032.
Bristol Records Office Pol/L/13/15.
Bristol Records Office Building Plan Volume 37 19f.
Buchli, V (2002) 'Towards an Archaeology of the Contemporary Past' *Cambridge Archaeological Journal* 12(1): 131–50.
Dewsbury, J D, et al (2002) 'Enacting geographies' *Geoforum* 33 (4): 437–40.
Grierson, J (1926) 'Review: *Moana*' New York Sun.
Hicks, Dan (2005) '"Places for thinking" from Annapolis to Bristol: situations and symmetries in "world historical archaeologies"' *Historical Archaeology* 37(3): 373–91.
Holtorf, C (2001) 'Fieldtrip theory: towards archaeological ways of seeing', in P. Rainbird and Y. Hamilakis (eds), *Interrogating Pedagogies: Archaeology in Higher Education*, British Archaeologial Reports, International Series 948, Oxford: Archaeopress, 81–87.
Holtorf, C (2005) *From Stonehenge to Las Vegas: Archaeology as Popular Culture*, Lanham: AltaMira.
Lefebvre, A (2003) 'Things temporal exposé, passages from Benjamin' *Journal for Cultural Research* 7(1): 47–60.
Lindegaard, D P (1992) *Brislington Bulletins No 1: 1066–1600*, unpublished ms.
Lindegaard, D P (1993) *Brislington Bulletins No 2: 1601–1699*, unpublished ms.
Lindegaard, D P (1994) *Brislington Bulletins No 3: 1700–1749*, unpublished ms.
MacPhee, G (2000) 'On the incompleteness of history: Benjamin's arcades project and the optic of historiography' *Textual Practice* 14(3): 579–89.
Marshall, J D (1999) 'Performativity: Lyotard and Foucault through Searle and Austin' *Studies in Philosophy and Education* 18: 309–17.
Massey, D (2005) *For Space*, London: Sage.
Matta-Clark, G (1976) *Substrait (Underground Dailies)* and *City Slivers*, NY, video/performance.
Matta-Clark, G (1977) *Sous-sols de Paris*, video/performance.
Merleau-Ponty, M (1969) *The Visible and the Invisible*, Evanston: Northwestern University Press.
Pearson, M and Shanks, M (2001) *Theatre/Archaeology*, London: Routledge.

Phelan, P (1993) *Unmarked: the Politics of Performance*, London: Routledge.

Piccini, A and Rye, C (forthcoming) 'Of fevered archives and the quest for total documentation', in Jones, S, Kershaw, B and Piccini, A (eds), *Practice-as-research in Performance and Screen Media*, London: Palgrave-Macmillan.

Pleasants, N (1999) *Wittgenstein and the Idea of a Critical Social Theory: a Critique of Giddens, Habermas and Bhaskar*, London: Routledge.

Reason, M (2006) *Documentation, Disappearance and the Representation of Live Performance*, London: Palgrave Macmillan.

Rye, C (2000) *Living Cameras: A Study of Live Bodies and Mediatised Images in Multi-Media Performance and Installation Art Practice.* Unpublished PhD. Edinburgh: Napier University.

Rye, C (2003) 'Incorporating practice: a multi-viewpoint approach to performance documentation' *Journal of Media Practice* 3(2): 115–123.

Rowe, J and Williams, D (1986) *Bygone Brislington* unpublished ms.

Shanks, M (2004) 'Three Rooms: Archaeology and Performance' *Journal of Social Archaeology* 4: 147–80.

Stampp, K M (1994) *Records of Ante-Bellum Southern Plantations from the Revolution through the Civil War*, Series L: Selections from the Earl Gregg Swem Library, The College of William and Mary in Virginia, Part 2: Jerdone Family Papers, 1736–1918, Bethesda: University Publications of America.

Stoddard, S (1981) *Mr Braikenridge's Brislington*, Bristol: City of Bristol Museum and Art Gallery with the assistance of the Friends of Bristol Art Gallery.

Thomas, J (2004) 'Archaeology's place in modernity' MODERNISM/modernity 11 (1): 17–34.

Walker, S (2003) '*Baffling archaeology*: the strange gravity of Gordon Matta-Clark's experience-optics' *Journal of Visual Culture* 2(2): 161–85.

Wylie, J (2002) 'An essay on ascending Glastonbury Tor' *Geoforum* 33: 441–54.

1633–34, Quarter Sessions at Bridgewater, Somerset Records Society.

The Privatisation of Experience and the Archaeology of the Future

Paul Graves-Brown

The attempt to privatize life, to suppose that it is within single self-achieving individuals that lie the infinite recesses of being and morality that shape and define life, is a phenomenon of narrow historical significance. It belongs to a particular, and brief, phase in the evolution of bourgeoisie capitalism, and is the phenomenon of peculiar, and temporary economic arrangements. All the signs are that this conviction about man will soon have passed away.

Howard Kirk *The Defeat of Privacy*

In this chapter I want to explore 'the privatisation of experience' (see Graves-Brown 2000; Spierenburg 1991) — the process by which human activities tend to move from the public to the private sphere. Can this be seen as a long-term trend in human history and can this tell us anything about our present and future? At the very least, placing current trends in context can counteract the presentist tendency to regard the contemporary world as qualitatively different from the past. Given limited space I will discuss the examples of housing and transport. The privatisation of death is discussed in Shilling (1993) and Spierenburg (1991), that of crime, punishment and the treatment of insanity in Spierenburg (1991), whilst the general discussion of the privatisation of social practice can be found in Elias (1994). I believe that other areas, such as entertainment and the 'media', show similar patterns.

The discussion of the long-term is problematic. Short of writing a book on the topic, one is forced to give a synthetic overview of any example, an approach which does not sit well with the particularistic accounts favoured in much recent archaeology. Moreover, any attempt to approach long-term trajectories must deal with the controversy surrounding determinism and teleology. Consequently I shall try to unpack some of the issues before turning to my substantive discussion. There are also some specific problems around the concept of 'privacy' that need exploration at this preliminary stage, and it is here that I shall begin.

Privacy defined?

Many recent authors have argued that individuality (or perhaps more accurately individualism) is a very modern concept with limited use in understanding past societies (see Fowler 2000; Tarlow 2000; Thomas 1998). I should, therefore, emphasise from the start that privacy need not be equated with the individual or individualism. Most societies define 'front regions' and 'back regions' of social space (Goffman 1959; Portnoy 1981). The back stage area, temporary or permanent, is the more or less exclusive domain of an entity, be it an individual, family, kin group, work group, etc. The front region is that in which such an entity interacts with society at large. This front region includes both 'privately' owned spaces, shops, living rooms, etc, and the wider 'public' space that all members of a society share. Dialectic within the 'back space' entity and between its denizens and the 'public' world create the rules and practices that delineate and define the nature of public–private demarcation. Equally, this dialectic can be seen as defining identity — setting the boundaries between self (individual or collective) and the Other.

Here, as Moore (1984) argues, the emergence of a defined public sphere of activity can be seen as the product of the need for co-operation. Where activities are co-ordinated or organised at a level above the back space/private entity, rules and practices arise which define the public in opposition to the private. In the Greek polis, according to Arendt (1958), the private world, that of the family, came to be seen as constraining, whilst the public world of the polis was seen to allow greater freedom of expression. Whilst the private domain remained the unit of production, the public debates of the polis defined social status. To be excluded from the activities of the polis was a *privat*ion — house arrest. It was only, in Arendt's view, in Roman society that privacy came to be seen as desirable.

In subsequent centuries, and in different cultures, the nature of privacy has been expressed in a wide variety of ways. What has certainly shifted, especially in the last 400 years, has been the locus of privacy — the emergence of individualism. Any number of accounts can be given of this process. I would argue that the predominant factors in European history have been the Reformation, the not unrelated emergence of the nation state and the transition from agrarian to industrialised economies. In one way or another, each of these factors shifted emphasis away from collective identities — church, village, family (although see Nisbet 1994) — towards the relationship of the individual with God, power or work. Leading from Moore's argument, one might say that the increasing importance of action and interdependence in the public realm progressively eroded the importance of (collective) privacy. The individual has a 'contract' with society at large, rather than one mediated by group membership, and hence privacy comes to inhere in the individual. It becomes, as Arendt puts it, a question of intimacy — of personal as opposed to collective space. Moreover, in virtue of its inherence in the individual, privacy also becomes mobile — it is no longer confined to the back spaces of the home.

Determinism and freedom

...obviously, individual people did not at some time in the past intend this change, this 'civilisation,' and gradually realise it by conscious purposive measures...

(Elias 1994)

The study of long-term trends has become unfashionable in recent archaeological writing. I see this as a quite proper reaction to the determinism and/or teleology that haunts previous accounts of the past. Since the Enlightenment fell in love with the idea of progress, temporal change has been interpreted as directional, not to say purposive (although see Nisbet 1994). Explanations of why this was the case have varied. Cultural historians saw change as the expression of the genius of certain peoples; evolutionary accounts from Herbert Spencer to the Neo-Evolutionists of the 1960s saw change in terms of 'the survival of the fittest' or adaptation. Childe viewed social change as the inevitable consequence of Marx's dialectic; functionalists and New Archaeology looked to ecology and related fields to explain the direction of change. With the advent of Post-Structuralism/Post-Processualism, archaeology rejected the *deus ex machina* of Neo-Darwinism and other deterministic theories. Archaeological remains were to be seen as contingent and contextual. Whilst, as noted above, the role of the individual has been downplayed, a sense of agency (and not necessarily individual agency) and free will is stressed in opposition to mechanism. But in the process, I suggest, archaeologists have denied themselves the possibility of addressing long-term trends — a field that *can* be approached without resort to determinism.

Norbert Elias was clearly aware of the pitfalls in charting the history of manners. His argument, as I understand it, was that the integrative forces that hold society together are the constant factor which drive social rules and manners to become increasingly complicated and ramified, one generation building on another. Braudel (1972), on the other hand, in discussing the *longue durée* and what he calls 'total history', takes a more pessimistic view, arguing that in practical reality individuals have very little freedom of action and are effectively swept along by the tide of history. I would argue that observable *longue durée* trends are a product of the simple fact that conditions and constraints, be they physical or social, remain the same. One need not appeal to external forces to explain what is essentially the inertia of continuity. An obvious example of this would be population growth. Economic affluence tends to promote population growth. Societies make practical and social accommodations to the fact of more people living together in order to avoid conflict, disease, starvation or whatever. But such accommodations tend to promote further population growth and so on. In some cases — the Maya or Easter Islanders spring to mind — the dialectic between societies and their context has unravelled. In other cases, such as the Black Death or the European invasion of the Americas, disease has wiped out large sections of human populations. Yet the essential dialectic between societies and the prevailing need to accommodate growing population and/or population density has been a more or less constant factor through the millennia till the present day.

However, this is not to accept Braudel's fatalism. As Dennett (1985) has suggested, free will does not imply that I can fly simply by flapping my arms. What we have is 'elbow room' — a freedom of action circumscribed by physical and social possibility. This circumscription might in turn be imagined as something like Waddington's (1966) idea of 'chreodisation' — that an individual or society can develop in a variety of ways, but is channelled by its circumstances. Thus, for example, once the 4'8¾" railway gauge had been chosen by Stephenson and implemented on most railways, the choice of another gauge, such as Brunel's 6' gauge, would be difficult and costly.

Moreover, apropos of the question of individuality, I would stress that free will is not contingent on individualism. As an agent every human being has free will, even if they do not conceptualise themselves as radically individual. This is a crucial point in understanding the history of privacy since changing ideas of freedom of action are implicit in the relationship between the public and private domains.

For a man's home is his castle…

From ethnography it seems reasonable to conclude that prehistoric shelters or dwellings did not offer any sense of privacy. Indeed as Moore (1984) argues, many traditional societies recognise no distinction between the public and the private — virtually all activities are carried out within the sight or hearing of other family or community members. Individuals can slip away into jungle or bush to perform bodily functions or sexual acts, or indeed to argue. Where the dwelling or village offers no 'back space' of its own, the *outside* of the village fulfils that role (Portnoy 1981). This situation persisted even in medieval towns and cities, where the advent of spring allowed lovers to escape the lack of privacy of the dwelling for the sexual freedom offered by the countryside (Mumford 1938). But even this can be circumscribed by what Moore terms 'socially available space'. Thus, for the Inuit, at least in the winter months, the fact that they live in a vast open space counts for little and virtually all functions are, perforce, carried out within the igloo. Similarly, among Pueblo Indians there seems to have been little inclination to carry out even the most 'intimate' activities in 'private'. In general, the daily round is such that most activities are conducted individually or in informal/familial groups. Only when there is a need for organised communal activities, governed by rules or other injunctions, does a distinction between the public and private emerge. Thus, as Moore describes, the net hunting of the Mbuti requires a co-ordinated placement of each family's net, thereby defining a distinct public realm of activity.

If we look at the shelters and houses built from the Upper Palaeolithic right through to the Iron age and beyond, they are dominated by round structures of one kind or another that seem to offer little opportunity of individual privacy. Indeed, the very form of the round building seems antithetical to privacy, whilst ideally suited to public events — e.g. amphitheatres or sports stadia. Although formally more suited to partitioning, rectilinear structures from the Neolithic LBK to the long-houses of early medieval Britain show little evidence of private space. As Hodder (1990: 69) says of the Neolithic in south-east Europe:

> it seems possible that the 'performances' associated with the use of figurines around the oven in the house were very 'public' in the sense that they were participated in by many members within the domestic or wider social group.

In fact in many cases the 'privacy' of the humans was further reduced by sharing their space with animals. Granted that, from the Neolithic at Skara Brae or Jericho there are nucleations of small dwellings, it seems reasonable that, as with the Pueblo Indians, these need not be indicators of any developed sense of private space. The Skara Brae rooms seem to confirm this in that each appears to have two beds in it. In none of these cases, I suggest, can one discern a distinction between 'back space' and 'front space' (Goffman 1959; Portnoy 1981).

Rather, as one of the fundamental principles of the privatisation of experience, it is only with the development of wealth, of affluence, that we see the emergence of clearly private spaces. Thus if we think of the 'palaces' of the ancient world or the Roman 'villa', we start to see structures segmented into multiple rooms, which offered privacy to their occupants, or defined public/private front/back areas (Spierenburg 1991). Such patterns can also be seen in religious buildings with inner sanctuaries that are the exclusive domain of priests. At the same time, in the written record of societies from Classical Athens to the emergent Chinese Empire, we begin to see philosophical and legalistic discussions of the distinction between public and private, and of the rights and obligations of the individual in relation to the polis, Emperor or whatever (Arendt 1958; Moore 1984; Spierenburg 1991). The point is, of course, that enhanced privacy requires infrastructure: water supplies, heating, means of waste disposal, sufficient agricultural and industrial production to construct and maintain private dwellings. But it also requires a kind of social infrastructure that defines and circumscribes the boundaries of the private and public domains.

In post Roman and medieval Europe, we see what appears to be a step back to a less private life. In my view, the Roman World had prefigured the mores of bourgeoisie capitalism. Thus, for example, the kind of hall described in Beowulf and excavated at sites such as Yeavering seems to offer little privacy except perhaps for the lord himself. Following Levi-Strauss (1983), these domestic arrangements are examples of the 'house' — a transitional state between kin group and state societies (see also Carsten and Hugh-Jones 1995; Spierenburg 1991). As in the Medieval/post-medieval sense of the 'house' of a powerful family, such an entity can incorporate affiliated families, retainers and other unrelated groups and individuals. One might even characterise this as the hypertrophy of the private sphere — the house as a microcosm of society at large and as an expression of the communal ideology of Christianity (Arendt 1958). Yet the context in which personal privacy existed remained very limited, as indicated by Elias' (1994) discussion of sleeping arrangements. Here, as late as the fourteenth century it was permissible for an unmarried man and woman to sleep (and I do mean sleep) in the same bed (see also Spierenburg 1991). It is only in later centuries that the manners surrounding who could sleep with whom became increasingly ramified and indeed the whole process of going to bed became so mannered that well bred individuals would rather talk of 'retiring' (Elias 1994).

Here again affluence brings about a change. With the expansion of agriculture that begins in the sixteenth and seventeenth centuries, we see the construction of many more substantial dwellings, albeit often on a modest scale, where separate rooms offer some degree of privacy. Such changes also reflect both the collapse of the feudal system and the weakening of the Church through the Reformation (Arendt 1958; Spierenburg 1991) — the overarching power of Christendom having largely precluded a distinct public political realm. In this sense the Reformation's insistence on the individual's relation to God is a metaphor for change towards a more privatised life. The end of feudalism, associated as it was with enclosure, paralleled the development of mercantile economies based on the growth of urban living. Indeed the growth of urbanism, from whenever we place its origins, must have been a primary force in the privatisation of experience. For clearly here Moore's 'socially available space' becomes an ever more pressing issue where the manners, rules and institutions governing behaviour are required to be ever more complex to accommodate high-density living. As Elias points out, the 'civilising process' is one in which it is necessary to take ever more elaborate steps to avoid confrontation and violence. For hunter gatherers, the ultimate response to conflict is simply to move away. In medieval times violence was casual and endemic (Elias 1994; Spierenburg 1991). But such luxuries could not be afforded as societies became increasingly integrated.

The social and economic forces of the seventeenth and eighteenth centuries produced a change that Spierenburg characterises as a transition 'from the house to the nuclear family'; the social unit of 'privacy' shrank from the extended family/multi-family group to the nucleus of a married couple and their children. Here, from the eighteenth century onward, industry played an increasing role. Industrial production promoted high-density living and broke traditional social bonds — people became workers, individual units of production. But beyond this, industrialisation also changed housing through the mechanisation of production. Beginning in the late eighteenth century, housing became a process of mechanical reproduction and repetition. In the great crescents of Spa towns like Bath, or in the development of London, we see the production of terraces of more or less identical buildings. The great nineteenth-century builders such as Thomas Cubitt entirely industrialised the building process from the production of bricks and the preparation of timber to the 'system build' techniques employed in construction (Hobhouse 1971). Such techniques of mechanisation, first employed to produce relatively high status dwellings were then translated into the production of mass housing for factory workers or miners, as well as the factories themselves.

The importance of mechanisation in the privatisation of experience cannot be underestimated. The easy reproduction of artefacts, be it through the invention of printing or building houses facilitates individual consumption. A reduction in unit costs makes privacy cheaper. One ultimate expression of this equation is the Corbusian 'machine for living in' as exemplified by the tower blocks of the 1960s and 70s. However the latter case indicates that there are limits on how far experience can be privatised 'on the cheap' — the mass housing of this period was sparing on the provision of social and/or 'front' spaces, whilst a failure to recognise the costs of maintenance led to the deterioration of what public space there was (see Chapman and Hockey 1999).

High-density, apartment living is successful in many of the world's big cities, particularly where there has been a return to inner city areas, but this has tended to work for the more affluent sections of society. A more general trend has been the continuing spread into suburbia and beyond. The invention of suburbs and the desire to escape the city is clearly a further development of privatisation. As with the development of the large suburban cemeteries (see Nash 2000), so the wealthy middle class began to escape to the suburban villa in the late nineteenth century, to be followed by vast numbers of the middle class in the 1918–39 period: not just an enclosed building within which we escape the Other, but one in which we are as far from our neighbours as possible. The fact that, in the UK at least, there is still such a huge demand for new housing suggests that people wish to live more and more separately in smaller and smaller groups. Indeed, projections in the late 1990s suggested that by 2016 there would be around nine million single occupancy homes in the UK. This compares with a fairly constant eleven million family dwellings, whereas in 1970 there were only around one million single occupancies (Chapman and Hockey 1999).

Transport

Animal and mechanical transport acts as an extension to human capabilities (McLuhan 1964; Graves-Brown 2000). Were early forms of transport public or private? Since animals generally carry a single rider this would, I suggest, tend to promote private ownership. Boats, with some exceptions, carry multiple people and require considerable input of time and materials in their construction. Indeed the building of a boat would usually be the kind of communal activity that Moore sees as the point of emergence of public life. Thus boats would tend to be public transport.

Given that water transport remained the predominant form until the nineteenth century, it seems fair to say that most transport would tend to be public until this time, albeit often privately owned. Again, this is a function of wealth and the level of social organisation. Whereas boats need infrastructure for their construction, their medium is essentially free (with the exception of canals). Land transport, on the other hand, requires a huge investment in infrastructure. Water transport invites, if indeed it does not necessitate, the economies of scale involved in carrying large numbers of people. Land transport does not.

Nevertheless by the late eighteenth, early nineteenth centuries we begin to see the necessary investment in terrestrial infrastructure; in Britain this first appears in turnpike roads, scheduled coaching services and the inns that served them. It is easy to underestimate the effect of this development. In my hometown of High Barnet, one of the first coach stops on the Great North Road, there were around thirty to forty pubs and inns serving coach traffic in the early nineteenth century. The next step, beginning in Britain but rapidly spreading to Europe and North America, was the construction of railways. Here again the issue of economy of scale determines that railways are a means of public rather than private transport.

As has often been observed, the railways acted as a powerful integrating force in public social life (McLuhan 1964). Through increased individual mobility, the standardisation of the measurement of time, rapid dissemination of information or indeed in the development of new ways of death (see Nash 2000), mechanised transport promoted a more homogenised society. This seems to run counter to the desire for increased privacy (see next section). However, there were elements of privatisation built into railway travel. From early on this included segregation by class, reminding us of the continuing relationship between affluence and privacy. But what is less well known is that until the 1940s, British trains also had 'ladies only' carriages. And in some countries, such as Egypt, this practice continues. Moreover, until the late twentieth century, British railway carriages were segmented into compartments that offered a more intimate situation. US railway carriages, however, are 'open plan', perhaps representing the more egalitarian episteme of American culture. It is also worth noting that transport infrastructure also facilitated privatisation of housing, as in the growth of suburbia noted above.

I have written at length elsewhere about the car culture (Graves-Brown 2000). The car is a perfect icon for the privatisation of experience in general, and for the development of a more mobile sense of privacy in particular. As Lefebvre (1971: 101) succinctly describes it:

> motorised traffic enables people and objects to congregate and mix without meeting, thus constituting a striking example of simultaneity without exchange, each element remaining within its own compartment, tucked away in its shell; such conditions contribute to the disintegration of city life.

Yet the origins of the car industry lie in a more publicly orientated direction (Flink 1977). The early market for cars in the USA lay with the relatively isolated farming communities of the mid-west. It actually allowed farmers and their families to more easily participate in social life. The extension of car sales to urban areas had the opposite effect. The car was, and remains, unsuited to the city, and by the early twentieth century most western cities already had developed public transport infrastructure. In such a context cars were sold as symbols of status and expressions of style, and Wolf (1996) suggests that car manufacturers in the USA deliberately undermined public transport systems in order to promote car sales. As in the continuously ramified world of private housing, so car culture takes transport beyond any sense of functional necessity. There is no need for one person per car, any more than single occupancy housing. The desire for intimacy, for the possibility to 'mix without meeting', drives the process forward.

The evolution of privacy

There is a general pattern in the development of privatised experience, which I believe these examples illustrate. In my view, two basic motivations underlie the desire for privacy: the desire to act freely, and the need to avoid confrontation with others. These motivations are facilitated or frustrated by constraining factors including 'socially available space', levels of population, population density and affluence. Where these constraints are negligible there is no need to distinguish between what is private and public. Only when social organisation requires a level of co-operation between groups or families does the distinction emerge between those activities that are private to the domestic unit and those that belong to the wider social domain. And, moreover, the emergence of privacy does not imply the kind of intimate personal privacy that we seek today.

In pre-industrial societies the private sphere gradually becomes more inclusive. The 'house' (*sensu* Levi-Strauss 1983) emerges as a social system which is more inclusive than kinship but which is in no way as integrated and interdependent as the modern nation state. This principle could equally apply to dwellings and transport — the ship as a waterborne house. It would also apply to manufacturing before the industrial revolution. The guild structures found throughout Europe were non-kin based organisations, yet lacked the level of integration to be found in modern industrial production. Yet ultimately, the standardisation of production, which has its origins as far back as Ancient Egypt, is predicated on intensive and extensive social integration and hence the domestic sphere, the original locus of privacy begins to be assailed. A man's (*sic*) home is no longer his castle — for he owes that home to the institutions of economy and state. The private sphere contracts to the nucleus of the family. It is, then, in reaction to the growth and power of the public domain that we see the emergence of a new notion of privacy — the intimate, mobile, personal and individual sense that, according to Arendt (1958), has its origins with Rousseau.

What is perhaps ironic here is that the well being of the private individual is increasingly predicated on the power of the public domain. This takes the form of both a standardisation of social rules and institutions, and the standardisation and mechanisation of material culture provision for the desires of the mass (e.g. the contradictions inherent in 'public' transport). In effect the process of production of the means to private life tends to erode that life through the homogenisation of cultural products. The desire for intimacy, for a radical individual then emerges as a reaction to the forces of uniformity. The development of interchangeable components was the foundation of industrial, mass production, but leads people to fear that they too are interchangeable parts. The people of medieval Europe may not have seen themselves in individualistic terms, yet much of their material culture shows the idiosyncratic variety of pre-industrial, unstandardised and non-interchangeable production. 'Modern' people see themselves as radically individual and yet their material culture is becoming globally homogeneous — we are 'different and original like everybody else'.

Returning to the question of individual free will, how is this to be reconciled? Firstly, as Braudel points out, concepts of freedom have changed over time. For many societies, the individual is not a free agent, as among the Azande a person can be controlled through witchcraft. Indeed it has been argued that people under such circumstances are not truly conscious individuals (Jaynes 1976). In a slightly different sense, Elias argues that the civilising process relies on a transition from external constraints to self-restraint. That social change involves the internalisation of rules. Thus in the military case, the modern army relies on the ability of junior ranks to take the initiative, to have internalised the ethos of the army, as opposed to being herded around in tight formations of 'clockwork soldiers' (De Landa 1991; Graves-Brown 2007).

For Arendt, this process is observable in totalitarian societies. In Nazi Germany, she says, the individual resolved problems of action by asking, 'what would the Führer do?'

Clearly then, the notion of intimate privacy, predicated on individualism, can serve both 'free' and totalitarian societies. The citizen of the totalitarian state is expected to turn privacy inside out — to internalise oppression. Yet is the privatised state we live in that much different? Are we prisoners of ourselves? Arendt believed that modern people were 'imprisoned in the subjectivity of their own experience', a view echoed in Marcuse's (1964) analysis of 'One Dimensional Man'. Benjamin (1970) christens this state 'self-alienation,' but we must be careful not to see the privatised individual as an unwilling prisoner of mass society in the sense that Marx talked of alienation, for clearly people actively desire this state. Technological developments in the last twenty to thirty years have led to what Baudrillard (1994) calls 'hyper-reality' — a form of imprisonment in the self which echoes Lefebvre's account of car culture 'mixing without meeting'. Or, as Robins says with respect to the internet:

> There is 'group mind' but no social encounter. There is online communion, but there are no residents in [cyberspace]...What we have is the preservation through simulation of the old forms of solidarity and community. In the end not an alternative society but an alternative to society. (Robins 1995: 150)

Where experience is increasingly enabled to be private, the possibility of shared experience, of a 'common world' (Arendt 1958) recedes. The public domain becomes a simulation.

Drowning by numbers? the future of privacy

Xander: How about a movie? They're showing 'em in theatres now. I hear it's like watching a video with a bunch of strangers and a sticky floor.

(Noxon 1998)

Where next? The hyper-real episteme is already spreading to India and China. Recent reports suggest that the number of cars in China will exceed that in the USA within the next twenty years (Goldman-Sachs 2003). But can the privatisation of experience continue? Will we eventually blast off into space to find the ultimate solitude? Malcolm Bradbury's Howard Kirk, quoted at the beginning of this article, claimed to believe that privacy had already been overthrown by the radical politics of the 1960s (but see below). This did not happen, yet today it might seem that the radical Other offers the greatest threat to privatised experience. The essential shock of 9/11 lay in the fact that, as Baudrillard (1995) has observed, America has no concept of the Other. Will the dispossessed overthrow hyper-reality, as many authors (e.g. Forster 1997[1928]; Orwell 1949) have predicted?

Conflict over the world's resources is in prospect (if not already happening). Peter Tatchell (pers. comm.) once claimed that there is simply not enough copper on the planet to give everyone mains water and electricity. Is it practically possible for everyone to live the affluent life that we have become familiar with in the last fifty to sixty years?

In my view the real nemesis of privatisation of experience will be that which underlies it: affluence and consumption. If nothing else the evidence from melting glaciers, sea ice and permafrost and the rise in global air and sea temperatures suggests that the by-products of our privatised experience will eventually bring about its destruction, and that the spread of this way of life (e.g. the ever increasing demand for oil) is accelerating the process.

What I find ironic is that the very nature of a privatised existence tends to make such a catastrophic outcome more likely. Although humans have always travelled considerable distances, rapid transport and other technologies render location irrelevant. Millions of tons of waste are hygienically disposed of, the victims of flood and famine are perceived only through the hyper-real media. As Shilling and Mellor (1993) have shown, the hyper-real world hides even death away from us. By its very nature, and of necessity, a privatised existence cushions one from the physical consequences of existence. Whilst the people of Easter Island had to live with the consequences of their actions, today they would probably be evacuated by the UN. Unfortunately we cannot yet evacuate the entire planet.

Archaeologically, I suggest the mobile nature of modern privacy is both important and problematic. Setting aside what we know of the modern world, would its material culture allow us to detect the extent of privatisation? Most cars have room for at least four or five people, most new houses can accommodate three or four people. But we know that routinely they have one occupant; the fluid nature of modern society actually masks the extent of privacy. Conversely, the millions of mobile phones and i-pods™ might hint at our atomised way of life.

The material culture remains of mobile/nomadic societies are generally more evanescent than those of sedentary ones. Hence my discussion above has had to rely on ethnographic data to sketch aspects of the history of privacy. Yet the contemporary world is different; despite the massive amount of material evidence, we are more hunter-gatherers than inhabitants of a 'Global Village' (see Chatwin 1987). This is notably true of global capital, which can forage anywhere to turn a profit. As discussed, modern privacy is internalised; it is not imprinted in artefacts but inheres in the way (for example) mobile phone users assume a kind of virtual privacy when talking in public places. Privacy has moved up the 'ladder of inference' (Graves 1994) and thus, to some extent, become archaeologically invisible.

Postscript

'Is this your new book? I've been reading it.' 'You'd no business to do that,' says Howard 'It's not quite finished. It's private.' 'The attempt to privatize life is a phenomenon of narrow historical significance.' says Felicity.

(Malcolm Bradbury 1975: 91)

Acknowledgements

Thanks to Tom Cullis, Carolyn Graves-Brown, Cornelius Holtorf and Angela Piccini for reading and commenting. Thanks to Tom Cullis for innumerable conversations which fuelled the process.

Bibliography

Arendt, H (1958) *The Human Condition*, Cambridge: Cambridge University Press.
Baudrillard, J (1994) *Simulacra and Simulation*, Ann Arbor: University of Michigan Press.
Baudrillard, J (1995) *The Gulf War Did Not Take Place,* Sydney: Power Publications.
Benjamin, W (1970) 'The work of art in the age of mechanical reproduction', in Arendt, H (ed), *Illuminations*, London: Cape.
Bradbury, M (1975) *The History Man*, London: Arrow.
Braudel, F (1972) The Mediterranean and the Mediterranean World in the Age of Philip II, London: Collins.
Carsten, J and Hugh-Jones, S (eds) (1995) *About The House: Lévi-Strauss and Beyond*, Cambridge: Cambridge University Press.
Chapman, T and Hockey, J (eds) (1999) *Ideal Homes? Social Change and Domestic Life*, London: Routledge.
Chatwin, B (1987) *The Songlines*, London: Viking.
De Landa, M (1991) *War in the Age of Intelligent Machines,* New York: Zone Books.
Dennett, D (1985) *Elbow Room: The Varieties of Free Will Worth Wanting*, London Oxford University Press.
Elias, N (1994) *The Civilizing Process: The History of Manners and State Formation and Civilization*, Oxford: Blackwell (single volume edition).
Flink, J J (1977) *Car Culture*, Boston, Mass: MIT Press.
Forster, E M (1997[1928]) 'The Machine Stops' in *The Machine Stops and Other Stories*, London: Andre Deutch.
Fowler, C (2000) 'The individual, the subject and archaeological interpretation: reading Luce Irigaray and Judith Butler' in Holtorf, C and Karlsson, H (eds), *Philosophy and Archaeological Interpretation Perspectives for the 21st Century*, Göteborg: Bricoleur Press.
Goldman-Sachs 2003 *Third BRIC Report*.
Goffman, E (1959) *The Presentation of the Self in Everyday Life*, London: Pelican.
Graves, P M (1994) 'Flakes and ladders: What the archaeological record does not tell us about the origins of language' *World Archaeology* 26(2): 158–71.
Graves-Brown, P (2000) 'Always crashing in the same car', in Graves-Brown, P (ed), *Matter, Materiality and Modern Culture*, London: Taylor and Francis.
Graves-Brown, P (2007) 'Avtomat Kalashnikova' *Journal of Material Culture* 12(3): 285–307.

Hobhouse, H (1971) Thomas *Cubitt: Master Builder*, London: Macmillan.

Hodder, I (1990) *The Domestication of Europe: Structure and Contingency in Neolithic Societies*, Oxford: Basil Blackwell.

Jaynes, J (1976) *The Origin of Consciousness in the Breakdown of the Bicameral Mind*, Boston, Mass: Houghton Mifflin.

Lefebvre, H (1971) *Everyday Life in the Modern World*, Harmondsworth: Allen Lane.

Levi-Straus, C (1983) *The Way of the Masks*, London: Cape.

McLuhan, M (1964) *Understanding Media: The Extensions of Man*, New York: McGraw Hill.

Marcuse, H (1964) *One Dimensional Man: Studies in the Ideology of Advanced Industrial Society*, Boston, Mass: Beacon Press.

Moore, B (1984) *Privacy: Studies in Social and Cultural History*, London: Sharpe.

Mumford, L (1938) *The Culture of Cities*, New York: Harcourt, Brace and Co.

Nash, G (2000) 'Pomp and circumstance: archaeology, modernity and the corporatisation of death', in Graves-Brown, P (ed), *Matter, Materiality and Modern Culture*, London: Taylor and Francis.

Nisbet, R (1994) *History of the Idea of Progress*, London: Transaction.

Noxon, M 1998 'Into the Woods' *Buffy the Vampire Slayer*, Series 5, Episode 10, 20th Century Fox.

Orwell, G (1949) *Nineteen Eighty Four*, London: Secker and Warburg.

Portnoy, A W (1981) 'A microarchaeological view of human settlement space and function' in Gould, R A and Schiffer, M B (eds), *Modern Material Culture. The Archaeology of Us*, London: Academic Press.

Robins, K (1995) 'Cyberspace and the World we live in' *Body and Society* 1 (3–4): 135–56

Shilling, C and Mellor P A (1993) 'Modernity, self identity and the sequestration of death' *Sociology* 27(3): 411–31.

Spierenburg, P (1991) *The Broken Spell. A Cultural and Anthropological History of Preindustrial Europe*, London: McMillan.

Tarlow, S (2000) 'Comment on Fowler, C "The individual, the subject and archaeological interpretation"', in Holtorf, C and Karlsson, H (eds), *Philosophy and Archaeological Interpretation Perspectives for the 21st Century*, Göteborg: Bricoleur Press.

Thomas, J (1998) *Time, Culture and Identity: An Interpretative Archaeology*, London: Routledge.

Waddington, C H (1966) *Principles Of Development And Differentiation*, London: Macmillan.

Wolf, W (1996) *Car Mania: A Critical History of Transport*, London: Pluto Press.

Index

Aborigines, Aboriginal, 169, 170, 173-75, 177
advertising, 16, 50, 53, 139, 176
Africa(n), 165, 175, 176, 187
agency, 69, 78, 84, 92, 203
Algeria, 162, 166, 167
America, American, 18, 20, 52, 57, 60, 61, 66, 75, 77, 89, 97, 98, 101, 103, 104, 114, 164, 166, 170-72, 174, 177, 192, 203, 207, 208, 210; see also United States
animals, 17, 34, 41, 65-75, 83-85, 88, 117, 204, 207
Antarctic Heritage Trust, 84, 91, 92
Antarctica, 17, 83-86, 89, 91
anthropology, anthropologist(s), 10, 19, 41, 52, 61, 127, 165, 169
antiquarian(ism), 24, 33, 34, 131, 135, 137, 138, 187
antiquities, 38, 77, 188
Apollo rocket programme, 162, 164, 170
Appadurai, Arjun, 20
archaeo-appeal, 56
archaeologist(s), 9-14, 17, 18, 20-25, 37, 41, 43, 47, 49, 53-60, 76, 77, 95, 100, 102, 104, 105, 108, 109, 113-15, 141, 142, 183, 184, 187, 190, 203
archaeology: as adventure, 51, 53, 55-57; as metaphor, 17, 33-45, 58; as storytelling, 12, 13, 58-60; contemporary, 9-29, 36, 54, 78, 96, 108, 109, 165, 176, 177, 186; industrial, 18, 21, 22; medieval, 18; of ten minutes ago, 10; politics of, 14, 105, 109, 110; post-medieval, 18;

prehistoric, 14, 100, 101; historical, 9, 18, 100, 101
architect, 141
architecture, architectural, 21, 48, 49, 92, 113, 115, 124, 196
Arendt, Hannah, 202, 205, 209, 210
Ariane rocket programme, 163, 168, 170
art deco, 190
art, contemporary/modern, 11, 23-25, 34, 92, 102, 107, 113, 138, 141
artist(s), 10, 13, 15, 23, 24, 88, 120, 138, 139, 141
Asia, 50, 69
Athens, 38, 205
Atlantic Ocean, 18, 20, 188
Austin, David, 19
Australia, Australian(s), 61, 83, 87, 161-80
Austria, 140
authenticity, authentic, 35, 38, 49, 52, 61, 175
Babylon, 77
Barnes, Jodi, 9
Barnes, Julian, 47, 51
Bath, 206
Baudelaire, Charles, 192
Baudrillard, Jean, 210
Beck, Colleen, 9, 17, 95-111
Belgium, 83, 116
Benjamin, Walter, 10, 13, 186, 200, 210
Bergson, Henry, 194, 195
Berlin, Berlin Wall, 21, 22, 93
Blackpool Pleasure Beach, 53, 56
Bloomfield, Lincoln, 176
Boyle Family, 15, 16

215

Braudel, Fernand, 203, 209
Braun, Wernher von, 162
Bristol, 11, 18, 19, 185, 187-91, 193, 196
Britain, British, 71, 113-17, 127, 166, 167, 196, 204, 207
Brith Gof, 19
British Museum, 41, 77
Bronze Age, 186
Buchli, Victor, 11, 19-21, 78, 142, 187
Buddhists, 106
Burström, Mats, 12, 21, 17, 20, 22, 131-43,
Cambodia, 21
Canadian, 196
capitalism, capitalist, 165, 166, 171, 173, 201, 205
car cemetery, 12, 21, 131-43
car(s), 12, 16, 17, 91, 131-43, 189, 192, 208, 210, 211
Carter, Howard, 49
Chernobyl, 56
Chessington World of Adventures, 51, 53, 55
Childe, V. Gordon, 203
China, Chinese, 71, 77, 163, 205, 210
Christianity, 38, 205
city, cities, 9, 37, 53, 67, 175, 185, 187, 189-92, 204, 206, 208
Clarke, Arthur C., 162, 173
cliché(s), 49, 50
Cold War, 17, 22, 113-15, 120, 126-28, 163, 164, 173
colonisation, colonies, colonial, 56, 161, 165-71, 173-77
Commonwealth, 167
community, communities, 13, 20, 41, 66, 73, 95, 106-9, 113, 166, 173-76, 187, 193, 196, 204, 208, 210
computer, 56, 57, 59, 117, 127, 171, 175
conservation, 22-24, 69, 77, 85, 89, 113, 133, 142

consumers, consuming, 41, 50, 53, 59, 60, 86, 92, 183, 185, 187,
consumption, 49, 50, 176, 206, 211
Contemporary and Historical Archaeology in Theory (CHAT), 18, 19, 22
Corporations, 166, 171
Crawford, O. G. S., 24
Crossland, Zoë, 12, 23
Danielsson, Åke, 132-38
Däniken, Erich von, 53, 59
Darwinian, Darwinism, 165, 203
death, 22, 37, 38, 65, 70, 74, 76, 155, 188, 201, 203, 207, 211
decolonisation, 161, 165, 166, 170, 171, 176, 177
deep map, 145
Delphi, 124
Denmark, Danish, 53, 140
Dion, Mark, 24
Discovery Channel, 22, 50
Disney theme parks, 47, 49-53, 56, 60, 61
document(s), documentary: 12, 87, 93, 134, 176; written, 11, 12, 85, 142, 189; see also photography, radio, video
documentation, documenting, 12, 17, 18, 73, 91, 96, 97, 100, 101, 109, 110, 113, 127
Dogpatch USA, 54
dream(s), dreaming, 40, 41, 43, 52, 53, 57, 59-61, 103, 133, 149, 150, 152, 170
Drollinger, Harold, 17, 95-111
Earth, 10, 15, 16, 35, 83, 95, 103, 104, 108, 149, 150, 161-66, 169, 171-73, 176
Easter Island, 51, 203, 211
Edmonds, Mark, 19
education, 13, 58-60, 171
Egypt, ancient, 41, 49, 50, 53, 209
Elias, Norbert, 201-6, 209

England, English, 11, 47, 51, 61, 89, 113, 124, 138, 167, 173
English Heritage, 19, 24, 100, 113, 115, 127, 188
Enlightenment, 36, 202
entertainment, entertaining, 47, 52, 53, 56, 58, 59, 61, 201
ethnography, ethnographical, 10, 37-8, 204, 211
ethnologist(s), 10,
Europa-Park Rust, 53, 56
Europe, European(s), 18, 20-22, 50, 66, 161, 163, 165, 168, 169, 172-77, 196, 202-5, 207, 209
European Space Agency (ESA), 163, 165, 168; see also Ariane
event(s), 10, 12-14, 18, 22-24, 35, 40, 41, 66, 76, 85, 87, 93, 97, 100, 105-7, 145, 149, 151, 153, 176, 184, 196, 204
evolution, evolutionary, 40-42, 93, 165, 177, 201, 203, 208-10
excavation, excavate, 10, 13, 16, 22, 23, 25, 36, 40, 41, 49, 85, 145, 146, 148, 150, 151, 156-58, 170, 186, 189, 193, 205
Exmoor Singers, 115, 120-24
Experience Society, 17, 52-54, 56, 58, 60
family, families, 12, 15, 16, 53, 59, 67, 68, 109, 145-59, 170, 175, 185, 187, 188, 191, 201-9
fieldwork, archaeological, 21, 54, 73, 102, 105, 107, 109, 142
football pitches, 21
Ford Transit van, excavation, 10, 21
forensic archaeology, 10, 12, 23, 186
forgetting, 10, 22, 23
Foucault, Michel, 11, 13, 34
Fox, Cyril, 24
France, French, 71, 83, 125, 162, 163, 166
Freud, Sigmund, 17, 33, 36-43, 192

Furuvik Parken, Gävle, 53
Gadsby, David, 9
Gagarin, Yuri, 162
Geertz, Clifford, 10
Gemini rocket programme, 168, 170
genocide, 21, 23
geographers, 10, 21, 60
Germany, German, 49, 52, 53, 56, 58, 61, 83, 138, 162, 164, 166, 209
Gilmore, James, 52, 53, 59
Gladiator (movie), 48
globalisation, 161, 165, 170, 171, 174, 176, 177
God, gods, 34, 39, 56, 202, 206
golf, 54, 69, 168
González-Ruibal, Alfredo, 12, 23
Gorman, Alice, 17, 21, 161-80
Gould, Richard, 11, 20, 21
GPS, 93, 114, 175
graffiti, 87, 91, 93, 102, 103, 107
graves, 12, 21-23, 36, 83
Graves-Brown, Paul, 11, 14, 18, 19, 201-13
gravestone, 65
Greece, Greek, 50, 53, 56, 183, 202
Greenaway, Peter, 92
Greenham Common, 100
Greenpeace, 96
Grierson, John, 185
Ground Zero, 22
Halloween, 187, 191, 194, 196
Hamilakis, Yannis, 24, 78
Hawkes, Jacquetta, 24
heritage: 17, 21, 23, 47, 76-78, 91, 101, 107, 113, 127, 131, 137, 164, 175, 188; management, managers, 21, 58, 77, 90, 131, 135-37
Hicks, Dan, 9, 18
historian(s), 10, 14, 21, 22, 47, 51, 57, 61, 126, 127, 141, 203
history, histories: 10-12, 17-20, 22, 36, 39, 47, 58, 60, 61, 87, 91, 93, 96, 100, 101, 105, 113-15, 118, 124-27,

140, 141, 145, 147, 156, 164, 165, 202, 203; Disneyfied, 60, 61; family, 145-59; military, 100, 113, 114; of archaeology, 43; of human kind, universal, 40, 42, 201; of ideas, 134; political, 106
Holland, 116, 124
Hollywood, 51, 59
Holtorf, Cornelius, 9-29, 43-64, 70, 72, 78, 186, 187
home(s), 18, 19, 71, 73, 114, 132, 133, 145-59, 169, 188, 202, 204, 207, 209
human remains, 36, 106
human rights, 166, 171
hyper-real, hyper-reality, 210, 211
identity, identities, 19, 50, 59, 86, 165, 169, 173, 176, 202
imperialism, imperial(ist), 77, 83, 84, 165, 166, 170
India, 163, 210
Indiana Jones, 47, 50, 53, 56, 57, 59
indigenous people, 18, 101, 107, 161, 165, 170-74, 177
individual(s), 12, 23, 37, 39, 41, 54, 73, 76, 85, 106, 107, 122, 134, 140, 141, 171, 191, 201-10
individuality, individualism, 87, 201, 202, 204, 209, 210
industrialisation, 17, 171, 191, 202, 206
industry, industrial, 18, 21, 22, 52, 136, 139, 162, 165, 166, 169, 173, 177, 191, 205-9
Institute of Contemporary Archaeology, 15, 16
International Space Station, 163
Internet, 69, 75, 77, 138, 140, 171, 210; see also World Wide Web
Inuit, 204
i-pods, 211
Iraq, 65, 66, 77, 78, 127
Iron Age, 14, 204
Jamaica, 187

Jameson, Frederic, 34, 35
Japan, Japanese, 21, 83, 154, 162, 167, 173
Jensen, Rolf, 53, 57, 59
JORVIK, 61
junk, 131-38, 161, 174
Kazakhstan, 162, 166
Kennedy, John F., 172
Knossos, 36, 53, 56
Korff, Gottfried, 48, 52, 56, 61
landscape(s), 17, 20-23, 72, 83, 90, 96, 97, 100-3, 107-10, 116, 120, 127, 145-54, 156, 169, 175-77
Lara Croft, 57
Las Vegas, 48-53, 66, 72, 95
Le Corbusier, 206
leisure, 47, 52, 58, 59, 93, 134, 135
Levi-Strauss, Claude, 196, 205, 209
London, 41, 53, 71, 83, 120, 193, 206
Lucas, Gavin, 10, 11, 13, 14, 18-21, 36, 78, 142
McDonald's, 49
McLucas, Clifford, 19
Magnusson Staaf, Björn, 58
Malaysiam 50, 69
Mars, 163
Marx, Karl, 203, 210
Marxism, Marxist, 35
material culture studies, 19, 20
material culture, 11, 12, 14, 17, 19, 20, 25, 53-5, 65-80, 93, 101, 102, 107, 108, 141, 161-65, 176, 177, 188, 195, 196, 209, 211,
materiality, 11, 13, 17, 19, 23, 123, 129
May, Sarah, 17, 65-80
Maya, 53, 203
media, 18, 50, 57, 59, 66, 77, 93, 124, 131, 134-38, 171, 173, 174, 183, 184, 193, 201, 211
Medieval period, 18, 51, 76, 188, 189, 204-6, 209
memory, memories, 17, 23, 37, 40, 60, 109, 113, 114, 126-28, 131, 140,

142, 145-53, 155, 156, 196; see also remembering
Mercury rocket programme, 168, 170
Mexico, Mexicans, 140, 166
military sites, 17, 21-23, 66, 77, 100, 113-28, 167
Miller, Daniel, 20
Mir space station, 163
modernity, 17, 33, 35, 58, 192
Moon, 108, 162-64
Moore, Barrington, 204-7
museum(s), 19, 24, 38, 41, 48-9, 53, 56, 61, 77, 85, 86, 89, 91, 92, 119, 134-38, 161, 164, 170, 187, 188
music, 116, 122, 124, 125, 174, 184, 189
Mycenae, 36, 53, 56
Mystery Park, 53
mystery, mysteries, mysterious 49, 51, 53, 54, 56, 58, 59, 85, 87, 91, 114, 119
narrative(s), 14, 21, 40, 56, 83, 93, 94, 153, 161, 164, 186, 187
NASA, 163, 172, 174; see also Apollo, Gemini
Nash, Paul, 24
National Geographic Society, 50, 70, 84-85
National Trust, 113-15, 126
nation-state(s), 33-34, 161, 165, 170, 171, 176, 202, 109
Neolithic, 14, 184, 186, 204; see also Stone Age
Nevada, 17, 21, 53, 95-111, 114, 139
New Archaeology, 58, 203
New York, 192
New Zealand, 83-6, 89, 90, 140
newspaper(s), 16, 50, 56, 69, 73, 107, 134-37
nostalgia, nostalgic, 21, 51, 60, 138, 140
nuclear power stations, 21

nuclear weapons, nuclear tests, 17, 23, 95-111, 120, 122, 123, 127, 166, 170
Olympic Games, 161, 172, 173
Opaschowski, Horst, 52, 59
Orford Ness, 17, 113-20, 124-27
Orser, Charles, 22
painting(s), painter(s), 13, 37, 116, 138-41, 170
Palaeolithic, 204; see also Stone Age
Paris, 22, 52, 172, 192, 196
Parker Pearson, Mike, 20
patina, 93, 119
Peace Camp, Nevada, 9, 17, 95-111
Pearson, Mike, 12, 17, 19, 20, 24, 83-94, 184, 187
Peenemünde, 162
penguin(s): 83, 89; trampling sites, 84
Perec, George, 125
performance(s), 12, 13, 17, 19, 69, 71-74, 93, 114, 121, 122, 184-86, 204
performativity, performative, 12-14, 18, 19, 20, 24, 25, 84, 92, 187, 191
philosophers, 141
philosophy, philosophical, 13, 14, 19, 36, 101, 113, 138, 142, 186, 205
photographer(s), 85, 138, 140, 141
photography, photographs, 10, 13, 68, 75, 84, 85, 89-92, 146, 148, 184, 186
Piccini, Angela, 9-29, 183-99
Piggott, Stuart, 24
Pine, Joseph, 52, 59
poet(s), 140, 141
poetry, poetics, poetical, 93, 142, 194
Polish, 196
politics of the past, 14
Pompeii, 36, 37, 40
Popcorn, Faith, 57
post-processual archaeology, 203
post-structuralism, 43, 203
practice-led research, 12, 13, 18, 19, 24

219

prehistorian, 100; see also archaeologist(s)
pre-industrial, 209
preservation, preserving, 21-23, 40, 42, 78, 84, 90, 113, 116, 135-8, 210; see also conservation
privacy, 18, 201-13
psychoanalysis, 34, 36-43, 192
radio, 69, 114, 124, 138, 162, 174
railway(s), 8, 133, 203, 207, 208
Rathje, William, 10, 11, 20, 22
recreation, 59, 92, 134, 135
Reformation, 202, 205, 206
remembering, remembrance, 10, 15, 22, 23, 51, 52, 86, 114, 131, 140-2, 145, 146, 149, 150, 154; see also memory
Riksantikvarieämbetet (Swedish National Heritage Board), 137, 142
robots, 21
Roman(s), 50, 53, 189, 193, 202, 205
Rome, 38, 48
Roms, Heike, 19
Rousseau, Jean-Jacques, 42, 209
rubbish, 11, 37, 87-92, 102, 170
ruin(s), 36, 37, 42, 53, 113, 137, 140-142, 145, 149
ruination, 12, 76, 115
Russia(n), 106, 120, 165, 166, 173
Salyut rocket programme, 162
satellite(s), 161-64, 166, 168, 170-77
Saunders, Nick, 11
Saussure, Ferdinand de, 35, 39
Schiffer, Michael, 11, 20, 21
Schliemann, Heinrich, 36, 38, 40
Schmitt, Bernd H., 52, 53, 60
Schofield, John, 17, 21-3, 95-111, 127
Schulze, Gerhard, 52, 59
science, scientific, 14, 18, 33-36, 38, 43, 51, 57-59, 69, 83-85, 96, 162, 166, 170
scientists, 122, 166
sculpting, sculptures, 13, 76, 103, 119

Sebald, W. G., 114
Shanks, Michael, 12, 14, 19, 20, 22, 24, 87, 93, 137, 184, 187
shopping: 38, 191; arcades/centres/malls, 38, 49, 52, 54
Siberia, 69, 71
Siegfried and Roy, 66, 67, 72, 75
singing, 120-25
Skara Brae, 204, 205
slavery, slave(s), 11, 162, 187, 191
smell, 141, 152
sociologist(s), 10, 49, 52
Sorrell, Alan, 24
sound(s), 113-28, 147-56, 185, 197
South Africa, 53, 71
space exploration, 17, 18, 21, 161-80
Spadeadam, 113, 114
Sputnik rocket programme, 114, 161, 162, 171
stereotype(s), 50, 58
Stockholm, 138
Stone Age, 165, 177; see also Neolithic, Palaeolithic
story, stories, 10-12, 47, 50, 53, 54, 57-9, 65, 66, 69, 73, 76, 96, 97, 100, 105, 106, 109, 114, 116, 117, 132, 145-8, 152-6, 161, 164, 165, 177, 187, 197
structuralism, 35, 39
suburb(s), suburbia, suburban, 71, 185, 191, 206-8
Sun City, Pilanesberg, 53
Sweden, Swedish, 17, 20, 22, 58, 131, 133, 137-42, 145, 148, 152
Syncom satellites, 161, 162, 166, 171-77
tacit knowledges, 12
technology, technologies, technological, 18, 51, 60, 83, 93, 128, 161-80, 184, 185, 193, 210, 211
telecommunications, 17, 161-63, 171-74, 193

220

telephone(s), 14, 93, 106, 126, 127, 171, 175, 183, 211
television, TV, 13, 18, 19, 22, 50, 52, 56, 57, 59, 134-35, 162, 171-76, 193,
Thailand, 75
theatre, 71, 86, 87, 89, 210
theming, 17, 48-50, 52-54, 56, 60, 61; see also Disney theme parks
Theoretical Archaeology Group (TAG), 18, 19
Third World, 166
Thomas, Julian, 14, 17, 19, 20, 24, 33-45, 58, 192, 201
Thomsen, Christian J., 36
Tilley, Christopher, 20
time capsules, 84
time, 141, 142, 145-59
Tokyo, 161, 172
tool(s), toolkit(s), 10, 11, 16, 20, 25, 36, 37, 42, 52, 56, 86
Topography of Terror, Berlin, 22
touch, 50, 67, 87, 128, 134-37, 146-52
tourist attraction(s), 49, 138
tourist(s), 49, 50, 58, 84, 89, 91, 93, 134, 138
translation, translate, 13, 206
transport(ation), 18, 21, 50, 73, 83, 97, 104, 107, 113, 131, 201, 207-9, 211
trauma, traumatic, 21, 37, 41, 42
Trigger, Bruce, 33, 165
Troy, 36, 38, 40, 53, 56
Tuan, Yi-Fu, 60, 68, 74
Tutankhamun, 36, 40, 49
UFOs, 117
Ulin, Hulda, 145-59
Ulin, Jonna, 17, 145-59

United Kingdom (UK), 18, 22, 53, 56, 59, 100, 107, 162, 167, 168, 175, 193, 207
United Nations (UN), 161, 163, 166, 177, 211
United States (USA), 17, 18, 20, 22, 53, 54, 67, 70, 73, 74, 84, 89, 95, 101, 104, 105, 108, 139, 140, 161-66, 168, 172, 173, 176, 208, 210; see also America, NASA
USSR, 162-4, 166, 173; see also Russia, Salyut, Sputnik
V2 missile, 162
vandals, vandalism, 89, 114
video, 12, 13, 18, 115, 117, 118, 121, 122, 127, 173, 174, 183-99, 210
Vietnam War, 173
Viking(s), 56, 61
violence, violent, 12, 76, 97, 154, 174, 187, 206
Wainwright, Angus, 115, 116, 119
Wallace, Mike, 60, 61
Wilson, Louise, 17, 24, 113-28
witchcraft, 209
Wittgenstein, Ludwig, 13
Woodward, Christopher, 76, 141
Woomera, 161, 162, 166-70, 175, 177
World War I, 11, 21, 22
World War II, 22, 114, 161, 165, 166
World Wide Web, websites, 57, 70, 75, 77, 93, 106, 138, 175; see also Internet
youth culture, 21
zoo(s), 17, 21, 54, 65-80
1989, 21
9/11 (11 Sept 2001), 22, 209

Peter Lang · Internationaler Verlag der Wissenschaften

Udo Worschech

Alois Musil in the *Ard el-Kerak*
A Compendium of Musil's Itineraries
Observations and Comments from Surveys in 2005–2006

Frankfurt am Main, Berlin, Bern, Bruxelles, New York, Oxford, Wien, 2007.
103 pp., num. fig.
Beiträge zur Erforschung der Antiken Moabitis (Ard el-Kerak).
Edited by Udo Worschech and Friedbert Ninow. Vol. 6
ISBN 978-3-631-57348-8 · pb. € 29.60*

The volume gives a summary and evaluation of Alois Musil's travels in the *Ard el-Kerak*, the ancient Moabitis, during the years 1896 to 1902. References are made to his records and observations regarding Biblical sites and the customs of settled and nomadic tribes in the Kerak region at that time. The volume is also intended to give credit to the meticulous work of A. Musil (1868–1944) and the valuable information he gave about the geography and topography of the ancient Moabite territory. Musil faithfully recorded the Arabic names of all the landscapes, roadways, watercourses, wadis, and ancient ruins he encountered. These are still neglected in modern discussions about the archaeology and history of ancient Moab. This volume is intended to help researchers of the region to find their way, following in A. Musil's footsteps and, hopefully, gain more insights into this land from his work called *Arabia Petraea I*.

Contents: Alois Musil's travels in the *Ard el-Kerak* · Geography · Topography, customs and ancient settlements in Central Jordan · References to Biblical sites

Frankfurt am Main · Berlin · Bern · Bruxelles · New York · Oxford · Wien
Distribution: Verlag Peter Lang AG
Moosstr. 1, CH-2542 Pieterlen
Telefax 0041 (0) 32 / 376 17 27

*The €-price includes German tax rate
Prices are subject to change without notice
Homepage http://www.peterlang.de